Pretty in Pink

The Golden Age of Teenage Movies

Pretty in Pink

Jonathan Bernstein
St. Martin's Griffin ⚓ New York

To my parents

SPECIAL THANKS: Heather Shroder, Biz Mitchell, Ross Jones, Todd Williams, Lori Majewski, and Shelley Bissessar.

Photos courtesy of the Everett Collection.

Design by Bonni Leon-Berman
Photo editor: Shana Sobel
Production editor: Mary Louise Mooney

Library of Congress Cataloging-in-Publication Data

Bernstein, Jonathan.
    Pretty in pink : the golden age of teenage movies / by Jonathan
Bernstein. — 1st St. Martin's Griffin ed.
        p.   cm.
    ISBN 0-312-15194-2
    1. Teenagers in motion pictures.   2. Young adult films—
United States—History and criticism.   I. Title.
PN1995.9.Y6B45   1997
791.43'652055—dc20   96–44748
                                                        CIP

10 9 8 7 6 5 4 3

Table of Contents

Pretty in Pink

Introduction

Loners, Stoners, Princesses, Cheerleaders, Geeks, Jocks and Dweebs

"When the causes of the decline of Western civilization are finally writ, Hollywood will surely have to answer why it turned one of man's most significant art forms over to the self-gratification of high schoolers."

—review of *The Breakfast Club*, *Variety*, February 13, 1985

Somewhere in the middle of the nineties, we stopped castigating ourselves for the excesses of the previous decade. Hindsight removed the taint from the eighties. No longer were we doing extended penance for all those years of avarice. No longer did we have to share a guilty complicity for lolling back and allowing Reagan and Thatcher to feast like carrion on the flesh of the underclass. Somewhere in the middle of the nineties, it all became so clear; the shoulder pads, the flashy cars, the lurid colors—the eighties were the fifties, an AIDS-free adventure playground with the promise of prosperity around every corner. It seems, in retrospect, like our last age of innocence. Now the emotion we feel when we

look back is less shame than a mingling of amusement, embarrassment and affection. But though benedictions have been bestowed on almost every eighties artifact, from the Trumps to the Thompson Twins, Dynasty to the DeLorean, one essential area has gone largely uncelebrated.

Whenever a quorum of cineastes and semioticians gathers to discuss and dissect the great eras of moviemaking, the eighties rarely elicit celebratory cheers and group hugging. Rather, a mention of that decade tends to provoke the rolling up of sleeves and spitting on hands as a precursor to escorting those contentious years outside and pounding the living shit out of them. The eighties, goes the conventional wisdom, was the decade when Hollywood gave up any pretense of engaging the emotions and challenging the intellect, concentrating solely on meeting the demands of the marketplace. It was a time dedicated to catering to the basest whims. It was a time when substance abuse, sadism, promiscuity and voyeurism were promoted as desirable character attributes. It was a time when movies were made for kids, and dumb kids at that. Dumb, horny, crater-faced, metal-mouthed, 14-year-old boys who lurked around the multiplex or the video store or the rec room.

Adolescent desires have been mirrored by the movies since the first flickering images were projected against a white sheet. The Gish sisters, Lillian and Dorothy, tossed their ringlets and mouthed silent entreaties against cruel and monstrous antagonists back in the silent days. The Depression years were marginally enlivened by the spunk of miniature adults like Mickey Rooney, Judy Garland, Jackie Coogan and Freddie Barthlomew, as well as the rambunctious but ultimately redeemable ensembles of Dead End Kids, Bowery Boys, East Side Kids and Little Tough Guys. Throughout the forties and fifties, studio publicists utilized the million-selling screen fanzines to foist battalions of gleaming adolescent types on a swooning cinema-going public. Teenybop audiences wanted either to inhabit or violate the sweaters of Tuesday Weld, Piper Laurie, Sandra Dee, Debbie Reynolds and Natalie Wood. As the end credits rolled they knew they were going to end up either with or like a moody icon, a Dean, a Brando, a Clift—or a lightweight charmer, a Tony Curtis, a Tab Hunter, an Elvis or a Rock Hudson. By the sixties, teens were mainly represented by the squealing and snarling ciphers filling the beach romps and biker flicks churned out by indie titans like Roger Corman, Bert I. Gordon and Samuel Z. Arkoff. The period running from 1968 to 1976, low on teen movies, has been celebrated as one of the most fecund in American cinema history. It was a time when a handful of gifted visionaries stamped their signatures over a number of pictures that reflected the national mood. In films like *M*A*S*H*, *Nashville*, *The Conversation*, *Last Tango in Paris*, *Joe*, *Carnal Knowledge*, *Sunday Bloody Sunday*, *Five Easy Pieces*, *Klute*, *Scenes from a Marriage*, *The Last Picture Show*, and *Taxi Driver*, we sense the fear, paranoia, frustration and uncertainty of America post-JFK, post-Vietnam and post-Watergate. Those days of risk, individuality, art and responsibility disappeared down the gullet of a giant rubber shark. Steven Spielberg's *Jaws* may have been as rich in character and narrative as it was in big, bone-crunching thrills but it can be held directly responsible for initiating the ritual of the Big Summer Movie and the demand for endless spectacle. In 1977, *Star Wars'* intergalactic dogfights yanked a new generation of virgin cinemagoers away from TV screens and pinball arcades and into theaters. As the seventies trundled to a close, a process of natural selection was being performed on movie attendees of a certain age. Thrillride movies (*Superman*), gross-out movies (*National Lampoon's Animal House, Cheech and Chong's Up in Smoke, Caddyshack*) and slashers (*Halloween, The Hills Have Eyes*) were beginning to proliferate, and adult audiences were beginning to microwave their own popcorn.

Thus we arrive at the eighties, the decade when the teen movie comes into its own. This was the time when the spawn of the boomers had pockets bulging with pocket money, and they were happy to lavish that coinage on all manner of electronic babysitter, from Pac-man to Pong to *Porky's*. Suddenly, adolescent spending power dictated that Hollywood direct all its energies to fleshing out the fantasies of our friend, Mr. Dumb Horny 14 Year Old, because he was the one demographic whose patronage could be relied upon to give a film a big opening weekend. (The luxury of hindsight allows us to savor the irony that the feted and fawned-over execs of the day, the Ovitzes and Eisners, were driven to Rolaids and relaxation courses by the caprices of teens flipping coins over which sex comedy or slasher on which to waste their money.) Soon, the multiplex played home to a white-bread world populated by an unruly mob of alienated outsiders, rich, privileged emotional cripples, horny high schoolers, computer whiz kids, loners, stoners, princesses, cheerleaders, geeks, jocks and dweebs, all of them demanding their due in terms of attention, respect and empathy.

Where once movie teens railed passionately against an uncaring society, against the bomb, against the draft, against The Man, the new breed of fictional adolescents worked themselves into a fever over *not being popular*. These teen tribe members were brought to life by a fresh-faced cabal of young actors marked out for greatness by their winsomeness, precocity and lineage. In this decade of divorce and dysfunction, adults became the enemy. If they weren't entirely absent (how many hundreds of films used "my parents are away for the weekend" as a plot point?) they were stumbling prehistoric buffoons or corrupt intransigent fascists standing in the way of the hero or heroine achieving their desires. Said desires were almost always of a sexual nature, though the borrowing of a car or the search for a suitable prom partner were equally weighty issues.

Interestingly, for a period characterized by the adoption of greed as a national pastime, conspicuous consumption does not play a huge part in the teen movies of the times. *Risky Business* aside, many of the eighties teen flicks expressed a yearning for a pluralistic schoolyard where wealth was no longer an impediment to the interaction of previously segregated social strata, where the jock could lie down with the geek and where the punkette could break bread with the princess. In fact, John Hughes, the writer-director-producer with whose name the eighties teen movie genre is most inextricably linked, spent most of his tenure among the lockers railing against cliques and caste systems. I can't claim such lofty moral aspirations on the part of the decade's standby subgenres, the T&A movie and the slasher. But, deadening as these breeds of movie can be—people getting laid and people getting killed for getting laid—they resonate in the minds of a generation as formative cinematic experiences.

Not only did untold millions of adolescents come of age watching these films, but they got to relive and replay the fart gags, food fights and fumbling first times on innumerable occasions. Simultaneous with the spread of teen-aimed movies were the rise of home video and the saturation of cable (specifically MTV, which aired countless soundtrack hits whose videos were little more than trailers for the movies from whence they came). Which is to say, disposable as most of these films were intended to be, the shit never went away. Midway through the seventies, nobody, save for some shifty types, was searching the midnight movie circuit for old Annette Funicello beach films. A decade after its release, a piece of fluff like *Just One of the Guys* is still a cable staple, replayed enough for it to seem like a fondly recalled hit (which it wasn't) and a valuable social document (which it certainly isn't). Superior movies, like the Hughes cycle, have become enduring classics of their kind. After all, every year throws up a fresh batch of brats about to get laid, get drunk, crash daddy's car and worry about the prom.

So is this volume intended as a shameless, rose-colored wallow in nostalgia or a serious attempt to deconstruct an era in which the appetites of the marketplace resulted in an extended period of artistic bankruptcy? Absolutely the former. Though this is by no means an exhaustive collection—I fully expect to be waylaid in the streets by aggrieved completists haranguing me for omitting *Hot Sluts* or *Pizza Dudes Vacation*—I'm digging deep into the teen toilet bowl. I hope the calcified corpses I recover are wide-ranging enough to induce both smiles and winces of recognition. If the repressed memory of hours frittered away gawping at a *Real Genius*, a *Last American Virgin*, a *Better Off Dead* or a *Hardbodies* is sent simmering back to the surface after mention in these pages, well then, my mission is accomplished.

The selection of teen movies churned out during the eighties was ample enough to include some of the crappiest pictures ever perpetrated—the work of filmmakers baffled by and contemptuous of their audience. But it also included some—*The Breakfast Club, Fast Times at Ridgemont High, Pretty in Pink, The Sure Thing* and *Heathers*, to name a few—that were good enough to act as a beacon illuminating the whole fraught process of adolescence. At any point in our lives, the need to have our existence validated is always hovering over us, but during adolescence, the yearning is particularly acute. I'd like to believe that the better examples of the field helped to salve some of the anxieties of their audience, playing a part in reassuring them that not only might they emerge unscathed from the end of their sentence of teen servitude, but that these were times to cherish. That the best of these movies can transcend its genre I can attest, recalling emerging, moist and sniffling, from a screening of *The Breakfast Club* in my hometown of Glasgow, Scotland. I was touched. I was emotionally shaken. I was 24. Which sort of gives the lie to Ally Sheedy's oft-quoted line, "When you grow up, your heart dies." Or it means I never grew up, which is the downside of watching too many of these stupid movies. . . .

Gross Misconduct

1

Grossouts, Goofballs, Virgins, Vomit, Boners and Bikinis

f you remember the 1986 Alan Alda film *Sweet Liberty* for anything other than it being 107 minutes snatched cruelly out of your
life, chances are you'll remember it for the scene in which an unc-
tuous director (played by Saul Rubinek) outlined his three laws of
moviemaking in the eighties. To succeed in the current environment,
he explained, a film must contain three crucial elements. It must feature 1) Property being destroyed, 2) Authority being defied, and
3) Someone being stripped naked. The listing of these tenets was
intended as a jab at the prevailing climate wherein taste, irony, sub-
tlety and Alan Alda movies were nearing extinction and bodily emis-
sions were received by paying audiences as manna from on high.

Whenever I peruse an op-ed piece by some concerned commenta-
tor expressing qualms about the pernicious influence of contemporary pop culture and labeling items like *Dumb and Dumber* and
Beavis and Butt-head key culprits in the shaping of an even more
brutal and stupid America, I find it hard to resist the urge to bawl:

"Have a good snooze, Van Winkle?" Where was this hand-wringer a decade ago when movie screens were awash in rivers of regurgitation, when pee, snot and doody flowed freely and when decent upstanding citizens could, at any given moment, be caught whacking off in the can?

Just as The Beatles had Motown and the girl groups on which to construct their foundations, so the teen movies of the eighties had *Animal House* and *Caddyshack.* From the former film came the irresponsible flinging around of food that millions of starving children could put to good use and the knowledge that one's elders and betters existed to be mocked, humiliated and ultimately destroyed. From the latter came a floating chocolate log. From such heady influences came the ingredients for the species of movie comedy labeled by some Grossout, others Goofball and still others, Tits 'n' Zits. The basic construct of this subgenre seemed to have been carved in stone: a group of young males—stud, sensitive, blimp, blustering but inexperienced foul mouth—in feverish pursuit of sex. While slews of semisoftcore films adhered rigidly to this blueprint, there were others that paid lip service to the concept of responsibility, attempting to teach life lessons along the way. Sometimes the sensitive guy would find true love and the stud would come to the rueful conclusion that hurried, heartless, empty animal intercourse is an unfulfilling experience. The fat guy and the buffoon learn nothing in any telling of the scenario. The examples we will relive in this chapter all received theatrical release, but the most appropriate environment to appreciate them was a darkened living room, decorated by the detritus of convenience food, in the company of mumbling drunks with hands shoved down their pants.

As previously intimated, the shadows of *Animal House* and *Caddyshack* loom large over the eighties, but sizeable as their influence was, the form and function of the Grossout, the Goofball and the T 'n' Z was defined by two pioneering teen comedies. These we shall salute in the following subsection.

Original Sins

Deep in the Florida Everglades lurks a ramshackle cathouse, a grime-caked white-trash sin bin, overseen by an irascible slagheap answering to the name of Mr. Porky.

Porky's (1981) was the *Pulp Fiction* of its day inasmuch as it altered the notion of what could be put onscreen in the name of entertainment, and its influence could be felt in lesser works for years to come. Facing what would seem to be insurmountable odds—low budget, no stars, Canadian origins and a collection of reviews that were less hostile than disbelieving—*Porky's* made an unexpectedly big stink at the box office, providing the first slab of concrete evidence that the adolescent consumers of the eighties were dancing to the beat of a different drum. Ironically, this founding father of squalid sex

comedies isn't even based in the era for which it would write the rule book. Directed by Bob Clark, who also has a preteen classic to his name in *A Christmas Story, Porky's* is set in 1954 in Angel Beach, South Florida, where a bunch of Neanderthal hose monkeys—Tommy the bête noire of gym mistress Miss Balbricker, Tim the raging anti-Semite, Mickey the redneck, Meat ("Why do they call you Meat?," dimples an unsuspecting ingenue), Billy and the elfin comic relief Pee Wee—are foaming with testosterone. Desirous of release, they travel 70 miles away from the safety of their beach town to Porky's shack of ill repute, where they are swiftly relieved of their cash and then their confidence. First, Porky has them dropped in the foul, croc-populated waters of the Everglades, then his brother, the sheriff, smashes their headlights and extracts a stinging fine. That may be the plot of the movie, but that's not what it's *about.*

From its opening moments, focusing on the towering edifice that is Pee Wee's morning wood (he injures himself rolling over to hide the beast from his mother who suddenly walks into the bedroom, then he whips out a growth chart and is crestfallen, certain that his endowment is shrinking), *Porky's* either had you nailed to your seat snorting with amazed laughter or fumbling for your car keys. If you remained in a seated position you paid witness to the ground being broken in the Grossout Hall of Fame. How low could *Porky's* go? In the first act, the ensemble's smuggest pair of sadists, Billy and Tommy, play a ridiculously intricate prank on their compadres, luring them into the backwoods with arousing promises of the skilled ministrations of sex professional Cherry Forever. Seconds after the dupes have dropped trou for inspection by the wry hooker (to Pee Wee: "What do you use for a jockstrap? A peanut shell and a rubber band?"), they're chased naked and screaming into the night by a cleaver-wielding black man splattered with what looks to be the blood of Billy and Tommy. Long after the two wags have fessed up to their complex scam, a screeching Pee Wee is still scampering in a pink and shriveled state down the highway till he's pulled over by cops who smirkingly demand to see his driver's license.

Then there is the running gag of junior gym teacher Coach

Bracket's desperation to discover the reason his shimmering distaff counterpart Miss Honeywell (Kim Cattrall, the only *Porky's* player to go on to anything like regular employment) is nicknamed Lassie. He finds out when he drags her up to the boys' locker room and she becomes so howlingly inflamed by the torrid aroma of lingering boy sweat that he has to cram a jockstrap in her mouth. But more, much more than this, the defining *Porky's* set piece, the moment burned into the memory circuits of a generation, and the moment which threw down the gauntlet to a million villains looking to get into the teensploitation business, was the legendary girls' shower room scene. This is where Angel Beach's roaring boys squat peering through holes punched in the walls behind the shower room, thus affording them a free, full-on, towel-flicking, buttocks-lathering peep show. "I've never seen so much wool," hyperventilates Pee Wee. "You could knit a sweater. It's got to be the biggest beaver shot in the history of Florida." At that exact moment, the squashy rump of a big-boned bather blocks Pee Wee's view. "Move it, lard ass!" he bawls, breaking the boys' cover.

A salient reminder that we're observing another age comes from the girls' reaction. They *like* the fact that they're being watched, posturing for their voyeurs' entertainment. Tommy responds by sticking first his waggling tongue, then his wiggling dick through the peephole. He fails to see the entrance of his eternally forbidding nemesis Miss Balbricker, who dispatches her charges. It takes a few moments for Tommy's organ to come between her crosshairs, but when she spots it (it's cheerfully chirping, "I'm Polly the Penis and I just love to have fun"), she takes immediate and decisive action. She grabs hard and holds on with a double-handed grip. The Big Yank is followed by a scene with Balbricker in the dean's office demanding justice ("I've got him now and I'm not going to let him slip through my fingers") in which the actors portraying teachers are called upon to pantomime hysteria for so long and so loudly that they must have been coughing up blood and particles of lung by the time "Cut" was called.

Porky's thin sliver of plot contained its more serious passages. Principally, there was the case of Tim. Pounded and abused by his leather-clad, boozing badass dad ("He tore a guy's ear off"), Tim attempts to take out his frustrations on Jewish high-schooler Brian Schwarz, but Brian is no whining Woody Allen asthmatic type. He shrugs off Tim's catcalls of "kite" (sic), but doesn't stand down from a schoolyard face-off. "When you're Jewish you either learn to fight or you take a lot of shit. I don't like to take shit." So saying, he flattens Tim. This provides the impetus for Tim to reject his loser of an old man and bond with the former target of his prejudice. Brian is also instrumental in the movie's climax. Still smarting from the rough handling he received at Porky's hands, Mickey the redneck sets out for the Everglades to seek revenge. He returns a bleeding pulp. His colleagues decide payback is overdue. Utilizing a combination of trucks, boats and chainsaws, they destroy Porky's. (A moment of pathos ensues when the owner surveys the wreckage of his establishment and wheezes: "It's gone. Porky's is gone.") There's a chase back to Angel Beach where Mickey's brother, the sheriff, shoots out the lights of Porky's car and extracts a fine. The conquering heroes are met by a marching band and the cheers of their peers. As the movie concludes, Pee Wee almost gets laid.

When set against the welter of soggy sex farces that would spring up in its wake, *Porky's* seems like a model of restraint and even, kind of . . . *classy.* Atrocities like the *Screwballs* and *Hardbodies* series were packed with 28 year olds grimly going through the teen pussyhound motions. The cast of *Porky's* actually seemed to be enjoying themselves. Dan Monahan, the sprite who played Pee Wee, brought a giddiness to a role that, in the hands of other actors, would have you renouncing your membership in the species. Although a Guy Movie to the nth degree, it boasted a couple of memorable female roles. Canuck screen vet Susan Clark strolled sardonically through her scene as Cherry Forever. (About Pee Wee, she sneers: "We're going to have to tie a board across his behind or he's liable to fall in.") Kaki Hunter, who plays Wendy Williams, the inspiration for Pee Wee's attempted devirginization, performs the same function in *Porky's* that Julia Louis-Dreyfus does on *Seinfeld.* On absolutely equal terms with the boys, she's able to mock and humor them, even when they pull the geriatric workplace prank of asking Wendy to find a friend of theirs. Her unfazed shrug after repeatedly yelling "Has anyone seen Mike Hunt?" is a charming moment.

Two sequels, *Porky's 2: The Next Day* (1983) and *Porky's Revenge* (1985), followed. The first revolves around the boys' attempt to save their drama class production of *Romeo and Juliet* after a coalition of Christians, KKK members and city councilmen object to a Seminole Indian being cast as the male lead. The second had Mr. Porky (absent from *The Next Day*) return with the intention of blackmailing the school's basketball coach for gambling debts. By this time, most of the cast looked like they were only sticking around to pay for their own kids' expensive orthodontic work. Though *Porky's* was eventually superseded by a decade's worth of teen comedies, whenever a locker-room raid was on the horizon, its imprint was unmistakable.

Fast Times at Ridgemont High* (1982) is more than just a Grossout pioneer. In its variegated vignettes are many moods, nuances and flavors, almost as many as in the components of the Sherman Oaks Galleria in which its ensemble lurks and works. But if you consider the scenes which made the biggest and most immediate audience impressions, and those which still have influence at this very moment, you will think of 1) Sean Penn saying "You dick!" to Ray Walston, 2) Phoebe Cates fellating a carrot and 3) Judge Reinhold wanking in the crapper. So it is that *Fast Times* takes its place in the pantheon.

In the seventies, Cameron Crowe was one of *Rolling Stone*'s star reporters. He was 16, an almost unheard-of age at which to hold down a position of influence at a magazine staffed by wizened men of letters. But Crowe radiated a boundless enthusiasm for the stuff that made the graybeards wince. The Eagles, Frampton, Fleetwood Mac, you name it, he raved about it, and without the ironic distance that makes today's seventies boosters such insufferable company. The luster of Stevie Nicks was quick to dim and Crowe discovered what it takes most American rock writers a lifetime to learn: theirs is no fit gig for a grown-up. He left behind the pressures of the bimonthly deadline and, for the purposes of a book project, went into deep cover at an unnamed American high school (thought to be Clairemont High in San Diego), still fresh-faced enough at 21 to pass unnoticed among the student body. A year's worth of observed and overheard language, fashion and lifestyle choices formed the content of the Teen Like Me exposé *Fast Times at Ridgemont High.* The book quickly became a movie. Written by Crowe and directed by Amy Heckerling, *Fast Times* was a launching pad for a shoal of young actors including Sean Penn, Jennifer Jason Leigh, Judge Reinhold, Phoebe Cates, Eric Stoltz, Forest Whitaker, Anthony Edwards and Nicolas Cage.

Establishing a teen movie convention, it takes place in a world entirely uninhabited by parents. Establishing another convention, it takes place in a world almost solely inhabited by whites. (The awed reaction to Forest Whitaker's fierce football star is almost subtle compared to the sense of Otherness with which blacks are regarded in subsequent films.) It is, of course, most immediately memorable for Sean Penn's audience-slaughtering performance as the sweet-natured, brain-fried surf savant, Jeff Spicoli. Spicoli—the man who, while talking on the phone, will beat himself about the head with a shoe ("That was my skull, I'm so wasted"). Spicoli—the man who will wreck Charles Jefferson's car but show no fear, even though Jefferson's younger brother predicts certain death ("Relax, my old man is a TV repairman, he's got an ultimate set of tools. I can fix it"). Spicoli—the man with a respect for history ("So what this Jefferson dude was saying is, We left this England place because it was bogus. If we don't get us some cool dudes, pronto, we'll be bogus, too . . ."). From his choking enunciation to his beautifully staged classroom duels with Ray Walston's Mr. Hand ("C, D, F, F . . . what are you people, on dope?"), Spicoli is up there with Belushi's Bluto as a bad influence of heroic proportions. The character has continued to reverberate down the years, detectable in the personas of Bill and Ted, Wayne and Garth, Pauly Shore and Kato Kaelin.

If Spicoli was *Fast Times'* hit, Jennifer Jason Leigh's Stacy Hamilton was its heart. "Brad, your sister's turning into a fox," observe associates of senior Judge Reinhold as his little sib passes by. And therein lies her dilemma. While simmering with womanly desire, she's still awkward and self-conscious (and still packing a little baby fat; a pre-Madonna pot pokes out now and then). Her best friend Linda (Phoebe Cates), the epitome of sophistication and experience, is appalled at Stacy's late development ("God, Stace, you're *fifteen*!"). Attempting to fall into step with the sexual status quo, she gives her number to a sluglike salesman who eats at the mall pizzeria where she works. He takes her to the make-out rendezvous, The Point, and slobbers on her while she stares at the ceiling. She agrees to go on a date with bashful Mark "Rat" Ratner (Brian Backer), a colleague at both Ridgemont High and the mall (he's the assistant to the assistant manager at the multiplex). The Rat is buoyed with advice from his weasely friend Mike Damone (Robert Romanus) the scalper ("When it comes to making out, whenever possible put on side one of *Led Zeppelin 4*"), but blows the date big time, taking Stacy to a swank eatery and then forgetting his wallet. Nevertheless, she asks him back to her home (her parents are—of course!—away for the weekend). They sit in her bedroom leafing through a photo album and then she offers herself to him. He starts to respond, then makes a mumbling excuse and flees her bedroom. It's too much for him!

Stacy rebounds to Mike, whose professional gregariousness ("Can you honestly tell me that you forgot the magnetism of Robin Zander or the charisma of Rick Neilsen? *I Want You To Want Me*? *The Dream Police*?") seems to cross out the possibility of his being clumsy or inexperienced. In the event, he knocks her up. Although he grudgingly agrees to give her a lift to the abortion clinic, he leaves her in the lurch. It's left to brother Brad, whom she tells she's going bowling, to take her. When she emerges, Brad's waiting for her, sympathetic and nonjudgmental.

Brad's luck with life and love is scarcely better than his sister's. When we first clap eyes on him, he's a Golden Boy, glowing with self-confidence ("I'm a senior now. I'm a single, successful guy"), a hot car, a loving girlfriend and a position of importance at All American Burgers. He dumps the girlfriend, thinking he's restricting himself from the many vistas of womanhood that are his for the taking. He loses the plum job at the burger dispensary after being drawn into a war of words with a short-tempered customer. Soon, he's reduced to working in a seafood joint and forced to wear a pirate uniform. Then, when he spies the lovely, bikini-clad Linda reclining by his pool, he rushes upstairs to pleasure himself and is caught in the act by the star of his grubby fantasies. "You're telling me the fun is over," he will bitterly tell a career officer. "I'm still waiting for the fun to begin."

Though Spicoli gets all the laughs, *Fast Times'* sympathetic treatment of Stacy, Brad and Mark Ratner's precarious progress through their teenage years belies the movie's come-on title. Time is flying, but not everyone's having the fun they're supposed to be having.

A semisequel penned by Crowe, *The Wild Life* (1984), attempted to replicate *Fast Times'* structure, placing its protagonists in post–high school situations. Eric Stoltz had the Brad-type role of the bright guy with the big future that falls

apart the moment he moves into his swinging bachelor pad. Lea Thompson, Stoltz's estranged girlfriend, is Stacy a few summers down the line: a waitress having an affair with a married cop. The Sean Penn, big-hearted bonhomie quotient is provided by beefy brother, Chris, as a cheerful wrestler. It's no catastrophe but how highly can you recommend a movie whose most memorable moment is a fleeting cameo from Ron Wood during a party scene in Eric Stoltz's swinging bachelor pad?

We Don't Need No Education
School Movies

Screwballs (1983) is the madman in *Porky's*' attic. When the prerelease buzz about the positive testing of Bob Clark's film registered on Roger Corman's antenna, the veteran carpetbagger determined to rush out something almost exactly the same. Cribbing from Clark's shooting script, *Screwballs'* writer/producer team, Linda Shayne and Jim Wynorski (they hired Canadian director, Rafael Zielinski, who lacked what suddenly came to be seen as the light comedy touch of countryman Bob Clark), set their piece in 1965 in the environs of T&A High. There, a quintet of droolers enliven school days by pretending to be doctors and extending breast examination to interminable lengths. T&A's last surviving virgin, Purity Busch, fails to see the funny side and lands the boys with detention. For this, they swear, The Bitch Must Pay! Among the high jinks is a strip bowling contest during which a nerd gets his member caught in a ball yet still manages to execute a strike. This one's really a relic from the rollicking days before date rape became a consideration. Appropriately for a movie containing so many shower scenes, the viewer feels grubby throughout. A sequel, *Loose Screws* (1985), contained exactly one joke. Here it is: the requisite allocation of stud (here called Hardman), fat guy (Marvin Eatmore) and dweeb (Hugh G. Rection) are sitting round a cafe table bemoaning their imminent expulsion. "This is the last straw," exclaims one. "No, there's

Gross Misconduct

plenty more," chirps a waitress, depositing a fresh selection of straws on the table. You had to be there.

For anyone who's ever gotten a wedgie, had their head stuck down a toilet bowl, their sexuality called into question in mixed company or their hair used as a handy storage space for a still-soggy ball of chewing gum, two school bully–bashing movies went part of the way to easing the agony. (Years of expensive therapy went the rest of the way.) In *My Bodyguard* (1980), cringing little Clifford (Chris Makepeace) turns the tables on nogoodnik Moody (Matt Dillon) when he engages hulking Linderman (Adam Baldwin), previously Moody's instrument of torture, to be his hired muscle. Ultimately, Clifford learns to stand up for himself but the few scenes where the schoolyard power is suddenly within his grasp are sweet indeed.

Three *O'Clock High* (1987) is an altogether weirder proposition. Straight outta film school and sizzling with technique, director Phil Joanou imbued his high school *High Noon* with all the dazzling and disorienting effects at his disposal. The camera spins and swings, the cast all act like zombified versions of teen stereotypes. The only natural element in the movie is the mounting distress of its hero Jerry Mitchell (Casey Siemaszko). The whole school is ablaze with rumors of new transfer Buddy Revell (Richard Tyson), a notorious psycho, whose homicidal exploits are exaggerated with each telling. Jerry, a nose-to-the-grindstone straight arrow, is persuaded by his best friend, the editor of the school newspaper, to do a "Welcome Buddy!" piece. In an effort to ingratiate himself, Jerry pumps the bad dude's hand. Only then do we find that, more than all the other things that set him alight, *Buddy hates being touched!* So much so that he vows to annihilate Jerry in the parking lot at . . . three o'clock high! Jerry descends through several levels of Hell, stooping so low as to pilfer from the till of the student store he manages in order to buy off the bully. In the end, though, the underdog has to stand up for himself, taking a few lumps and then, in front of the whole school, knocking Buddy unconscious with a sneakily concealed knuckle-duster. Not only is Jerry's use of a hidden weapon lauded as a triumphant example of brain over brawn but, in the closing moments, he's suddenly catnip to all the teen sex kittens who'd previously disdained him.

More male wish fulfillment permeates two notorious older woman schoolboy fantasies. First, *Class* (1983). Spotless Rob Lowe and baffled Andrew McCarthy are prank-playing preppies, as adept at vomiting and voyeurism as any attendee of T&A High. McCarthy, though, is still unsullied. That is, until a spot of solo barhopping brings him into contact with an older woman—and not just any older woman, but Jacqueline Bisset, whose pinups fueled the straining and squeaking of a million midseventies single bedsprings. Before you can say "Here's to you, Mrs. Robinson," she's impaling herself on him in the middle of a glass elevator. Come Christmas, rich kid Lowe, in a display of largesse, insists McCarthy, a man of more modest means, join him at his sprawling family home. The visit is a rousing success until McCarthy meets Lowe's ravishing mother who is, of course, La Bisset. (Lowe, McCarthy and Bisset in one movie? Timber!) He's dumbstruck, slack-jawed and boggle-eyed. In fact, he's the same as he is in every movie.

The thrill of nailing his best friend's mom wanes quickly for McCarthy. But the movie plays a cruel trick, on both him and us. Bisset won't leave him alone. *Class* appeared before the *Fatal Attraction* woman-from-Hell cycle, so she's not razoring the crotches out of his shorts. Instead, she sneaks into his bedroom at night, feels him up under the dinner table and follows him back to school. Mention is made by Lowe's father, Cliff Robertson, of his wife's neuroses, but it is never ascertained whether she's a nut, a drunk, a stalker or some sort of crazy free spirit. Once her proclivities are revealed, she's simply removed from the picture and the real climax nail-biter is whether Lowe will forgive McCarthy and they can go back to being preppie friends again. Go on, guess.

Much less vile, though no less prurient, is *My Tutor* (1983). As so often happens, a concerned Dad (Kevin *Invasion of the Body Snatchers* McCarthy), hires a hot, pouting thirtyish knockout (Caren Kaye) to get his head-in-the-clouds son, Bobby (Matt Lattanzi, onetime Mr. Olivia Newton-John) to hit the books. The conjugation of French verbs quickly becomes an exercise crackling with sexual tension. Not only does the instructress ease Junior's mounting frustration (he spends the first half of the movie trawling around biker bars and brothels), but she unshackles him from the weight of his dad's ambitions, encouraging him to pursue his dreams of studying astronomy. *My Tutor* earns points for leavening its smut level with a certain sweetness. It also contains a scary performance from Crispin Glover as Lattanzi's Horny Toad bud.

If I could go back to school knowing what I know now. . . ." That pitiful impulse experienced by so many of us as we long to escape adulthood was exploited in a couple of movies. In the opening moments of *Hiding Out* (1987), we're asked to accept the premise of Jon Cryer in glued-on beard and wig as a stressed-out Wall Street power guy. Suddenly, his world of fast cars and pliable brokerettes is overturned when he witnesses a mob killing. He's whisked into the world of witness protection. Then his guardians are killed. He goes on the lam, winding up at the high school of his teenage cousin. He jettisons the ludicrous facial fuzz and registers at the school under the name Maxwell Hauser (fabricated *Usual Suspects*–style from a nearby can of coffee). Considerably more credible as a fresh-faced 16 year old than he was as a grizzled 27, Maxwell Hauser has a modicum of adult wit and restraint which makes him seem like a repository of cool in the eyes of his new classmates. He's even put forward as a candidate for the school presidency against the angry white male whose girlfriend (Annabeth Gish) he's just filched. *Hiding Out* is no more than an okay cable time-waster but Jon Cryer's unerring affability stays the normally itchy zapper finger. He carries the picture on a pair of scrawny shoulders (as, to a lesser extent does the always-on-the-cusp Keith Coogan as his cousin), even when director Bob Giraldi, notorious for his lavish pop videos, had him cavorting through the empty high school corridors, pirouetting and whooping like a chimp.

Actor Arliss Howard, memorably creepy in the TV movie *I Know My First Name Is Steven,* was a strange choice to pass for teen, but there he is in *Plain Clothes* (1988) as a cop investigating the murder of a teacher after his brother has been nabbed as chief suspect. Howard adopts the name Nick Springsteen, moistens English teacher Suzy Amis with some erotic verse reading (Casey Siemaszko did this in *Three O'Clock High,* too) and keeps some classmates on the straight and narrow. He also gets his brother off the hook. In the end, George (Norm!) Wendt did it!

With its generous allocation of soft-focus shower shots and long, lingering close-ups of unclad female flesh, *Private School* (1983) rented through the roof to an audience willing to disrupt the movie's narrative through judicious use of the Pause and Slo-Mo functions. Matthew Modine stars as the poor schnook caught between good girl Phoebe Cates, who wants to wait while all around her are boffing their brains out, and lascivious wild child Betsy Russell, who wants him to abandon himself to the moment. In keeping with the film's late-night premium cable soft-core tone, Sylvia Kristel shows up as sex teacher Regina Copuletta. She gets to keep her clothes on, probably because no one wanted the target audience to be put off its popcorn by all that old, sagging, wrinkled flesh.

Cherry Forever?
Loss of Virginity Movies

Awake-up call to the world," they called it. "An amoral and unflinching examination of adolescent sexuality." I refer to Larry Clark's 1995 film *Kids,* rhapsodically reviewed by the majority of movie scribblers as a cautionary tale for our times. I say that's a lot of hooey. For any teenager living outside the New York metropolitan area, a viewing of *Kids* was an invitation to sneak out the back door and board a bus to the big city where a bunch of brats were having a high old time. The boys in *Kids* got any girl they wanted, robbed shops and never got caught, had instant and endless access to booze and drugs and walked straight past the line of losers into nightspots where everybody knew their names. For a real study of the teenage horrorshow, one so consistently raw and squalid that it made half its audience want to lop their cocks off, there is only one movie, *The Last American Virgin* (1982).

One of the reasons Cannon, the indie movie studio run by Israeli exploitation specialists Menahem Golan and Yorum Globus, attained its mideighties status of mini-major was the success of its Lemon Popsicle series. Though largely unseen in America, these movies (threadbare titillation set in the fifties, executed in a style that aimed for Porky's but achieved Benny Hill), packed European cinemas, largely on the backs of TV-advertised soundtrack albums stuffed to the gills with early days rock 'n' roll standards. The series' director, Boaz Davidson used its components—sex-seeking stud, shy guy and gutbucket—as the basis for *The Last American Virgin*. But there the similarities end.

As soon as you catch a glimpse of the titular hero, Gary (the never-heard-of-before-or-since Lawrence Monoson), you can't stop your shiver of identification. He tries to look cool, but cool clothes don't hang right on him. He's got a big nose and a high voice. He can't get a handle on his emotions. He's real. Even though most of the situations he's stuck in are beyond farcical, his anguish and infatuation never fail to assert themselves. From the moment the film begins, when he's sitting in a garish cafe with his friends, Rick, the predatory hedonist (Steve Antin), and David, the fat guy (Joe Rubbo, great fat guy name!), and he catches sight of his dream girl, Karen (Diane Franklin), he's lost. But he's also lost in a world where sex with strangers is easy and accessible to everyone but him. When he accedes to peer pressure and provides his parents' home as a location to nail the unappetizing trio from the opposite table, he's stranded on the couch with a surly fat girl ("Don't start that small talk with me, it's not going to get you anywhere.") while his friends make out in the upstairs bedrooms. One of the more surreal scenes in cinema history follows as Gary catches Victor, the high-school nerd, engaged in the fine old teen movie tradition of peeping through a hole into the girls' shower room. Gary insults Victor's manhood and a penis measurement contest ensues ("The man with the biggest tool wins the pool."). A student scrupulously measures all the organs and Victor is the victor with a throbbing nine inches. "It's nine and a half!" he claims. "We're not including your balls," he's told. "Neither am I," he retorts.

Gary pursues the lovely Karen, letting the air out of her moped tires and then charmingly offering her a lift to school. They connect sufficiently for him to ask if she has a boyfriend, but she stays coy. She's less coy at the crazy new wave pool party that night where Gary sees her in the arms of his best friend, Rick. The lights dim, the smooching starts and Gary stands sucking on a bottle of Wild Turkey. He gets lachrymose

and unsteady, aching for the love of his life who's suddenly a million miles out of his reach.

Just as the penis measurement scene seemed like it was conceived to fuck with the expectations of the audience, the subsequent plot turn was even more confounding. On his pizza delivery route, Gary is chased around by a shriekingly caricatured Hispanic nympho. He flees but returns with friends in tow. She services Rick the stud, then eyes David hungrily, purring, "Come to Carmella, my big burrito." We are then privy to an unbelievable fat guy sex scene with the big boy thrashing around like a whale, revealing vast expanses of flabby white ass. The senorita's sailor boyfriend arrives home before the hapless Gary is forced to take sloppy thirds.

Gary's crush on Karen and resentment of Rick grows with every passing humiliation. First, he's forced to go on a double date with them and Karen's quirky girlfriend Rose (*Twin Peaks'* squeaky Kimmy Robertson), then Rick asks him for the keys to his grandmother's empty house so he can be alone with Karen. Gary mindfucks Rick, deriding him for wanting to play house with Karen, when he could be out scoping the streets for hookers. Amazingly, this has the desired effect of keeping Rick away from Karen. In a genre boasting its share of teen-friendly hookers-with-hearts-of-gold, *The Last American Virgin* presents its audience with the most unpleasant and intimidating whore in living memory. "You move like you don't want to get laid," she snaps at Gary, "You ain't still a virgin, are you?" She attempts to manipulate him manually, then gives up, sneering "You've got a lot to learn, little boy." Gary stumbles away and vomits. The others avail themselves of her services and are subsequently struck down with scorching cases of crabs.

Gary's delaying tactics are ultimately to no avail. "Rick took her out to the football field to bust her cherry," Victor the nerd cheerfully tells Gary when he sees Karen's moped parked outside the cafe. Sure enough, Rick will come in later, giving a blow-by-blow account of the event. Gary drives away in his pizza delivery van, tears streaming down his big nose. But he will soon come across Rick and Karen in the school library. "I already told you that we're through," Rick is telling her, "so get the fuck away from me, you're embarrassing the shit out of me." Karen's pregnant. Gary rises to the occasion. He takes her to his grandmother's empty house, sells his stereo and borrows money from his employer at the pizza service to pay for her abortion. He comes to the hospital with a Christmas tree and teddy bear for her. He's told his parents he's gone on a skiing trip so he can spend the next few days with Karen, sleeping on the couch while she recuperates. He finally tells her that he loves her and they embrace.

The next day is her birthday. Gary has a locket inscribed with the words *To Karen with Love* inscribed on the back. He turns up at her birthday party with the locket in his hand. When he walks into the kitchen to give it to her, she's kissing Rick. Their eyes meet but no words are exchanged. One last time, Gary drives into the night, tears in his eyes. And that's how it ends! No American movie would have a more down-beat climax till the advent of the similarly stomach-churning *Seven.* What sort of message could audiences at the time have possibly derived from *The Last American Virgin?* That it's a cruel, cold world? That selflessness and tenderness will be rewarded only by the betrayal of trust? A million after-school specials and preachy P.S.A.s couldn't have done a better job of scaring kids off the terrors of the flesh.

Following *The Last American Virgin* with a few lines about *Losin' It* (1982) is kind of like saying, "Yeah, the Sex Pistols were great but did you ever hear Mr. Mister . . . now *there* was a band." The usual quartet of high schoolers—stud (John Stockwell), sensitive (Tom Cruise), stupid (Jackie Earle Haley from *The Bad News Bears,* actually very funny and accoutred after *Come Fly with Me*–era Sinatra) and resourceful underage smart-ass (John P. Navin)—cross the border to Tijuana in search of hookers and Spanish Fly. Along the way, they're joined by runaway housewife Shelley Long, who's seeking a Mexican divorce. Stud Stockwell puts moves on Long but is rebuffed. Nice guy Cruise gets her before she reunites with hubby. Directed by Curtis (*The Hand that Rocks the Cradle*) Hanson, the movie is at least adroit enough to chastise the fun-seekers for treating Mexico like a dumping ground for their dirty little desires.

In the 1979 summer camp classic *Meatballs,* little Rudy (Chris Makepeace) was a lonely camper who wanted to go home till he was befriended by gonzo counselor Bill Murray. What a difference a few years makes. In *Meatballs 3* (1987), Rudy (now played by always-on-the-cusp Patrick Dempsey) is desperate to get laid, but crippled by his nerd status, faces a destiny of rejection. Luckily, he's got a guardian angel in the cross-eyed form of Sally Kellerman. She's a porn queen who drops dead on the job. Refused entrance to the gates of heaven on account of never having done a good deed, she's assigned the task of aiding Rudy in his attempt to find That Special Someone. The elusive Dempsey magic fails to crystallize here. Sally Kellerman actually didn't seem too humiliated by the demands of the role, which suggests an impressive degree of denial.

Which brings us to the bottom of the barrel. Then way beyond, to the special level of ignominy reserved for *Party Animal* (1983). The films of David Beaird—*My Chauffeur, It Takes Two* and *Pass The Ammo* to name a few—share a unified directorial signature, i.e., they all feel like they were made by a drunk. *Party Animal,* on the other hand, is the work of a madman. The title character is a campus loser, an unhappy wookie called Pondo Sinatra who can't get laid even in a college filled, as this one is, by *Swank* centerfolds. He makes a deal with a mute lingerie model who might be the devil: his soul in exchange for his virginity. Every moment in this movie is extraordinary. The cast are left desperately improvising as scenes sprawl on long past their natural parameters; there's one of the most ill-advised white-guy-in-a-black-bar bits ever filmed (yup, Pondo's in pimp gear, talking that fly shit); for no rhyme or reason, one sequence is shot in black and white. *Party Animal* is guaranteed to turn any social gathering into a suicide pact. (R. E. M. completists will be pleased to learn of their heroes' presence on the sound track to this monstrosity).

Beaches Ain't Shit
Spring Break and Summer Vacation Movies

Annette Funicello never got sand in her crotch. Frankie Avalon never roamed the sands in shorts that barely concealed a boner the size of a banana. That's why movies like *Muscle Beach Party* are rarely seen relics and shit like *Hardbodies* (1984) lives on in cable perpetuity.

When it's cold outside, murky, dank and depressing, *Hardbodies* may possess a recuperative travelogue quality. Any other time, it's a long, dark night of the soul. Endless volleyball montages, studies of the application of suntan lotion and thong close-ups are soundtracked by the keening of Loverboy tribute bands. The jiggling is so interminable you're desperate for something—anything!—to happen, but when an impoverished piece of plot actually develops, you're praying for a resumption of jiggle. *Hardbodies* is almost John Hughes–like in its open contempt for the old, the out-of-condition and the corruption they trail in their wake. Three fat, fortyish swingers turn up at a beach bursting with buff nugs. Finding their attempts to hook up ignored or spat upon, they engage the services of a waterfront Casanova. He shows them how to walk and talk, but then one of the old guys attempts to put the moves on their mentor's girlfriend and has to be punished. A much less complicated sequel followed.

The only Spring Break movie that has any kind of merit is *Fraternity Vacation* (1985). And when I say merit, I'm talking about a degree of merit so infinitesimal, technology has not yet produced a device capable of measuring it. Fort Lauderdale is, as ever, the destination for hordes of American teens, lemminglike in their determination to pour beer over each other, participate in teeny weeny bikini contests and generally regress to a primeval state. Which is fine if you're *there*. Among this movie's revelers is a crew that includes Tim Robbins (playing a character called Mother) and that odd little guy Stephen Geoffreys as geek incarnate Wendall Tvedt. While Wendall's affections are being toyed with by the hard-ass sheriff's daughter, Mother's boys are locked in combat with some rival frat scum, led by ex–*Dallas* pretty boy Leigh Mc-Closkey. Not only do they hate each other but they're vying for the affections of Hot Sex Babe, Sheree J. Wilson (another *Dallas* graduate, now attempting to act opposite Chuck Norris in *Walker, Texas Ranger*). The big twist at the end is that the sought-after hottie rejects the advances of the big men on campus, choosing instead to shower her affections on Wendall.

Dumb and Dumber
Stupid Movies

For me, stupidity in teen movies is synonymous with three words: Savage Steve Holland. The brief series of films that sprung from the imagination of this writer/director/animator were not big hits. They were not well reviewed. They weren't even very good. What they were, though, was filled past capacity with scattershot gags, acts of whimsy and triumphantly realized running jokes. When I hear plodders like Ivan Reitman and Garry Marshall hailed as Zen masters of comedy, I want to hawk up a rope of phlegm. Savage Steve Holland has funnier stuff going on in any given frame than these vets have mustered up in their entire filmographies. What he never had was a coherent movie. Savage Steve was a man enamored of the margins but bored by the blank canvas.

Better Off Dead (1985), the first and best of Savage Steve's canon—and a film which predates *Heathers* by three years in finding teenage suicide a suitable source of slapstick humor—is a perfect illustration of his dichotomy. The nominal plot has high-school ski team hopeful Lane Myer (John Cusack) dumped by Beth, the girl to whom he's made his home a shrine—the hangers in the closet bear her image—in favor of slope stud Roy Stalin ("I think it would be in my best interests if I went out with someone more popular," she explains). Lane variously tries to gas, hang and hurl himself to his death before deciding to regain his self-respect by taking on Stalin (whose brilliant moniker requires characters to say things like,

"Stalin's a hero!") in a race to the death down the treacherous terrain known as the K-12.

Savage Steve can't be shackled by such structural require-ments. He's too busy conjuring up nonsense like an over-enthusiastic adolescent magician. Fear of paperboys runs rampant throughout the movie. Lane's dad (David Ogden Stiers) begins the film rushing downstairs in a fit of panic, pulling on one of his wife's frilly robes, trying to open the garage door before the paperboy can smash the windows with the velocity of his pitch. Johnny the paperhood (he does his hair with a switchblade comb) will terrorize Lane, demanding the $2.00 he claims to be owed. Massed ranks of paperboys will take up Johnny's claim, pursuing Lane into the night like vengeful Klansmen. In the midst of the dumped Lane's misery he is frequently assailed in his car by a pair of Asian kids de-manding a race and deriding him over their loudspeaker, Howard Cosell–style ("The once bright champ is a portrait of mawkishness!"). His 8-year-old brother Badger sends away for ridiculous contraptions advertised on the backs of cereal boxes and comics—and they all work. Lane signs for the UPS delivery of Badger's book on *How To Pick Up Trashy Women,* and a few scenes later the tyke is surrounded by hot sluts. His best friend Charles (teen movie regular Curtis Armstrong, who also held down the comparatively adult role of Herbert Viola on *Moonlighting*) is a cartoon stoner, vacuuming up Jell-O cubes in the cafeteria and falling to his knees on the slopes, ex-claiming: "This is snow! It's everywhere! Have you any idea what the street value of this mountain is!" Lane tries to re-venge himself on Beth by drawing foolish caricatures of her, but the cartoon comes to life and abuses him ("You're a spas-tic nerdbag!"). "I'll show you," he snarls at the doodle, fool-ishly putting the moves on Chris Kremen, the girl who dates the basketball team . . . *the entire team.*

Salvation from humiliation comes in the shape of Monique, the foreign exchange student (Diane Franklin, the faithless wench from *The Last American Virgin*) marooned in the house of Lane's neighbor Ricky, a fat freak who sits at home all day with his crochet, his nasal spray and his monstrous mother.

(The portrayal of Ricky crosses the movie from cartoon pranks into David Lynch–like grotesquerie. He does have one shining moment, though, when he steps onto the dance floor looking like he's going to pull off the fat-guy trick of being limber on his feet. Instead, he belly flops on to the ground and lies motionless.) Many of the movie's stupid set pieces went nowhere and the climactic ski race, complete with triumphant blaring sound track, is perplexingly conventional, but *Better Off Dead* is one of the few teen flicks of the decade to eschew sentimentality and titillation, relying on sheer idiot entertainment. Long may its cable life endure!

The subsequent *One Crazy Summer* (1986), a bikini-free vacation movie set in Nantucket and again starring John Cusack (the De Niro to Savage Steve's Scorsese), an openly miserable Demi Moore, Curtis Armstrong (the Pesci to . . .) and Bobcat Goldthwait was a similar smorgasbord (even ending with a stirring boat race) but failed to wring as many unexpected laughs out of stock situations.

Rounding out the Savage Steve troika, *How I Got Into College* (1989) replaced Cusack with Corey Parker and featured a recurring joke wherein the A and B variables, famous from many mathematical problems, become live-action characters who torment the hero till he blows them up at the end. Which is to say, nothing else about the movie need ever trouble you.

Many scrawny and embittered screenwriters and directors sought retribution for the rejection, solitude and sand—literal and metaphorical—kicked in their faces during their formative years by using teen movies to rewrite their stories with happier endings. I happen to think that *Revenge of the Nerds* (1984) is *not* one of these movies. It panders to a non-nerd's idea of what might constitute an underdog fantasy. It methodically ticks items off a checklist that features such geek-associated paraphernalia as computers, pocket protectors, buck teeth and thick-rimmed glasses. It misses the yearning to belong and the overpowering sense of disassociation from those earmarked as similarly blighted members of the tribe. If the talent behind the movie had truly been in touch with the feelings of its subjects, its ending would have been a flash-forward fantasy where the nerd-tormentors now worked for their former victims instead of Robert Carradine's impassioned "We Are *All* Nerds" address.

That said, Carradine and Anthony Edwards imbue their spat-upon teen geniuses Lewis and Gilbert with a complete sweetness. Curtis Armstrong works chunky, bestubbled, phlegmy magic as Booger. Timothy Busfield's Poindexter seems more hilarious when you consider he was only a couple of years away from *thirtysomething.* Remember also Larry B. Scott's mincing black homosexual, Lamar, a stereotype so garish you'd think he was trying out for a Wayans brothers movie. Forget *Nerds'* barely felt message of universal suffrage and recall instead scenes like the one where the wonks have planted video cameras in the sorority house. Sprawled around, slurping down beer and stuffing themselves with Doritos and sniggering "Focus on the crotch! Do we have bush? We have bush!" the nerds finally, fleetingly, fit in.

The Fort Lauderdale–based sequel *Revenge of the Nerds 2: Nerds In Paradise* (1987) is only notable for giving Robert Carradine a romance with *Melrose Place*'s Courtney Thorne-Smith and the fact that it was directed by movie industry heavy hitter Joe Roth.

The premise of *Bill & Ted's Excellent Adventure* (1989)—time-traveling metalheads collecting actual figures of historical import to help them with their homework—borders on genius. Almost everything Keanu Reeves (Ted "Theodore" Logan) and Alex Winter (Bill S. Preston, Esquire) do and say is funny. (A highlight: the poker scene with Billy the Kid where Winter is told to show a poker face and bursts into a cheery grin.) The trouble is, there's a few too many stretches where they don't do anything at all. Watch it again and squirm in your seat at the length of the sequences where they hurtle through time, where they meet the rulers of the universe, and where Joan of Arc frolics on the waterslide.

This problem was solved with the sequel *Bill & Ted's Bogus Journey* (1991) which, in common with *Evil Dead 2: Dead by*

Dawn, Superman 2, Star Trek II: The Wrath of Khan and *Gremlins 2: The New Batch,* is better than the original. Highlights include B&T beating Death (William Sadler) at Twister.

One of the biggest selling editions of *National Lampoon* was almost entirely given over to a rambling, scabrous slice of fiction entitled "The Ugly, Monstrous Mind-Roasting Summer of O.C. and Stiggs" wherein two smart-ass white supremacists (the archetypal *Lampoon* heroes) hurl abuse at anyone who isn't them. Directed by Robert Altman during his long dry spell, the big-screen adaptation was made in 1984 but not released till 1987. The little-seen *O.C. and Stiggs* has garnered something of a reputation as a great Lost Teen Classic. This is not entirely deserved. The funniest moment comes in the first three seconds when the MGM lion roars, "O.C. . . . Stiggs." From there on, the sneering titular duo (Daniel Jenkins and Neill Barry) slouch their way through a story that has them declaring war on insurance magnate Randall Schwab (Paul Dooley) for canceling the old age insurance of O.C.'s grandfather (Ray Walston). The same elements that bedeviled *Popeye*—Altman's snatches of overheard conversation and overlapping dialogue that work so well in a naturalistic situation and so horribly in a fantasy—kill most of *O.C.*'s gags stone dead. The two mavericks don't indulge in prankage much more mind-roasting than outing a teacher and fixing a water faucet so it blasts Schwab's geekoid son (Jon Cryer). Everyone seems to be in different movies. That's good news when O.C. and his would-be girlfriend (Cynthia Nixon) break out into a top-hat-and tails dance number. It's very unfortunate when Dennis Hopper, in the middle of *his* long dry spell, shows up as a zonked fighter pilot.

White nerds. White geeks. White jocks. White princesses. White stoners. The cinema of eighties teens seem to be a triumph of ethnic cleansing. But, in the heart of this Norman Rockwell–like suburban dreamscape, a lone voice shattered the calm with ugly truths about racial divisions, bigotry and hatred. That voice belonged to C. Thomas Howell. In *Soul Man* (1986), he plays Mark Watson, a self-satisfied smart-ass with a big future and a place in Harvard Law School. Then, convinced by a therapist to put his own needs first, Mark's dad rescinds his offer to pay his son's school fees. All seems lost till Mark comes across a scholarship intended to make Harvard accessible for black students. One dose of miracle bronzing pills, one kinky Afro and Mark gets his place in school, cheerfully rationalizing his decision by saying "This is the Cosby decade. America loves blacks!" He's soon barfing up his words, introduced to reality by a white girl with Mandingo fantasies, the outlandish expectations of the school basketball team, the cops who throw him in jail on suspicion of having stolen his own car and the winsome presence of Rae Dawn Chong. *Soul Man* is as crass as a film can possibly be but, as the only feature of its era even to recognize the existence of another race, it has to be given credit for having its heart in the right place. But where was its kinky Afro'd head at?

Dead Teenagers

2

Boogeymen, Bloodbaths, Slashers, Psychos and Screaming Coeds

You're ugly and pustulent. You're oozing and repugnant. You're self-obsessed but apt to fixate on others. You're moody and uncommunicative. You act like you're going to live forever but you're eaten up with dread about death. You're . . . well, you could be the editor of *The New Yorker* but, for the purposes of this paragraph, you're Everyteen, morbid and miserable, paranoid and tragic, sick and scared. All those hours spent alone and brooding up in your bedroom, all those fetching black ensembles, the bad poetry, body embellishments and death-metal discography. You are, in fact, the audience whose appetite for the dark side caused the horror movie to thrive in the eighties.

The predominant school of terror during the era was, of course, the slasher, wherein a clutch of the young, dumb and comely were decapitated, eviscerated and used as examples of the efficiency of contemporary garden and kitchen hardware. Teens weaned on creature-feature midnight double bills finally got a chance to see

the gory deaths that previously only occurred offscreen. The slasher shared many similarities with the T&A movie. It was most often viewed in a darkened living room to the rhythmic accompaniment of Dorito chomping and groans of "That's fucked up!" Its casts were made up of recognizable high-school stereotypes, whose objectives were nearly always of a sexual nature. But there the genres parted company. Getting laid was the T&A's raison d'être. In the world of the slasher, the sex act unleashed unstoppable forces of darkness whose sole function was to rid the earth of pimply fornicators. Spectating on the hacking up of the popular, the beautiful and the promiscuous at the hands of some ski-masked misfit with a grudge was initially a rewarding evening's entertainment (and unbeatable as a source of first date physical contact); this was the *real* revenge of the nerds. The amount of sadism and cynicism that went into these movies increased apace, swiftly sucking the fun out of them. Franchise requirements dictated that every episode run along the same rails: a group of dupes was whittled down to one who managed to dispatch the bogeyman who, in the final seconds, showed signs of stirring back to life. Worse still was the way the viewer was made an unblinking accomplice in the rape and murder of women.

But the slasher survives, albeit on life support, to this very day due to the patronage of a peculiar consumer that came into being in the eighties: the Gorehound. The Gorehound is perpetually doomed to disappointment; you can see his letters every month in the splatter bible *Fangoria* ("I just saw *Friday the 13th, Part 7.* What a piece of crap. I thought 4, 5 and 6 were bad, but . . ."). He knows the films reek but he's besotted by the FX. He's enthralled by mutilations, amputations and thick, viscous, sticky, squirting blood. His heroes are makeup mavens like Tom Savini. The first time he tried, stuttering and mumbling, to purchase a pack of condoms was so he could fill them with raspberry sauce, stick them under a latex mask and simulate a gaping cheek wound. Hollywood recognized the existence of the Gorehound but consistently shat on him. His wages were frequently frittered on just-boil-and-serve sequels, failed attempts at horror-comedy crossovers and bigger budget flicks that skimped on the scares in an attempt to lure in the mainstream. Having said that, I must acknowledge the fact that many of my favorite horror movies were made in the eighties, playing to largely teenage audiences. But as these films—and I'm thinking of David Cronenberg's *The Fly,* Sam Raimi's *Evil Dead 2: Dead by Dawn,* Stuart Gordon's *Re-Animator* and *From Beyond* and George Romero's *Day of the Dead*—fail to address specifically teenage concerns or feature adolescents in any kind of substantial role, they are ineligible for inclusion. My hands are tied.

In the nineties, prepubescent audiences are moved to leave the nightlight on by R. L. Stine's *Goosebumps* series and Nickelodeon's *Are You Afraid of the Dark?* shows. Psychological serial killer studies have supplanted the slasher. The teen horror flick is largely moribund. But mold-encrusted though they may be, the franchises grind on. Somewhere, a few gorehounds still show up for the latest Jason or Freddy, hoping against hope that *this* one will deliver the kick that they remember from all those years ago . . .

The Treacherous Three
Pioneer Slasher Movies

No discussion of the slasher oeuvre could begin or end without mention of the night *he* came home. Simply put, *Halloween* is the shit. Even after you've sprawled semi-lidded through a million giftless knockoffs, John Carpenter's 1978 original still has the power to suck you in and keep you squirming in your seat. None of the films that followed had an ounce of *Halloween*'s atmosphere, its claustrophobia or its shock value. None of them had a heroine as resourceful or authoritative as Jamie Lee Curtis' embattled babysitter, Laurie Strode, none of them had a prophet of doom as peculiar as Donald Pleasence's Dr. Loomis. Most of them boasted Butchers from Hell like Michael Myers, but he was the first. From *Halloween,* a generation learned that the correct response to a suspicious sound of someone in the house is to go down to the basement in your underwear. From *Halloween,* we learned that the first scare was just the tease—there's nothing waiting behind the door—and, just as you've exhaled, the killer comes out from the bottom of the stairs, causing you to spill your drink onto your lap. From *Halloween,* we learned the shorts-soiling strength of a properly ominous score.

Unfortunately, those lessons were taken as gospel, and during the next decade, filmmakers looking to siphon a few fast bucks from the gorehounds (and *no one* ever went broke making a horror movie) rarely strayed from Carpenter's blueprint, with the result that the shiver of anticipation was rapidly replaced by sitcom familiarity. *Halloween* was as much a victim of its influence as the movies that came in its wake: *Halloween 2* (1981), with Rick Rosenthal taking over the reins from John Carpenter, featured an ingenious array of hospital-based homicides (the corpse of Michael Myers having come unexpectedly back to life) but lacked the *anything-can-happen-oh-shit* factor of the original. When an enemy cannot be killed, the victory of the last man or woman standing is an empty one.

The law of diminishing returns dictates that by the time a movie title is followed by a number or Roman numeral indicating that it has reached its third episode, watching it is an experience as rewarding as watching two raindrops as they dribble down a window. *Halloween 3: Season of the Witch* (1984) is worth mentioning, though, if only for the fact that it marks the sole occasion that a movie franchise has ditched its signature plot and characters, bringing in an entirely separate story under its rubric. In this one, the Silver Shamrock toy company plans to commemorate Halloween with a line of demonic masks that, once affixed, cause snakes and creepy crawlies to writhe out of the wearer's eyes, nose and mouth. "It's the best joke of all," hissed the toy boss, "a joke on the children." Audiences, however, were disgruntled by the lack of slash action and when the series resumed at the end of the eighties Michael Myers was back, unstoppable as ever, with Donald Pleasence's batty Dr. Loomis always just a few steps behind. (That situation will now sadly remain the same forever, as Pleasence died shortly after completing 1995's *Halloween 6: The Curse of Michael Myers.*)

In 1957, a camper named Jason Voorhees drowned at Camp Crystal Lake, a victim of neglect on the part of two camp counselors lost in the throes of passion. This was bad news because it signaled the start of the *Friday the 13th* series. Unlike *Halloween,* this franchise never had any heights from which to tumble. It was always a crude, barely competent exercise in pandering to an audience who would have been just as happy to see footage of meat being prepared, as long as blood flowed and sharp objects were utilized. Nevertheless, the first *Friday the 13th* (1980) is successful on its own terms, establishing a tone of idiot foreboding from the get-go with the sawing of Harry Manfredini's ssh-ssh-ssh-aah-aah-aah score. The story makes sense, too. The camp counselors (Kevin Bacon among them) are so perky, boisterous and adorable that you can empathize with the peevishness burning behind the hockey mask. And, before our collective goodwill was wiped away by a decade's worth of "aw, come *on*" Idiot Twist endings, the film's staggering climactic revelation that Jason's mad old mom was behind the carnage was met by dazed grins of acceptance. No way is *Friday the 13th* anything approximating a good movie, but you can't deny its ability to provoke starts, squeals and the sudden desire to view the movie through the cracks of your fingers. Only an audience of Amish could have been given the willies by the next episodes. The longevity of the series is due to its transformation into a crowd-participation vehicle. The knuckleheadedness of campers and counselors tempted to skinny-dip in Crystal Lake or go for a midnight walk in the woods was a signal for paying customers to hurl abuse at the screen.

Attempts to defibrillate the walking corpse occurred in 1982's Part 3 (filmed in 3-D so that knife was . . . *comin' at ya!*), 1984's Part 4 (billed as *The Final Chapter*, and boasting its most star-studded roster: Corey Feldman and Crispin Glover), 1986's Part 6 (*Jason Lives:* the cadaver is revived by a stray bolt of lightning) and 1988's Part 7 (*The New Blood:* one

of Jason's stalkees turns out to possess telekinetic powers and, as such, is a worthy opponent), but the series *was* its star, a lumbering moron adept only in the fields of slicing and dicing. Like Michael Myers, Jason survives into the nineties. The given explanation is that he has shrugged off bodily constrictions and ascended to a higher plateau of evil. Somehow, I can't imagine anyone in the multiplex having enough energy to shout back at the screen by that point.

As soon as you heard the *skreee* of Freddy Krueger's Ginsu fingernails along the pipes of his purgatorial boiler room, you knew there was a new sheriff in slash 'n' stalk territory. In Wes Craven's *A Nightmare on Elm Street* (1984), the sins of the fathers are visited on a group of suburban high schoolers when the child-murderer burned to death a decade ago by their vigilante parents returns to slaughter them in their dreams. This Krueger (played by Robert Englund) was no silent, masked emissary of Doom. With his barbecued visage, dirty striped sweater, rakishly tilted fedora and finger accessories, he was the personification of cackling malice. His killings were elaborately staged, hideously appropriate and capped by a lame quip. In the course of the series, he would dispatch the physically infirm, the drug addicted, the deaf, the asthmatic and the bulimic in creatively personalized ways. His wise cracking approach to teen-slicing made him an instant icon. It also quickly denatured the character, turning him into a Captain Hook–type ham.

Elm Street's first installment found Krueger at his least self-consciously cute. It also gave him a worthwhile adversary in Heather Langenkamp's Nancy, one of horrordom's more resilient heroines. While all around her were being hacked up, suffocated, swallowed by their waterbeds and bled dry in their dreams, Nancy stayed strong and, more important, stayed awake. She also became aware that the adult world could not protect her. Her police chief father (John Saxon) refused to believe in the return of the ghosts of his past. Her mother (Ronee Blakley) blurred reality with the bottle. Craven sets the scene for a *Rambo* climax, a kick-ass confrontation between tormen-

tor and teen. But even though Nancy fills her house with hidden tripwires and booby traps, the way she finally frees Elm Street of Freddy is to turn her back on him, refusing to believe in his existence. He subsequently vaporizes, denied access to a vulnerable subconscious. And then there's a dopey, tacked-on ending—the Elm Street kids are borne away yelping by a Freddymobile while Krueger sinks his nails into Nancy's mom—to set up the sequel. The professorial Craven would talk at length in interviews about studying dreams and the influence they wield in our lives, but his movie was a straight-ahead statement about self-reliance and the time to put away childish things.

The constraints of formula weighed heavily on the follow-up *Nightmares,* but they treated the viewer with less derision than the other tentpole franchises. Number two, *Freddy's Revenge* (1985), has some unexpectedly kinky kills, with a gym teacher being slowly stripped, bound, gagged and strangled by ghostly ropes. In number three, *Dream Warriors* (1987), Nancy returns as a child psychologist, specializing in dreams. Freddy finally gets rid of her but before she goes, she passes on the Freddy-bashing mantle to shy little Alice (Lisa Wilcox) who transforms into "The Dream Master."

Both Craven and Robert Englund attempted to use their *Elm Street* leverage to gain toeholds in the horror franchise industry. Craven floundered with *Deadly Friend* (1986) in which wholesome teen Kristy Swanson is knocked around once too often by her drunken dad. The neighborhood teen genius (*Little House on the Prairie*'s Matthew Laborteaux) resurrects her by sticking a computer chip in the back of her head. This transforms her into a killing machine who can throw a basketball at the local busybody with an impact that explodes her head like a watermelon. Of course, it doesn't take long for the wonk to realize, "I've created a monster!" and attempt to dismantle Swanson, who projects her reanimated state by moving like Pinocchio and enunciating in a "Please hold" monotone . . . *like she does in every movie*! Englund's attempt to get himself nice and comfy in the director's chair was *976-EVIL* (1988), wherein that odd little guy Stephen Geoffreys plays a high-school punchbag who unwittingly dials a phone number that connects him to Hell. Craven and Englund were reunited midway through the nineties on the redundant meta-movie *Wes Craven's New Nightmare,* in which Freddy attempts to kill his creators for bringing him back to do another sequel. The execution sucked, but the intent was honorable.

Little Monsters
New Treatments of Old Favorites

Bite Me

Teen Vampire Movies

From its teen-tempting tag line ("Sleep all day, party all night, it's fun to be a vampire") to its flouncing, fang-bearing, fashion-plate cast, seasoned gorehounds found something to loathe in every glossy, shock-free second of *The*

Lost Boys (1987). Not only did all the killings in this MTV horror movie occur offscreen, not only was Kiefer Sutherland's grinning kingpin villain clearly modeled on Billy Idol, but—and this is the crime that could get you the chair in some states—it provided the environment for the visionary alliance between Corey Haim and Corey Feldman. I recall being among the killjoys who dismissed the film on its release but either I've ditched the blinkers or become less discriminating over the years (evidence points to the latter) because *The Lost Boys* now seems a delightful deviation from the horror norm. Director Joel Schumacher, with his signature combination of scrupulous attention to set design and flickering interest in plot logic, delivers a movie several light years more lavish and loony than any woodlands slasher. It takes place in Santa Carla, a scuzzy West Coast beachfront community that's both a teenage paradise—it's dominated by a giant amusement park, and dotted with video emporiums and comic shops—and a crime capital. When just-divorced Lucy (Dianne Wiest) relocates her brood, Michael (smoldering Jason Patric) and Sam (Corey Haim, dressed like he just hightailed it off the set of the last Kajagoogoo video), to this burg, she pityingly notes its plethora of missing-children posters. Little does she realize that not all of these kids are lost; some of them are right here in her new hometown as part of a bare-chested, back-combed, body-pierced, bike-riding clan of engorged vampire stud puppies.

Schumacher takes Anne Rice's notion of vampires as the rock stars of their day and makes a big cheesy meal of it. Kiefer Sutherland, barely able to restrain himself from bursting into a chorus of *Rebel Yell*, is David, the head vampire go-go boy in charge, and as soon as he catches sight of Jason Patric's heavy-lidded vulnerability, he smells fresh meat. David vamps Michael, pulling him into a motorbike duel and enticing him to join his band of after-dark revelers. Facing initial resistance, David sics vampette Star (Jami Gertz at her most sumptuous. How come she never made it? She was always on the verge. In fact, she *was* verge) on his ass. Falling—and who wouldn't—for that lustrous gypsy tangle of hair and that impeccable bone structure, Michael follows Star into David's clutches where he's semi-initiated into the world of the hot, sexy and undead.

"Now you know what we are, now you know what *you are*," mumbles David through mouthfuls of scenery. "You'll never grow old and you'll never die. But you must feed!"

History, meanwhile, is about to be made as the two Coreys collide. Sam, wearing an ensemble so hideous—some manner of paint-spattered, ankle-length jacket—that it seems like a plea for mercy killing, saunters into a comic shop. He's spotted and rightly mocked by two dweebs in fatigues: the brothers Frog, Edgar and Alan (Corey Feldman and the never-heard-from-before-or-since Jamison Newlander). The razzing of Sam ceases when he displays a knowledge of fanboy ephemera. The Frog sibs, enunciating in *Dragnet* monotones, warn the newcomer of Santa Carla's vampire activity. He's skeptical but his attitude changes when he gets a look at his brother. Michael is pale, listless and permanently shielded by dark glasses. But there's something strange about him, too. He's developed a taste for raw meat and, in unguarded moments, he floats free from the grip of gravity. Like Louis in *Interview with the Vampire,* he won't take that last vital step and slake his thirst for human corpuscles. Star feeds him at first, but soon his vampiric tendencies are so developed that he almost takes a chomp out of his little bro before the snarling family pooch intercedes. "You're a creature of the night, Michael. My own brother, a goddam shit-sucking vampire. You wait till Mom finds out," bawls Sam, shaking Michael out of his delirium.

Up to this point, the movie's been careening crazily between the torment and posturing of the macho vamps and the teeny-bop goofing of the Frog boys, with a little of Dianne Wiest's tentative genteel romance with Edward Herrmann's avuncular video-store owner thrown in. Then it all falls apart gloriously. There's squirt guns filled with holy water. There's poison-tipped crucifixes. There's good vampires versus bad vampires. There's an Idiot Twist at the end when Edward Herrmann's avuncular video-store owner turns out to be the patriarchal vampire who wants the twittering Dianne Wiest to be the mother to his extended undead family, creating kind of a bloodsucking Brady Bunch scenario (which, in itself, is a fantastic premise for a movie and here I am just throwing it out there to the wolves). Clearly, another Idiot Twist is required and, luckily, one turns up right on cue courtesy of Barnard Hughes, as Wiest's crusty old pop who drives a truck straight through his living room wall, staking Herrmann in the process. "One thing about living in Santa Carla I never could stomach," he growls, "all the damn vampires."

As I intimated, I was among the bores who cold-shouldered *The Lost Boys* on its maiden voyage, repulsed by its preening hunks and lack of rotting flesh. A decade later, I'd stand in line for a movie as exhilarating and through-the-roof stupid.

A sterling defense on behalf of Old School horror was mounted in *Fright Night* (1985). Wholesome high-schooler Charley (William Ragsdale) becomes consumed by his conviction that the handsome, suave and charming guy

who moved in next door is actually *a vampire.* His attempts to draw out neighbor Jerry (Chris Sarandon) result in Charley being regarded as a strung-out dope fiend possibly on the verge of severe mental burn-out. Only one person believes him, but unfortunately, it's his weirdo gorehound friend Evil Ed (played to the sniveling hilt by that odd little guy Stephen Geoffreys). As it turns out, Jerry the Gent is, indeed, a creature of the night and he quickly inducts Evil Ed into his legion. Charley only knows one place to turn for help: to the campy old ham who used to host the midnight TV horror show, *Fright Night.* But the thesp, Peter Vincent (Roddy McDowall) has been ousted from his spot because the rotten kids just want to see psychos in ski masks hacking up screaming coeds in bikinis. The actor wants nothing to do with this seemingly disturbed kid but finally brings his knowledge of vampire lore to bear on freeing the neighborhood of the ghoul next door. But *not* before Jerry gets to make a hot panting acolyte out of Charley's previously demure girlfriend (Amanda Bearse, from TV's *Married With Children*).

How would you rather die: burning or drowning? It's a tough call, and an almost equally impossible task is choosing between two of the eighties' most puerile vampire vixen teen comedies. Both *Once Bitten* (1985) and *Vamp* (1986) star *dames grande* enough to know better: Lauren Hutton in the first, Grace Jones in the other. The first features one guy (Jim Carrey) who should be funny, but isn't. The second features two guys (Chris Makepeace, Robert Rusler) who shouldn't be funny, but are. The second loses points for treating Long Duk Dong almost as shabbily as *Sixteen Candles.* The first gains points by giving Carrey a feisty girlfriend (girlfriend to Hutton: "He doesn't want you because you're evil and mean. He wants me because I'm sweet and nice, so *fuck off!*"). I declare a tie. They both suck.

Hungry Like a Wolf

Teen Werewolf Movies

Huge leaps forward in the field of anthropomorphic technology had been achieved by the time Stephen King's short story "Cycle of the Werewolf" went into production as *Silver Bullet* (1985). We had gazed in awe at man-to-animal transformations in *An American Werewolf in London, The Company of Wolves, The Howling, Wolfen* and even Michael Jackson's *Thriller* video. Which is to say that after making us sit through 90 minutes of little wheelchair-bound Marty (Corey Haim) babbling about how werewolves are tearing up his small town and his blustering Uncle Red (Gary Busey) saying how he doesn't want to hear no more foolish talk about werewolves, you better be ready to show us some *fancy* motherfuckers. The guy in the moth-eaten Wile E. Coyote suit was not worth the preceding emotional investment.

Michael J. Fox made *Teen Wolf* (1985) before *Back to the Future,* but it was released afterwards. Suddenly, he was a media-straddling megastar and, like a cold sore on a first date, this blemish appeared to blight his moment of triumph.

I don't know how far from being a werewolf movie a film with the word *wolf* in its title can actually be, but *Teen Wolf* does a remarkable job in distancing itself from its supposed subject. Its assemblers obviously didn't want to alienate Michael J.'s core sitcom constituency with any upsetting imagery but, hell, they'd seen Tina Yothers in a halter top. After that, everything else was Christmas.

Boo!

Teen Ghost Movies

Idon't know if the term *The Wraith* (1986) immediately springs to mind when you think of Charlie Sheen. He prompts thoughts more along the lines of The Client, The Defendant or The Guy At The Bar Who Wants To Buy You And Your Friend A Drink, You Are Over Eighteen, Aren't You . . . ?

Nevertheless, there he is, a wraith called Jake, materializing mysteriously in a Turbo Interceptor with tinted windows on the outskirts of a small Arizona patch of dirt in the grip of intimidation by Packard (Nick Cassavetes) and his fearsome band of celebrity offspring (including Griffin O'Neal, famous for having his front teeth knocked out by dad, Ryan). Packard's gang get their twisted kicks forcing the locals to take part in chicken races and then stealing their cars.

Jake's Turbo piques the chief hood's interest. The fact that the newcomer seems to be trying to make time with his girlfriend (Sherilyn Fenn) makes him crazy. But Packard's time as arbiter of the fates of others is just about up. His band is quickly being squashed by the sleek Turbo which, no matter how they try to shoot it, stomp on it or set it alight, just keeps on rolling. That's because neither car nor driver are of this world. Jake was killed by Packard's gang a long time ago and now he's back from beyond to even the score. He is . . . the wraith. Nope, something about that still doesn't sound right.

White Zombies

Teen Zombie Movies

Wanna know about movies filled with slack-jawed, hollow-eyed, brain-dead catatonic kids? Well, that's why you bought this book! But as far as films where the zombification process is actually a pertinent subject matter, three titles come to mind. There's the slapstick of Dan O'Bannon's *Return of the Living Dead* (1985) wherein putrefying punks with names like Spider, Scuzz, Trash and Suicide go on a brain-sucking rampage through Louisville. There's the poignancy of *Night Life* (1990) in which a kid called Archie (Scott Grimes) has to contend with his glamorous job helping the local mortician (John Astin). He also has to cope with the fact that the best friend for whom he nurses a deep and gnawing yearning (Cheryl Pollak) is involved with El Sleazo Older Dude. Worst of all, he is the target of torment by a local gang of sneering hoods. Things get better when the bad guys are splattered in a car crash. Ironically, Archie has to tend to their bashed-up bodies. Even more ironically, they come back to semilife. More ironic still, they persecute Archie much more viciously in death than they ever did when they were alive. *Night Life* pulls a double bluff on the Idiot Twist when, after having busted up all the zombies, he's alone with the girl of his dreams and she starts to seem a little slack in the jaw, a little hollow in the eye. Oh shit, she's . . . "Just kidding," she says.

Finally, there's the relatively smart *Night of the Creeps* (1986). Two fraternity pledges, desperate-for-acceptance Chris (Jason Lively) and spunky cripple J.C. (Steve Marshall), are under orders to steal a corpse for a frat party. The stiff they wheel out of the morgue is actually a host to a strain of alien slug that shoots into people's mouths, incubates in their brain and turns them into . . . *the walking dead.* Soon, the campus is infested with zombie jocks. J.C. is among their victims, forcing Chris to replace him with similarly spunky cheerleader Cynthia (Jill Whitlow) and hard-ass campus cop Cameron (Tom Atkins). The latter has the best line in this, or indeed any other teen zombie movie, when he bangs on the door of the sorority house and growls: "Girls, I've got good news and I've got bad news. The good news is, your dates have arrived. The bad news is, they're all dead."

What About Blob?

Teen Blob Movies

Coppola's *Dracula*? Branagh's *Frankenstein*? Forget 'em. For a rousing big budget revival, look no further than Chuck Russell's *Blob* (1988). Blessed with more creative killing capability and a better-developed personality than Jason or Michael Myers, The Blob was a government created and sanctioned glob of carnivorous goo. Watch amazed as the pink stuff engulfs and devours the population of a small town, sucking them down plug holes, through windows, congealing them in their cars and sliming them inside their own protective suits. Watch even more amazed as teen fuckup Kevin Dillon saves the day by freezing The Blob.

Modern Horrors
Contemporary Frightfests

I'm going to scare the hell out of you!" declared Stephen King in the trailer for his simultaneous directorial debut and swan song, *Maximum Overdrive* (1986). Emilio Estevez starred as the ex-con doing his probation as a cook in a North Carolina truckstop when a comet smashes into Earth, turning all mechanical objects into lethal, human-skewering weapons. It starts promisingly with soft-drink dispensers suddenly cannonballing their loads into the skulls of thirsty consumers and kitchen knives hacking up unsuspecting housewives. Then we're back in that truckstop, which is now hemmed in by a circle of growling semis, and King throws the movie away with a bunch of siege-mentality clichés. If you stand there and say you're going to scare the hell out of us, you better be ready to show us dentist drills and power tools and machines *fucking shit up*!

There was more to the eighties than a bunch of limp-dick English synth-pop weenies. Lest we forget . . . *the eighties rocked*! Ozzy bit the heads off bats. Priest in court, suspected of influencing some midwestern kids to blow off their faces. Concerned Christians screwed up perfectly good turntables dragging records backwards in attempts to detect the subliminal commands. Coverdale and Kitaen (the Kurt and Courtney of their day). The mousse. The horned fist salute. The time could not have been righter for a teen horror movie to exploit and ridicule the metal nation and its collision of phalluses and Fundamentalist censors. *Trick or Treat* (1986) is not that movie. Directed by Charles Martin Smith (Terry the Toad from *American Graffiti*), it tells the story of spurned sad sack Eddie (Marc Price, who played Skippy, the spurned sad sack on *Family Ties*). Eddie's only escape from high-school hell is through the screeching racket of Sammi Curr. Sammi promptly drops dead but a friendly DJ (Gene Simmons) gives Eddie a tape of his idol's last, unreleased, recordings. Eddie plays the tape and Sammi (Tony Fields) returns to huge-haired, thunder-crotched life with electricity crackling through his veins and Satanic superpowers that increase in intensity every time he teases a fresh batch of power chords out of his axe. In the beginning, this is good. Sammi throws volts at the bullies who were messing with Eddie. When a televangelist (Ozzy Osbourne, looking like he is about to fall off his chair) rails against the scourge of metal, Sammi reaches inside the TV and fries him. Eddie comes to realize that the resurrected rocker is *evil* and must be stopped. So he flushes him down the toilet. *Trick or Treat* achieved the impossible: it insulted its audience's intelligence. (Shit soundtrack, too, by nonvaunted no-hopers, Fastway.)

"When You Grow Up, Your Heart Dies."

③

The John Hughes Movies

They fuck you up, your mum and dad," wrote grouchy English poet, Philip Larkin. "They may not mean to, but they do." John Hughes was not generous enough to add the qualifying suffix. The string of movies he variously wrote, produced and directed during the eighties were shot through with the explicit understanding that adolescence was too precious a time to be contaminated by the interference of The Enemy Within, a.k.a. Mom and Pop. All representatives of adult authority were characterized in the Hughes canon as cringing, vindictive, foul-smelling, prehistoric, bewildered and spiritually undernourished. But when it came to the progenitors of his protagonists, Hughes let loose the dogs of war. Parents were tyrannical in their expectations. They were criminal in their neglect. They were simpleminded. They were devious. They were archaic in their remove from modern times. They were pathetic in their attempts to acclimate themselves to the new age. In short, they were across-the-board unqualified to shepherd their offspring through the choppy waters of the teen years. That's why

Hughes felt justified stacking the deck in his characters' favor. His teen leads were smarter, hipper, more sensitive, more articulate and, at all times, morally superior to their adult oppressors. They were also almost entirely denizens of an upper-middle-class white-bread world and the agonies which assailed them seemed tame even at the time—no drive-bys, no drug addiction, no physical abuse, no gangs—but the way they were magnified into melodrama made empathy inescapable.

John Hughes was the Phil Spector of the teen movie. He took a bubblegum genre and served it up on a silver platter. There were writers and directors who were responsible for better, funnier, sadder, sweeter and more deeply felt films during the era, but there were none whose signatures were more indelibly scrawled over their output (much as I revere Savage Steve Holland, I'm not about to make grandiose auteur claims on his behalf), there were none whose movies were such diabolical contraptions of contrivance and honest emotion, and there were none who went back to the well so many times.

"High school was not this key point in my life. It wasn't traumatic. Basically, it was over real quick." John Hughes made these statements which, for some reason, remind me of a river in Egypt. Someone who hadn't devoted a few too many hours to brooding over the evil of the cliques separating him from his potential best bud/dream girl would *not* have made these movies. The series of films that started with *Sixteen Candles* and concluded with *Some Kind of Wonderful* are extended exercises in wound licking and "what if?" Maybe the adolescent Hughes never had to remove cleats from his butt or gum from his hair, but he made a tour of duty in the war zone we know as Outside Looking In. He also had no commercial need to churn out teen flicks; he had already earned his spurs penning two hits, *Mr. Mom* and *National Lampoon's Vacation,* the latter being one of the handful of classic nonteen comedies of the last two decades (you've got ten fingers, start counting: *Groundhog Day, A Fish Called Wanda, Spinal Tap* . . . I bet you don't need to pull the other hand out of your pants).

Hughes basically spent the eighties in the inner-demon cleansing business, continually replaying and refining that magical moment when the barriers were removed, the masks fell to the floor and social circumstances were no longer strong enough to separate teen soulmates. What spun his movies into a galaxy of their own was the way he was able to sugar his core of hurt with a variety of flavors culled from early adult life. From his days as a 100-jokes-a-day freelance gag writer came a repertoire that turned every script into a jack-in-the-box, spring loaded with enough zingers to make comparable comedies seem like speech therapy sessions for slow children. From his days as an advertising copywriter came a proficiency with a finely turned epigram. From his days as the editor of *National Lampoon* came a taste for mean-spirited sadism with particular emphasis on the aged, the infirm and anyone of other than American extraction. Add a glutinous dosage of sentimentality to the mix and you've got a combination guaranteed to induce heartburn and despair outside the target area.

Hughes' unwieldy stew of influences made for some mood-swinging movies that occasionally defied both credulity and goodwill (what's up with that *Ferris Bueller* scene where Cameron kicks his dad's Ferrari out the window? And *The Breakfast Club*'s dance sequence?). Teen audiences, though, willingly spooned up the argot, the angst, the fluorescent checkerboard apparel and the wall-to-wall, every-second-blaring, Anglo synth-weenie dominated sound track. Above all, they went wild for the casts, many of whom were performing at the absolute pinnacle of what were often very limited capabilities. Most of these kids may have been self-regarding little monsters, they may have been pumped full of drugs and they may have deserved their subsequent rapid declines in popularity (speaking of which, if you factor in Macaulay Culkin's personal problems and the premature death of John Candy, you could construct a serviceable Curse of Hughes conspiracy theory). But then you look at a dud romantic comedy like the 1995 remake of *Sabrina,* knowing it was made by consummate professionals, and you think, None of these people believe a word they're saying. You go back to the Hughes movies and the actors are delivering his lines like they're bringing the tablets down from the mountain.

A decade after its release, you've got Courtney Love in *Spin,* trumpeting *The Breakfast Club* as "the defining moment of the 'alternative' generation." You've got Sponge in the Buzz Bin with "Molly (Sixteen Candles)" (even though they swear it's not about La Ringwald). You've got the novels *Boy Culture* (by Matthew Rettenmund) and *Our Noise* (by Jeff Gomez) referencing *The Breakfast Club* as a significant teenage touchstone ("Back then, it was the closest thing we had to Virtual Reality," writes Gomez). You've even got the *Weird Science* syndicated TV show. Okay, I know it's not a Lifetime Achievement Award from the Academy, but it's something of an indication that the Hughes movies seeped into the consciousness of their intended audience and that their influence continues to be felt. The six films that follow contain moments of heart-pulping pathos, moments of pig-brained stupidity, moments of sniveling self-pity and moments of unmatchable cruelty, all of which often occur in the same scene. They also contain evocations of adolescence so affectionate that they cause to you to fall into step with their author's view that the subsequent years are all downhill.

How does Molly Ringwald express mortification? Let me count the ways. The rolling of the eyes. The chewing of the lips. The appalled exhalation. The jaw dropping in disbelief. The flinching. The lowering of the head signifying a wish to be swallowed up by the earth. *Sixteen Candles* (1984) martyred the flame-haired freckle-face many times over but it also acted as her coronation as Crown Princess of teen flicks.

In this first collaboration between director and muse, Ringwald stars as Samantha Baker, who wakes up on the morning of her 16th birthday dispirited to find that no major physical changes have transformed her into a big-boobed babe. "You need four inches of bod and a great birthday," she mutters, descending the stairs to face her family and the fuss she's sure they're going to make of her on this, her special day. But Samantha's birthday occurs the day before her sister Ginny's wedding to Rudy the bohunk and the entire household is focused on the upcoming nuptials. Sam's 16th causes not a ripple, not a mention. Nothing. Nada. Zero. Zip. She stares disbelievingly at her mother (Carlin Glynn), who's packing her off to school without so much as a packed lunch, "Don't give me that pouty look of yours," sighs Mrs. Baker. Sam is appalled; "I can't believe this. They fucking forgot my birthday."

Her appalled disbelief will get an exhausting workout as the day wears on. First, she scrawls her desire for sensitive hunk Jake Ryan (Michael Schoeffling, kind of a marked-down Matt Dillon) on a confidential sex survey note, which will find its way into his possession. Turns out he's noticed her interest in him and mentions to a gym colleague that he might reciprocate. "She's obviously too young to party serious," scoffs the jock. "Maybe I'm interested in more than a party," says Jake wistfully. Standing in the girls' locker room, Sam stares miserably at the womanly fullness of Jake's prom-queen girlfriend, Caroline (Haviland Morris), knowing she couldn't come within the same universe of desirability. But, on the noxious voyage of misery that constitutes the school bus ride home, Sam attracts the unwanted attention of someone whose heart beats a little faster when he sees her flinch. The ominous four-note *Dragnet* theme acts as a stunning introduction to a character sometimes called Ted but universally renowned and reviled as the Geek (Anthony Michael Hall). Pint-sized and pale-faced, his barely-formed features dominated by a huge pair of sheepish eyes, the Geek plants himself in the seat next to hers and starts sniffing her. "What's the story," he attempts to drawl, "You got a guy?" She turns on him. "Three big ones and they lust wimp blood so quit bugging me or I'll sic them all over your wienie ass."

Just as the *Dragnet* theme heralded the approach of the Geek, once Samantha gets home, the familiar tinkling tones of the *Twilight Zone* signature tune indicate that the comfortable and familiar is about to get uncomfortable and strange. Grandparents! Two sets of grandparents have occupied the Baker home for the wedding. The first set are unsightly in their underwear and their litany of ailments. They show no sign of remembering her birthday. As they're sleeping in her room, she flees to be assailed by the second set. "She's gotten her boobies . . . *and they are so perky!*" exults her grandmother, reaching out a grasping pair of hands to meet the new arrivals. Sheltering in her brother Mike's room, she moans, "I can't believe my grandmother actually felt me up." Suddenly, an Asian head looks down from the bed above. It's Long Duk Dong (Gedde Watanabe). You may think this Chinese exchange student with his decimated English is the most disgraceful stereotype perpetrated since the days of Stepin Fetchit, or you may reason that Hughes deals with many other Caucasian characters—the grandparents, Sam's narcissistic sister Ginny (Blanche Baker), her bohunk fiancé and his seemingly Mob-tied family, the girl in the neck brace (Joan Cusack) and the Geek's techno-loser buddies—with equal malevolence. Whichever side you take, there's no denying that moments like the one where a grandparent is gleefully recounting Dong's many uses as an indentured servant, the one where the suburban Baker kids are openly giggling at the foreigner's attempt to enunciate and the one where little brother Mike (Justin Henry) tells his mother to

"When You Grow Up, Your Heart Dies."

boil the sheets and the mattress after Dong's gone, grace the film like melanomas on an otherwise unmarked visage.

Sam's unhappy birthday continues to get worse. At a school dance, the Geek tells his bizarre friends Bryce (John Cusack) and Cliff (Darren Harris) that by the time the night is over, he and Sam will interface. Oblivious to his machinations, Sam gazes mistily at Jake who is slow-dancing with Caroline to Spandau Ballet's "True." Suddenly, shockingly, he looks up from the goddess in his arms; staring straight into Sam's eyes, his lips form something of a smile. That's the exact moment the Geek chooses to make his move. Throwing himself in front of Sam, he launches into a hip-shaking, crotch-thrusting frenzy. She withstands a few seconds of his convulsions then, overcome with mortification, rushes off and slumps down in the school corridors, overcome with sobs. Bryce and Cliff mock the Geek's rejection but he's cool: "Don't spazz out . . . the situation'll come online." They demand proof that he can get even the time of day from Sam. They demand underpants. He takes their challenge and saunters off, his confidence shattered by their specification: "*Girl's* underpants." His confidence is further eroded when he is approached by Jake who, as a jock, is known to pound nerds like him. But Jake wants to know about the girl the Geek was dancing with. Reverting to professional evaluator of female potential, the Geek sums up Sam: "Smallish tits, decent voice, smells pretty good, she drives me crazy."

Sam sits disconsolately in the body of a car in the school workshop. The Geek shatters her solitude and attempts to apologize for humiliating her ("I had no idea you couldn't dance"). She finds herself confiding in him about her birthday. He's sympathetic: "I'd freak if my family forgot my birthday." Touched by her vulnerability and willingness to interact with him on a sort of human level, he says, "Would you feel better if you knew one of my secrets?" She looks dubious, but he carries on, "This information can not leave this room, ok? It would devastate my reputation as a dude." He pauses before delivering the astonishing truth: "I've never bagged a babe. I'm not a stud." She shrieks with laughter, then shows him a little sympathy. He takes the opportunity to attempt to mount her. She swats him away and when he asks if it would be totally off the wall for her to have sex with him, she flushes and confides in him. "Your asking me is not as off the wall as why I won't." She explains she's saving herself for Jake. The Geek freaks: "Jake's my boy! . . . He asked me about you." Sam explodes with happiness. She can't believe it. She's about to rush off and put herself in his line of vision when the Geek asks to borrow her panties, so he can hold his head up around his dipshit friends. Seconds later, freshmen are paying a buck a shot to get a peek at her undies.

While the lovely Caroline is rounding up a posse of favored seniors for a party at Jake's place—his parents are away for the weekend—Sam is working up the nerve to talk to him. Just as he notices her, she crumbles and melts away. "I can't believe

I'm such a jerk," she berates herself. "I can't believe I gave my panties to a geek." That night, while she's trying to sleep on the sofa, her father (Paul Dooley) comes down to apologize for missing her birthday. Seeing something else is wrong, he presses her to unburden herself. She wails out her misery over Jake. "It just hurts," she wails. "That's why they call them crushes," he reasons. At the same time, Jake, while sifting through the wreckage of his party-strafed home, finds the Geek stored under a glass coffee table. They talk jock-to-dweeb about his disaffection with Caroline: "She's beautiful and she's built and all that but I'm not interested anymore . . . I want a serious girlfriend, somebody I can love that's gonna love me back." They make a swap, Jake gets Sam's panties, the Geek gets to drive Caroline home in Jake's dad's Rolls Royce. She's so blitzed she doesn't know where she is, but suddenly turns playful, and after stuffing birth-control pills down his throat drops her head down into the Geek's lap and breathes "I love you." He stares straight at us: "This is getting good."

The day of the wedding arrives. Sam's sister Ginny gets her monthly bill a little early and has sedated herself with several fistfuls of muscle relaxants, thus reducing her to a limbless, giggling, uncoordinated mass of Jell-O. Caroline wakes up in Jake's car outside the church and next to a freshman wearing head gear the size of a TV aerial. It seems they did it. But did she enjoy it? "I have this weird feeling I did." Jake races to the Baker household where the hungover Long Duk Dong tells him Sam's marrying an oily bohunk. At the church, Ginny can't even make it down the aisle. "You know what I liked best," Caroline tells the Geek, "waking up in your arms." They kiss at the very moment Jake appears outside the church. He makes a clean break with Caroline and is there to pick up Sam and give her back her panties. That night, sitting on the dining table, a birthday cake between them, they celebrate Sam's Sweet 16th. "Make a wish," he tells her. "It already came true," she whispers.

Not until *Natural Born Killers* came along did a movie devote so much open affection to its central characters while being so consistently contemptuous of all those around them. John Hughes leads Molly Ringwald through *Sixteen Candles* like a devoted dad proudly but protectively displaying his daughter. He treats Anthony Michael Hall like a freak until the moment his character and Ringwald's bond in the body of a car. Thereafter, Hughes switches gears, bundling up the rest of the film in a pink ribbon and gifting it to Hall. Despite the Long Duk Dong dilemma and Hughes' inability to provide a big rousing laugh-packed climax—the wedding scene should go off all-guns-blazing, instead it barely raises a titter—the movie confirms its creator as a Spy in the House of Teen. Its finest scene—the Ringwald/Hall bonding session—also paved the way for the enforced social intercourse that would characterize his next feature.

Saturday, March 24, 1984,
Shermer High School
Shermer, Illinois 60062
Dear Mr. Vernon,
We accept the fact that we had to sacrifice a whole Saturday in detention for whatever it was we did wrong—and what we did was wrong—but we think you're crazy to make us write an essay telling you who we think we are. What do you care? You see us as you want to see us: in the simplest terms and the most convenient definitions. You see us as a brain, an athlete, a basketcase, a princess and a criminal. Correct? That's the way we saw each other at 7 o'clock this morning. We were brainwashed."

The portentous boom of Simple Minds' bass drum over the Universal logo, followed by the introductory quote from eminent philosopher David Bowie (" . . . and these children that you spit on/as they try to change their worlds/are immune to your consultation./They're quite aware what they're going through") tipped cinemagoers the wink that what was to follow was not another soundtrack-shilling bout of high school high jinks but Something Special. In *Sixteen Candles,* Hughes displayed a David Attenborough–style delight in excavating and exhibiting the teen tribes secreted in suburbia. In *The Breakfast Club* (1985) he continued his anthropological theme, this time enclosing a quintet of representatives from disparate social groupings in a controlled environment, delving beneath the tribal markings in search of an underlying common humanity. In his choice of lab rats, he was well served. Anthony Michael Hall is Brian, the nervous, pale, gangly (Hall had sprouted a good three inches since *Sixteen Candles*) anal brain. Molly Ringwald, fetching in a soft leather and suede ensemble, is Claire, the envied, despised and desired, popular, privileged Daddy's girl with a repressed yearning to Be Bad. Emilio Estevez is Andrew, the buff, baffled varsity wrestler. Ally Sheedy is Alison, witchily sexy in a grunge-prescient bundle of baggy, shapeless sweaters and scarves, face obscured by a collapsed spiderweb of hair, almost autistic in her repertoire of tics and unfathomable actions. Then there's Judd Nelson as John Bender, the Iceman, the antagonist, the instigator, the agent provocateur, the swaggering, sneering bad boy "full of dick and penis and scrotum and testicle" (Courtney Love again) who masks his vulnerability by lashing out at others before they can pour scorn on his innate sensitivity. Their captor for this nine-hour sentence of educational servitude is Dean of Students Richard Vernon (Paul Gleason), the embodiment of all that is rotten, decaying and worthless in adulthood.

As soon as the library door swings shut behind Vernon, the battle lines are drawn. The two good kids, Claire and Andrew, sit together bemoaning the unfairness of their sentence. Bender the big-cocked wild-side denizen (but what's up with that Madness pin?) pushes Brian the wiener off his seat just to establish his no-quarter-given, no-shit-taken credo from the start. Alison the weird girl sits at the back engulfed in her voluminous parka. They may have ridden out the entire period of detention as islands unto themselves but for Bender's obnoxious attempts to stir up some communal bullshit. He's cut dead, first by Claire, which has the effect of sparking an ache for her that he tries to mask as hatred, then by Andrew, who tells him, "Bender . . . you may as well not even exist at this school." This has the effect of unleashing Bender's inner Incredible Hulk, a confrontation-craving beast, hell-bent on taunting and humiliating his cellmates. He sprays derision at

Andrew ("I wanna be just like you. I figure all I need's a lobotomy and some tights.") and Brian ("Dork, you are a parent's wet dream . . . neo-maxi-zoom-dweebie."). He reserves the heavy artillery in his splenetic arsenal for Claire. "Claire . . . It's a fat girl's name. . . . I can see you really pushing maximum density." She gives him the finger and he revels in her reaction. "Obscene finger gestures from such a pristine girl." She makes the mistake of indicating that she might not be so pristine. "Are you a virgin? I bet a million dollars that you are," singsongs Bender, launching into the sort of panty-moistening mockery for which the Artist Formerly Known as Prince was once justly famed. "Have you ever been felt up over the bra, under the blouse, shoes off, hoping to God that your parents don't walk in, over the panties, no bra, blouse unbuttoned, Calvins in a ball on the front seat past eleven on a school night . . . ?"

It is Bender who dictates the movie's inexorable direction when he asks Claire, "Who do you like better, your old man or your mom?" to which she replies, "Neither, they're both screwed." The seed of this parental probing will flower further when Bender is riffing on his colleagues' lunch selections. He sneers at Claire's sushi box ("You won't accept a guy's tongue in your mouth and you're gonna eat that?"), Andrew's healthy-as-a-horse choice, Alison's Cap'n Crunch and Pixie Stix sandwich, and then he zeroes in on Brian. "Soup, apple juice, p b and j with the crusts cut off. . . . Did your mom marry Mr. Rogers?" Bender launches unbidden into an impersonation of the happy family life of Brian. "What about *your* family?" asks Andrew. Synthesized storm clouds gather on the soundtrack. Audiences shrank back in their seats as if Jason was about to hack his way through the door. But something far more fearsome was about to occur. We were about to get a glimpse of the Bender beneath the bluster. "Stupid, worthless, no good, goddamn freeloading son-of-a-bitch, retarded big-mouth know-it-all asshole jerk," he thunders in the assumed tones of Bender *père.* "What about you, Dad?" he then yelps, reverting to the voice of blameless Johnny B., flinching like he's recoiling from a blow. Andrew expresses some skepticism. "You don't believe me?" Bender rolls up his sleeve to reveal a discoloration.

"It's about the size of a cigar . . . this is what you get in my house when you spill the paint in the garage." And so, the once-smirking punk becomes the first of the five to reveal his true colors.

Once his colleagues have partaken of Bender's doobage ("Yo, wastoid, you're not gonna blaze up in here," objects Andrew, but his protestations quickly go up in smoke), they, too, join him on the island of exposed emotions. "My home life is unsatisfying," reveals Alison, whose witchy weirdness turns out to be a defense erected after years of being ignored by her parents. She also claims to be a nymphomaniac, which inspires a dissection of the sexuality of the lovely Claire. Is she experienced or unsullied? "It's kind of a double-edged sword," postulates Alison. "If you say you haven't, you're a prude. If you say you have, you're a slut! It's a trap. You want to but you can't, and when you do you wish you didn't. . . .or are you a tease?" "She's a tease," says Andrew flatly, prompting a classic Ringwald reaction shot of open-mouthed mortification. "Sex is your weapon. . . . You use it to get respect." The leering Bender twists the knife: "Are you medically frigid, or is it psychological?" Claire is suddenly faced by a baying mob demanding to know, is she or isn't she, has she or hasn't she? "No!" she shrieks. "I never did it!" "I never did it, either," murmurs Alison with crack comic timing. "I'm not a nymphomaniac, I'm a compulsive liar." Going on to reveal some of the longing beneath the layers, she whispers, "I would do it, though. If you love someone, it's okay. . . ."

Andrew leaps into the pit of revelation, explaining the reason for his Saturday morning imprisonment. "I taped Larry Lester's buns together. . . . You know how hairy he is? Well, when they pulled the tape off, most of the hair came off, and some skin, too. . . . The bizarre thing is, I did it for my old man. . . . I got the feeling that he was disappointed that I never cut loose. . . . When I was sitting in Vernon's office, all I could think about was Larry's father and Larry having to go home and explain what happened to him and the humiliation, the fucking humiliation he must have felt, it must have been unreal. I mean, how do you apologize for something like that? There's no way. It's all because of me and my old man. My god,

I fucking hate him. 'Andrew you've got to be number one! . . . Win! Win! Win!' You son of a bitch. . . . I wish my knee would give." This inspires Brian to tell his traumatic story of how he failed to make the ceramic elephant-lamp that was his shop project light up.

The impediments to their intimacy seem to have broken down. They've been stoned and stupid in front of each other. They've confessed and sympathized. But they're not out of the woods yet. The group are whimsically discussing their special talents ("I can tape all your buns together!" declares Andrew, obviously having forgotten his earlier contrition), when Bender ominously hisses, "I wanna see what Claire can do." She's hesitant, but her newfound friends encourage her to demonstrate her hidden skill. She sticks her lipstick down into her cleavage, drops her head then looks up, lips newly reddened. The subsequent appreciative laughter is curdled by Bender's sneering, slow handclap. "My image of you is totally blown." The others turn on him. "What do you care?" he bleats. "I may as well not even exist at this school." Claire tearfully tells him she has just as many feelings as he does. Big mistake. Huge. *No one* has as many feelings as Bender. "You're so pathetic," he rages, a nostril-flaring, finger-stabbing, eye-popping riot of insecurity, self-loathing and adoration, "Don't you ever, ever compare yourself to me. . . . I like those earrings, Claire. Are those real diamonds? Did you work for the money for those earrings? Or did your Daddy buy them for you? . . . Do you know what I got for Christmas this year? It was a banner fucking year at the old Bender family. I got a carton of cigarettes. The old man grabbed me and said, 'Hey, smoke up, Johnny.'" "My God, are we gonna be like our parents?" wonders the shell-shocked Andrew. And here Alison delivers the line that caused some patrons to insert fingers in ears and la-la loudly till the movie was over and others to wonder if someone had got hold of their secret diaries. "It's unavoidable. It just happens. . . . When you grow up, your heart dies." The neglect, abuse and general wrongheadedness practiced by their heart-free parents has brought these five people closer then they ever imagined they'd be.

But are their emotional bonds tighter than their social ones?

Brian gives voice to the underlying question: "What is gonna happen to us on Monday when we're all together again? I mean, I consider you guys my friends." Claire doubts they'll ever be buddies in a nondetention scenario. Andrew is appalled at her retort but Claire stands firm. The simmering Bender boils over again. "You are a bitch. . . . You don't got the balls to stand up to your friends." Claire tries to pin the hypocrite tag on Bender, telling him that he wouldn't take Alison or Brian to hang out with his burnout cronies. Bender, one last time, goes *berserk.* "Don't you *ever* talk about my friends. You don't know any of my friends and you don't look at any of my friends, and you certainly wouldn't condescend to speak to any of my friends. So you just stick to the things you know—shopping, nail polish, your father's BMW, and your poor, drunk mother in the Caribbean. Just bury your head in the sand and wait for your fucking prom." Brian can't believe what he's hearing. "Then I have to assume that Alison and I are better people than you guys, huh, us weirdos. . . . I just want to tell each of you that I wouldn't do that, I wouldn't and I will not." Claire tells Brian it's different for him because his geek friends look up to her entourage of the wealthy and the genetically favored. "You're so conceited, Claire," laughs Brian. Struck, maybe for the first time, that this might be true, Claire claims that she hates to go along with everything her riends say and that Brian could never understand the incredible pressure of being popular. Brian begins to blub. "You think I don't understand pressure, Claire. Well, fuck you. Fuck you. . . . I'm here because Mr. Ryan found a gun in my locker. . . . I can't have an F. I can't have it and I know my parents can't have it. Even if I ace the rest of the semester, I'm still only a B." Asked if it was a handgun, Brian sheepishly responds, "It was a flare gun. It went off in my locker." Displaying more of that crack comic timing, Alison jumps in with the reason for her presence at detention: "I didn't have anything better to do."

This diffuses the tension. Unfortunately, it diffuses it to the degree that Hughes sticks in a completely spurious dance montage showing off the kids' syncopation and soloing skills. A mollified Bender returns to the storeroom where Vernon had banished him earlier. Claire, demonstrating the power of popularity, persuades Brian to write the detention essay for the whole group. Then she takes a long, hard look at Alison. What follows is the scene that sickened those in the audience who nodded tearfully at the truth of "When you grow up, your heart dies." This is the moment where Claire uses her innate knowledge of accessorizing and cosmetics to effect a makeover on Alison, revealing that the ugly-duckling swaddling was hiding a swan. As much as Bender's histrionics chafe, the remaking of Alison stands as *The Breakfast Club*'s biggest blunder. Before, she was a unique and unnerving character. After, she was just another simpering, pretty high-school girl with the hots for a jock. You may think you hate Courtney Love but imagine how cheated you'd feel if she cleaned up her act. The effect here is similar. As angelic synthesizers flung lilies in her path, the newly prettied-up, hair-in-a-bow, clean-white-blouse-wearing Alison presented herself to the gawking Andrew. As this coupling is occurring, Claire sneaks into the faculty office with a filthy look in her eyes. She approaches the transfixed Bender and kisses his neck. "Why'd you do that?" he mutters, "'Cause I knew you wouldn't," she says, smiling.

Back in the library, Alison and Andrew make out while Brian slaves over the essay. Claire removes one of the earrings that were the cause of a previous Bender explosion and gives it to him. "You know you said before how your parents use you to get back at each other," he says, "Wouldn't I be outstanding in that capacity?" And so they go into the cold afternoon, Alison and Andrew, Bender and Claire, Brian by himself but with the satisfaction of having recorded their epiphany that there's more to them than just simplistic definitions.

"Dear Mr. Vernon,
We accept the fact that we had to sacrifice a whole Saturday for whatever it was you thought we did wrong, but we think you're crazy to make us write an essay on who we think we are. You see us as you want to see us, in the simplest terms and the most convenient defini-

tions. But what we found out is that each one of us is a brain and an athlete, a basket case, a princess and a criminal. Does that answer your question?
Sincerely yours,
The Breakfast Club"

What an overwrought, exasperating film. Parts of *The Breakfast Club* ring so true that you'd swear John Hughes was editing in footage from security cameras. Other parts ("Smoke up, Johnny") are like an eternity trapped in dinner-theater purgatory. Though the movie's detractors, of whom there are, I believe, several, cite *The Breakfast Club*'s wholesale dumping on parents as the root of all adolescent afflictions as a grotesque example of pandering, I accepted it with ease. It's not like the film takes place in a holding cell with dealers, terrorists and serial killers bonding and blaming their parents (which is, in itself, a fantastic premise for a movie, and here I am just throwing it out there to the wolves). The Shermer High Five are buckling under angst which can be credibly attributed to the impossibly high—or low—expectations of their folks. Obviously, much more problematic is the way they express that angst. Judd Nelson's Bender is the train pulling the movie and it's his bombast that most *Breakfast Club* critics recall when they reach for the Mylanta.

Though his opening scene's obnoxiousness was entirely entertaining, he was the only one of the group whose descent into self-pity elicited no sympathy. When Emilio Estevez and, especially, Anthony Michael Hall opened themselves up to public scrutiny, few viewers could have failed to succumb to the sob rising in their throats (and if you did, apparently your heart had died). Didn't we know people just like that? Weren't *we* people like that? And if we weren't, wouldn't we be nice to them if we ever came into contact with them?

Had Hughes, ever ecologically minded in the recycling of his plots, been fully attuned to the desires of his audience, he would have whipped out a *Breakfast Club 2: Monday Morning* sequel in time for the next semester. This is a movie that screamed out for a follow-up episode, because even though it froze on Bender triumphantly punching the air, who *really* believed his relationship with Claire could get over his insecurity and the peer pressure of her friends (I know that's what *Pretty in Pink* and *Some Kind of Wonderful* were both about, but still . . .)? And would Alison really have ditched her old, weird ways? A decade later, I'm still guessing. As riddled with faults as it undoubtedly is (I mean, they just start *dancing* . . .), *The Breakfast Club* featured the best work that any of its cast would ever do and it stands as maybe the most powerful example of its genre.

So what do you little maniacs want to do first?" purrs *Weird Science* (1985)'s Lisa, the mainframe genie magicked up by Gary and Wyatt, the two computer geeks desirous of something to fill the void in their thrillfree lives. Seconds later, Lisa's in the shower and so are Gary and Wyatt, pressed up against each other, standing in their shorts, gazing dumbfounded at the lush acreage of fabulous womanhood undulating inches away from them. They are not alone in their discomfort; John Hughes is also in that shower in his shorts, utterly confounded by his creation.

No one is better than Hughes for wringing comedy out of mundanity. Think of the way he strip mined ordinary circumstances for slapstick in *Planes, Trains & Automobiles, Home Alone* and the *Vacation* movies. Remember that extended scene of boredom in the early stretches of *The Breakfast Club*? Judd Nelson sets fire to his boot and lights his cigarette off the flame. Anthony Michael Hall shifts his crotch then suctions his pen top to his upper lip. Emilio Estevez plays with the hood of his sweatshirt. Ally Sheedy wraps a thread around her finger, cutting off the circulation, then sketches a landscape which she decorates with a dandruff sandstorm. Removed from the everyday world, Hughes starts to struggle. *Weird Science* is glaring testimony to the limited workings of his imagination. "I want her to live. I want her to breathe. I want her to aerobicize!" declares hormonally imploding Gary (Anthony Michael Hall—still growing) of the perfect woman he and timorous accomplice Wyatt (gravel-voiced Ian Mitchell-Smith) are creating from input as varied as the shape of a centerfold, the brain of Einstein, the ingenuity of Houdini and the ironic cool—remember this is 1985—of David Lee Roth. The duo jack their computer up to a Barbie doll, strap a pair of bras round their heads and are rewarded by a freak electrical storm that amazingly gives life to their addled notion.

The result is Lisa (Kelly Le Brock, acting with her lips), the Hot Sex Bomb as Fairy Godmother. They've created a monster, but they don't know what to do with her, so she makes it her mission to bring popularity to her stumbling, mumbling mentors. She changes their geekwear to sharp duds, morphs their clanking excuses for cars into chick magnets, then works on instilling some confidence into the quaking pair. This first step on this journey involves a scene that became teen movie de rigeur ever since the *Animal House* boys foolishly dropped in unannounced on Otis Day and The Knights. Lisa takes Gary and Wyatt to a down-and-dirty blues dive where, of course, on their entrance, the music ceases and every mostly black head turns their way. "What's a beautiful broad like you doing with a *malaca* like this?" demands one of the pimp-attired regulars, seeing Lisa with the uncomfortable Gary. "It's purely sexual," she replies, breaking the tension. This paves the way for Hall to reprise the Mudbone impersonation he debuted in *The Breakfast Club,* only this time at excruciating length.

Soon Lisa teaches the still-timid Wyatt how to kiss with his mouth open and delivers a stirring squeeze to his hitherto untouched buttcheeks while doing so. She also takes vengeful note of the way his vicious militiaman brother Chet (Bill Paxton, broader than Broadway) knocks him about. She even allows herself to be flaunted as a sex toy to score points off the boys' high-school tormentors, Ian and Max (Roberts Rusler and Downey Jr.) when the smirking studs follow her like puppies only to see her slide into Gary's car and submit to his slobbers. "She likes the rough stuff, what can I do?" He shrugs at them, savoring the sound their jaws make as they hit the curb. Lisa's outstanding contribution to the establishment of her creators' self-esteem comes with her decision to throw a big, loud, wild bash. Wyatt whimpers that he doesn't want a party in his house—his parents are, of course, away for the weekend. She tells him, "If you want to be a party animal, you have to learn to live in the jungle." Then, in the movie's one flat-out funny scene, she goes to pick up Gary and confronts his par-ents, coming on smug and obnoxious like a female Ferris Bueller as dressed by Retail Slut. "I've whipped up this nasty little soiree," she tells Gary's aghast dad. "Sex, drugs, rock 'n' roll, chips, dips, chains, whips, a couple of hundred high-school kids running round in their underwear." When dad objects to her presence and goes to call the cops, she pulls a gun on him before escorting Gary out the house and wiping his parents' memory circuits.

In a genre where interminable party scenes are a requirement, *Weird Science* boasts maybe the most murderous and endless party scene of them all. A million and one ideas that probably snapped, crackled and popped on the printed page entirely fail to catch fire on screen. The whole high school converges on Wyatt's house. Ian and Max offer the skinny twits they call girlfriends to Gary and Wyatt in exchange for another perfect woman. They forget to hook up the Barbie doll to the computer and create a nuclear missile instead. Another freak electrical storm causes 8 × 10s to come alive, traps a teen inside the TV and sucks most of the contents of the house up the chimney. Wyatt's crusty grandparents arrive and Lisa puts them in suspended animation and sticks them in the closet. She then ponders the challenge of bringing out Gary and Wyatt's inner strength. This is accomplished by conjuring up a biker gang of raging mutants (*The Road Warrior*'s Vernon Wells and *The Hills Have Eyes'* Michael Berryman among them) to crash the party and scare the kids. The psychos grab Ian and Max's whimpering girlfriends and this, finally, brings the boys to ass-kicking life. "Let me tell you something," snarls Gary. "You don't come into my friend's house, riding your motorcycle, smashing things up. You're going to apologize to all these people." The Mohawk draws a gun but Gary grabs it, pulls out the gun Lisa used on his dad and pushes it into the party crasher's face. "You can leave in peace or you can stay and die," he hisses. "That's my boys," twinkles Lisa. And suddenly, they're men of respect. Not only that, but Ian and Max's two sappy girlfriends, Hilly and Deb, are theirs for the taking. Deb wonders how Gary could ever want her when he's got someone as shatteringly gorgeous as Lisa.

Here's where Hughes pulls out his crayon to underline the movie's message: "Lisa is everything I ever wanted in a girl before I knew what I wanted. If I could do it over again, I'd make her just like you." Wyatt expresses the same sentiments when he kisses Hilly and applies the buttcheek squeeze halfway into the act. Though Lisa's ultimate vengeance on Chet raises a smile—she turns him into a fecal version of Jabba the Hut—*Weird Science,* a film that could have been *this* much fun, is a thudding disappointment. Ironic, then, that a movie whose creator couldn't conjure up sufficient plot to fill ninety minutes of screen time would subsequently become a weekly TV show utilizing and jettisoning multitudes of storylines, almost all of them more ingenious than the source.

Pretty in Pink (1986) is the one that put Molly Ringwald on the cover of *Time.* It's ridiculously sentimental, utterly inconsequential and only a sharp tug on my nostril hairs can bring me quicker to tears. Hughes writes and produces (onetime music-video helmer Howard Deutch directs) another story of social pressures; this time it's poor but honest girl meets rich but backbone-free boy. How impoverished is Ringwald's Andie Walsh? So poor that she *literally* lives on the wrong side of the tracks (one shot of the film shows a train chugging past the Walsh home). She shares this modest accommodation with her defeated, do-nothing dad, Jack (Harry Dean Stanton, looking like he'd wandered onto the wrong set but couldn't muster up the energy to move). "Daddy, wake up," she urges his lifeless husk, "I want you to go see the woman about the job." A vintage slacker, he's skilled at changing the subject. "Is school good?" Andie shakes her head. "It never is." He inquires further, "You been asked to the prom?" A sore point. "No." Trying to perk her up, he says, "Let me see this outfit. Is this your latest creation? . . . What did this cost you?" She beams and says, "Fifteen dollars for the shoes, and I made the rest."

Andie, sadly, has no place in the eighties. Her ability to whip thrift-store samples into a head-turning little number goes unadmired in an environment where designer originals are the only indicators of a person's worth. Worse still, she's forced to attend a school with a built-in ruling class. While the punks and the peasants sniff glue and shoot the shit in the scummy schoolyard, the pampered progeny of the privileged (the "richies") lord it over them. "Where'd you get your clothes," sneer a cabal of richie bitchies in Andie's history class. "Five-and-dime store? Attractive." When her teacher dumps a shitload of extra homework on the harpies as punishment for their unshackled snobbery, Andie pleads for leniency on their behalf. The rich girls *demand* that their punishment be reinstated. They *hate* her.

Andie has further richie irritation in the shape of Steff. It's a shame some carnival act went and christened himself Vanilla Ice because the moniker is much more appropriate to describe the style and stance of James Spader. This actor is the absolute embodiment of smooth cruelty, and he was never more hissably irresistible than in *Pretty in Pink.* Emanating contempt and lassitude from every pore, his Steff seems much less like a high-school student and more like a studio exec cruising the schools for some pliable talent till the whole Heidi Fleiss thing dies down. Leaning back against Andie's crappy car, Steff peers snake-eyed at her from over his shades. "Andie, you look ravishing," he oozes. She freezes like she's trapped by some grotesque predator (which, of course, she is). "I'm talking about more than sex here," he smirks. She tries to get into her car. He waggles his scary tongue at her. "You're a bitch." As she goes, he mocks, "I'd go and see a doctor 'cause that condition of yours could get a lot worse."

On the other side of the coin from Steff's malicious intentions is the hopeless devotion of goofball pipsqueak Duckie Dale (Jon Cryer), who scampers like a puppy by her side, endlessly declaring his fealty ("May I admire you again later today?").

Andie's position as conscientious objector in the class war is about to be put to the test when a rich slice of white meat called Blane (Andrew McCarthy) spots her ambling into school. Her presence makes such a mark on him that he shows up at the grubby New Wave record shop in which she toils after school and tries to act inconspicuous flipping through the racks while the store's trend-damaged owner Iona (Annie

Potts in a not-terribly-hilarious running gag) terrorizes a shoplifter with a staple gun. Andie pretends not to notice Blane pretending not to notice her, but she tenses inside and out when he affects a casual stroll up to the counter, asking her advice on the quality of a Steve Lawrence album. Blane does something even cuter in computer class next day, logging onto her screen and posting a picture of himself. She chews her lips in delight. That night, she lies in bed staring at the phone, begging, "Please call, please, please, please," but only getting the usual 400 messages from Duckie. Finally, Blane ventures into the dark side of the school, coming on as tentative as Hugh Grant in the mosh pit, but summoning up the courage to ask Andie out that Friday night.

The forces of darkness conspire to puncture this potential romance before the date has even taken place. Steff, riven with concern, tells Blane he saw him talking to the redhead with the bee-stung lips. "My best friend's conversing with a mutant . . . it's your life, it's none of my business." Blane, his spine turning into a string of spaghetti, whimpers, "You really don't think she's got something?" Steff shoots him that blank-but-deadly stare. "No, I really don't."

The big night of the date, Duckie, more lovestruck by the second but unable ever to communicate his feelings to Andie in anything other than performing-monkey manner, shoots into the record shop and does a choreographed, down-on-my-knees, gotta-jump-back-and-kiss-myself-one-time, lip sync to Otis Redding's "Try a Little Tenderness." It's a showstopping number and its timing is exactly wrong because Andie has to tell the twerp she can't hang out with him because she's seeing Blane. "You're gonna go out with this guy? He's gonna use your ass and throw you away. I would have died for you. . . ." splutters the Duckman, the foundation of his world crumbling. Andie tries to mollify him. "If I hate him because he's got money, that's the exact same thing as them hating us because we don't." Duckie is not only not mollified, he crosses the fine line that separates childlike from bratty. "I live to like you and I can't like you anymore. So when you get your heart splattered all over hell, and you're feeling really low and dirty, don't run to me to help pump you back up because maybe, for the first time in your life, I won't be there."

For their big date, Blane wants to take Andie to a party smack in the heart of richieville. She's reluctant but he waxes heroic. "If you're above it, I'm above it. . . . We've gotta deal with this." The bash is in the sprawling elegance of Steff's family home (his parents are, of course, in Europe) and is filled to bursting with bored buff blond nazis guzzling Cristal and making out on the stairwell. Andie is well aware she's in enemy territory ("Nice pearls. This isn't a dinner party, honey," hiss some nasty girls). Every time blank-faced Blane opens a door he accidentally exposes Andie to more fleshy decadence. Finally, he stumbles in on Steff, who's rolling around with Andie's history class bête noire, Bennie (Kate Vernon). Steff, relishing the discomfort, insists the miserable pair take a load off. After some moments of being sneered at by Bennie, Andie wants to leave.

Blane is contrite ("I made a mistake. I overestimated my friends") and attempts to make amends by insisting they go somewhere she feels at home. Unfortunately, the dingy cellarful of noise she frequents is now under the ownership of the drunken, bruised and entirely obnoxious ego of the Duckman, whose bitterness and attempts to transfer his wounds drive Blane and Andie into the night. Finally, he offers to take her home, but she asks him to drop her off at Trax (the record store). He tells her it's no trouble to drop her at her door. "Don't you understand," she blurts out, "I don't want you to see where I live, okay?" Just when you think this Blane guy is an empty vessel, he suddenly says the right thing. "If I was in a Turkish prison, I'd have a great time with you." Then he asks her to the prom and it's all over. She kisses him fully and deeply. A moment later, she rushes into the house and screams with joy. Dad, of course, is still up—almost comatose, but still up. "He asked me," she squeals. "You in love?" She gushes, "I think I am. . . . His name's Blane, he's a senior, so beautiful. He's a richie . . . he drives a BMW. I'm not sure they're going to accept me. . . . It's not just his friends, it's my friends, too. It's everybody. I'm just not real secure about it." The old rogue is all understanding. "A good kiss can scramble anybody's brains." Then he turns pensive, "I'm sorry that I'm the one you have to talk to about these things." Andie shrugs off his reference to the mother who abandoned them both: "I'm not. She couldn't have said it any better than you."

But Andie's happiness is set to be short-lived. Steff hauls Blane over the coals for lowering the tone of his get-together. "I thought it was very uncool of you last night. It was way out of order to foist her on the party. Nobody appreciates your sense of humor. In fact, we're all puking from it. . . . If you've got a hard-on for trash, don't take care of it around us." Lowering the boom on Blane, Steff continues, "Your parents, they're really going to be thrilled. I've seen your mother go to work on you, Blane, it's vicious. When Bill and Joyce get through with you, you won't know whether to shit or go sailing. . . . If you want your little piece of low-grade ass, fine, go on and take it, but if you do, you're not gonna have a friend. . . ."

Making out with Andie in the stables of his family's country club, Blane make a stumbling attempt to declare his emancipation from social constrictions. "Corporate families replaced royal families. I'm the crown prince of McDonagh Electrics. . . . I could just tell them all to go to Hell. . . . This is going to happen, OK? I really want this to happen." His panicked eyes tell a different story. Next time he hears from Andie, he's lying on his bed listening to her bewildered voice on his answering machine, wondering why he never answers her calls and if they're still going to the prom.

Compounding her misery is the lurid pink dress her Dad gives her as a prom surprise. "It reminds me so much of your mom," he sighs. "She always wore pink." This pushes Andie over the edge. She accuses her father of deliberately missing job appointments and attacks him for dwelling on the past. "Why can't you just forget her. . . . She's never coming back. . . . I loved her, too, you know, she just didn't love us back. . . . I knew it all along. I mean, when I was five, I felt it. . . . I was fourteen and I knew it, you were fifty and you didn't." This has the effect of shaking dad out of his funk. "Since when is a daughter supposed to know more than her father," he murmurs and then he says—*he actually says*—"I've just been a blind fool."

Andie gets to humble another blind fool when she spots Blane in the corridor. "Why haven't you called me . . . What about prom, Blane?" His eyes dart all over the place. He starts to sweat and fidget. He starts babbling about having had a bad day and getting into trouble for the time they made out in the stables. He even insults her with that old standby "A month ago I asked someone else and I forgot." Andie goes bananas. "You're a liar. You're a filthy fucking no-good liar! You don't have the guts to tell me the truth. . . . You're ashamed to be seen with me. . . . You're terrified your goddamn rich friends won't approve." She beats him about the head and shoulders, then runs off. "Forget about it, man," sympathizes Steff, gleefully. "The girl was, is and will always be nada." Duckie, skulking nearby, overhears this slur and, like an enraged chimp, hurls himself at Steff, flailing away, his love and loyalty returning to the surface.

Andie becomes the embodiment of grace under pressure. She takes Iona's prom dress and the lurid pink gift from her father and, with her artistic bent, converts them into something that is less a garment than a statement: a cool, pink, fuck you, a sexy suit of armor deflecting the stares and sneers she knows will come her way when she walks into the prom . . . *alone!* "I'm just gonna go in, walk in, walk out and come home," she tells her admiring dad, who has, after her lecture, got himself together, put the picture of his wife facedown in the drawer and started hitting the pavement in search of an honest day's work. "I just want them to know they didn't break me."

The self-esteem that was surging through her veins suddenly looks to be leaking out her ass as she draws ever closer to the throbbing beats and squeals of delight signifying prom-in-progress. She stands rooted to the spot, a miserable vision in pink, tempted and tossed aside by a thoughtless rich prick. Just a stupid girl who thought she could rise above her station. And then like a goofball knight in flip-top glasses, the Duckman, resplendent in some sort of rockabilly baroque number, materializes by her side. She rushes, tearfully, to embrace him. "May *I* admire *you*?" she gasps. They take simultaneous deep breaths, summon up some reserves of courage, Duckie says "Let's plow" and they enter the fray.

As originally filmed, *Pretty in Pink* climaxed with Andie and Duckie's triumphant appearance at the prom. They outlooked, outclassed and outdanced everyone there. Their poor but honest moral superiority gnawed deep into the corrupt souls of the richies who were forced to deal with their own worthlessness. Apparently, test audiences balked at this outcome. They wanted to see the poor girl get the rich boy of her dreams. They didn't care about the dignity of the oppressed.

For years, fans of the film have expressed dissatisfaction with the altered outcome, feeling that the wrong guy gets the girl. And I too, empathizing automatically with the lovelorn goofball, thought the Duckman was gypped. But look again at that last scene. Andie and Duckie enter the hall to the accompaniment of OMD's plangent "If You Leave." Blane, who's come by himself, sees them and this motivates him to cut the ties with his Iago. "You buy everything, Steff, but you couldn't buy her and that's what's killing you. . . . She thinks you're shit and deep down you know she's right." Blane leaves the suddenly deflated Steff and approaches the nervous pair. He shakes Duckie's hand like a *mensch*. Then he gazes sadly at Andie. "You don't need me to say I'm sorry." She says, "I'm fine." He looks at her. "Oh well, if that's true, then I'm glad. . . . I believed in you . . . I just didn't believe in me. I love you. Always." And with that, he leaves. Andie doesn't move. Duckie rises to the occasion in one of movie history's great instances of self-sacrifice. "Andie, he came here alone. You're right, he's not like the others. If you don't go to him now, I'm never going to take you to another prom ever again, you hear me? This is an incredibly romantic moment and you're ruining it for me." She throws caution to the wind and rushes out. Which leaves a rueful Duckie, pondering his future solitude . . . for about half a second, till he sees a blond babe (Kristy Swanson) beckoning to him from the dance floor. He mouths "Moi?" She nods, and it's such an improbable occurrence that he breaks the fourth wall and gives us a "You believe this?" look. Out in the parking lot, rain is lashing down on Andie and Blane who are locked in a kiss so powerful and healing that she drops her handbag. And the OMD song is *still* playing. Sorry, there's something in my eye. Look, I'm all for identifying with the underdog, but *this* ending is right up there with the all-time great five-hankie classics.

I have only good things to say about *Pretty in Pink.* Strip away the pastel colors and the hip Brit sound track and it's an old-fashioned romance that functions beautifully. Howard Deutch's hand on the tiller frees the movie from John Hughes' predilection for slapstick and abrupt shifts in mood, making it the most cohesive of all his teen-aimed output. Molly Ringwald may have been saddled with the part of a saint but she dug deep into her armory of pained reactions, flinching, wincing, blushing and gasping with enough conviction to fully merit her brief ascendancy to Everygirl status. Even Annie Potts, whose part is otherwise excess to requirements, has a bright shining moment when she gets to deliver the line that ranks as runner-up to "When you grow up, your heart dies." Made nostalgic by Andie's prom preparations, she sighs. "Why can't we start old and get younger?" Strange to think that a song by a group as seedy and unsentimental as the Psychedelic Furs inspired a film as sweet and sappy as this.

Adamly, Adamowski, Adamson, Adler, Anderson, Bueller . . . Bueller . . . Bueller . . . Bueller . . . Bueller . . ." Just like Bonnie Tyler, the Hughes movies were holding out for a hero. After filling his films with the neglected, the abused, the neurotic, the anal, the demented, the despised, the vulnerable, the lonely and the lost, it was time to roll out a teen Terminator. Hot on the heels of forays into the realms of comedy, drama, science fiction and romance, Hughes went for broke with his *Kane,* his *Godfather,* his *Malcolm X,* his epic: *Ferris Bueller's Day Off* (1986).

In Matthew Broderick's Ferris Bueller, he gives us a mythic figure, an angst-free adolescent brimming, to an almost unbearable degree, with confidence and resilience. Adults and authority figures are, to him, no more than video-game villains vainly attempting to impede his progress to the next level. Not only is he unmarked by the parental pressures that crippled every other kid in the Hughes canon, but he is, in point of fact, a master manipulator of mom and dad. This is borne out in the opening seconds of the movie where his folks fret over his

"When You Grow Up, Your Heart Dies."

still, sweating form. They demand that he spend the day recuperating, much to the chagrin of his embittered he-gets-away-with-everything-it's-not-fair sister Jeannie (pre–nose job Jennifer Grey). "If I was bleeding out my eyes, you guys'd make me go to school," she kvetches. Once the coast is clear, Ferris bounces out of bed, exclaiming, "Incredible. They bought it. One of the worst performances of my career and they never doubted it for a second."

Cranking some cutting-edge Sigue Sigue Sputnik—remember, this is 1986—he makes the camera his confidante, delivering his spiel like a seasoned Borscht Belt traveler. "The key to faking out the parents is the clammy hands. It's a good nonspecific symptom. . . . Fake a stomach cramp and when you're doubled over moaning and wailing, just lick your palms. It's a little childish and stupid, but then, so is high school." He then adopts a demeanor of infomercial sincerity to deliver his justification for bailing. "Life moves pretty fast. If you don't stop and look around once in a while, you could miss it."

This philosophy is in no way shared by his best friend Cameron Frye (Alan Ruck) who is, in every way, Ferris' opposite. Cameron is basically every fucked-up Hughes ensemble staple rolled into one whining ball. He's so hopeless and oppressed, so poleaxed by fear, depression and a myriad of imaginary ailments, he can't even get out of bed. "Pardon my French"' says Ferris, "but Cameron is so tight that if you stuck a lump of coal up his ass, in two weeks you'd have a diamond." Ferris, though, has a Saturn salesman's skill in persuading people around to his point of view and the pale, skinny Cameron, permanently tensed to expect the worst, is soon on board for the big day off.

Ferris has, apparently, stopped to look around on some nine occasions this semester, severely testing the patience and credulity of Dean of Students Edward R. Rooney (Jeffrey Jones, master of the slow burn). This latest bout of absenteeism hits Ed where he lives. "What's so dangerous about a character like Ferris Bueller is that he gives good kids bad ideas," he tells his assistant Grace (dingbat nonpareil Edie McClurg). "He's very popular, Ed," she informs him. "The sportos, motorheads, geeks, sluts, buds, dweebies, wastoids, they all adore him." It's early in the day but Ferris has already established himself as the Bugs to Ed's Fudd, the Road Runner to his Coyote. First, he wipes his attendance record from the dean's files via computer, then he breaks his slinky girlfriend Sloane (Mia Sara, briefly rescuing her career from the wreckage of Ridley Scott's *Legend*) out of the big house.

Lacking a set of wheels ("I asked for a car and I got a computer, how's that for being born under a bad sign?") and unwilling to devalue their day of leisure tooling around in Cameron's piece of shit, Ferris is aroused by the presence of Old Man Frye's vintage Ferrari. "My father loves this car more than life itself," moans Cameron. "A man with priorities so far out of whack doesn't deserve such a fine automobile," retorts the smug felon, easing himself into the driver's seat and shuddering with pleasure. He rolls the vehicle out of its showcase shrine. Cameron is forced to run after the car (whose license plate reads NRVOUS).

"I did not achieve this position in life by having some snot-nosed punk leave my cheese out in the wind," says Rooney, by now fixated on making an example of this fugitive. "Fifteen years from now when he looks back at the ruin his life has become, he's going to remember Edward Rooney."

For his day on the town, Ferris becomes a pitchman for the Chicago Tourist Board, dragging babe and buddy up the Sears Tower, to Wrigley Field, a museum, a swank restaurant (where he pulls his "I'm Abe Frohman, the sausage king of Chicago" prank) and finally to the German-American Appreciation Day parade where he commandeers a float, serenades Cameron with "Danke Schoen" and then leads the thronged city streets in a rousing rendition of "Twist and Shout." Ed Rooney's day does not go so swimmingly. First he nabs the wrong victim ("*Les joux sont faits.* Translation: the game is up. Your ass is mine," he says to the back of someone who turns, reveals *her*-self not to be his prey, regards him with derision, then sucks up a strawful of Pepsi and hoses him down). Then he turns up at the lovely Bueller estate where he loses his shoe in the garden mulch, gets attacked by the family dog and is finally kicked into unconsciousness by Jeannie Bueller, who mistakes him for a prowler.

"When You Grow Up, Your Heart Dies."

Up to this point, *Ferris Bueller* is A Good Time. It totally achieves the two-pronged objectives of the genre: it makes the teenage sector of the audience exult in the triumphs of one of their own and it brings out a twinge of nostalgia in those outside the demographic. But Hughes is fully in the driver's seat, which means that it's only a matter of time before the film goes skidding off the main drag into some uncharted territory. That moment comes when Ferris looks at the odometer and realizes that the friendly parking lot attendants have taken the chariot for a joyride. "Here's where Cameron goes berserk," Ferris tells us. Not just ballistic, Cameron falls into a state of catatonia, during which time Ferris reveals that his motives for press-ganging his friends into his day off were less anarchic than altruistic. "All I wanted to do was give him a good day," says Ferris of the vegetable formerly known as Cameron.

"We're going to graduate in a couple of months and then we'll have the summer. He'll work and I'll work, we'll see each other at night and the weekends. Then he'll go to one school and I'll go to another. Basically, that will be it." Yup, it's "When you get old, your heart dies" time again. Ferris has been attempting to install in his friend the fearlessness and lust for life that runs through his own veins before he stumbles unprepared into the looming, corrupting adult world. And there's something else: "Cameron has never been in love. At least no one's ever been in love with him. If things don't change for him he's going to marry the first person he lays and she is going to treat him like shit, because she will have given him what he has built up in his mind as the end-all, be-all of human existence. She won't respect him, because you can't respect someone who kisses your ass." Jesus, enough already. If that's the case, and it has been in no way alluded to up to this point, why not *have the poor bastard meet a girl?* The madness continues when Cameron stages what appears to be a suicide attempt, letting himself fall into a swimming pool. As the horrified Ferris tries to revive him, Cameron grins, revealing it was all a prank. Immediately, the three friends start splashing around happily in the pool.

Hughes' treatment of the slit-eyed mass of resentment that is Jeannie Bueller is considerably smarter. Hauled into the cop shop on the grounds of making a prank phone call (Ed Rooney scrambled out of the Bueller home as she was reporting his presence), she's sat next to a bleary-eyed substance abuser (Charlie Sheen, throwing himself into the part again). His hoodlum looks and incisive character appraisal ("Your problem is you. You want to spend a little more time dealing with yourself and a little less thinking about your brother") make giggling mush of her.

The Cameron Saga reaches an indigestible climax as he does some primal scouring. "I sort of watched myself from inside. I realized it was ridiculous, worrying, wishing I was dead, all that shit, I'm sick of it. This was the best day of my life." Then he finds that their attempt to reverse the odometer has failed. His father will know he's touched the car! Rather than reduce him to nervous trepidation, the prospect sets him ablaze. "I gotta take a stand. I'm bullshit. I gotta take a stand against him. I am not going to sit on my ass as the events that affect me unfold and determine the course of my life. I'm going to take a stand and I'm going to defend it." With that he lets fly at the car, kicking it, unleashing the pent-up frustration. "Who do you love? Who do you love? You love a car!" Standing back, breathless, he stares at the fender he's just dented. "Good. My father will come home and he'll see what I've done and he'll have to deal with me. I don't care . . . I can't wait to see the look on the bastard's face." Then the car crashes off its stand and rolls out the back of the showroom window, falling to the ground far below. Stunned, the trio survey the wreckage of the formerly sumptuous Ferrari. Ferris quickly volunteers to take the heat for him. But Cameron knows this is his moment, his once in a lifetime. Shot in adoring close-up, he demands his right to take the heat. "I want it and I'm going to take it. When Maurice comes home, he and I will have a little chat. It's cool. It's going to be good." *Free at last! Free at last!* At the risk of repeating myself, why not have the poor bastard meet a girl? That would have been considerably more beneficial to the movie's last-days-of-innocence theme and would have contributed a lot more to Cameron's self-worth than the symbolic destruction of his oppression.

It's a sign of how exasperating a filmmaker John Hughes

often was that he could have audiences antsy and embarrassed in their seats during the whole Psychology of Cameron segment and then set what seemed like a doomed enterprise back on its feet with an exhilarating ending. After ascertaining that Cameron has sprouted a sufficiently hefty set of *cojones* to face the future, Ferris is horrified to find the time is 5:55. Five minutes before his parents get home. He races and leaps over the manicured lawns and rolling back gardens of Chicago suburbia. He makes it to the back door with seconds to spare, grabs under the mat for the key, only to find it in the hand of Ed Rooney. "How does another year of high school sound?" Ferris's reserves of smarm and gift for improvising his way out of tough circumstances both choose this moment to fail him. He's hanging out to dry when . . . "We've been worried sick about you," coos Jeannie Bueller. "Go upstairs and get in bed." She turns to a disbelieving Rooney. "Can you imagine someone as sick as Ferris trying to walk home from the hospital?" She ushers Ferris into the house. "Oh, Mr. Rooney, you left your wallet on the kitchen floor." She nails him with a vicious smirk of victory, tosses the wallet into the mulch and closes the door to hear Rooney's yelps as he's attacked once again by the family mutt. Ferris resumes his prone position nanoseconds before his adoring parents return to make a fuss of him.

As the credits roll, Ed Rooney trudges, bloody, torn and beyond bitter down the plush suburban streets, little realizing his humiliation is not quite over. The school bus draws up alongside him. He stares at it for a long moment before boarding and sitting next to a little girl who offers him a Gummi Bear ("They've been in my pocket. They're real warm and soft."). He looks to the heavens for salvation and is answered by the overhead graffiti: "Rooney eats it." Ferris, a smart-ass to the end, comes out of the bathroom and finds us, the audience, still glued to our seats. "You're still here? It's over, go home."

In *Ferris Bueller,* John Hughes' directorial stance comes perilously close to that of the parent who wants to be your buddy. Consider this: he makes a rowdy, exuberant, bursting-with-energy movie about three kids who skip school to go to a museum. He wants you to root for his leads but also throws in a private worry about their lack of values ("What are you interested in?" says Sloane to Cameron. "Nothing," he says. "Me neither," she says, laughing.). And he spends way, way too long fixating on the Cameron problem. The movie's greatest asset is that planet of charm we call Matthew Broderick.

The Ferris delineated in the original shooting script is a malign cross between J. M. Barrie's printed-page, parent-hating Peter Pan and the young hippy-bashing Johnny Rotten. That version of Ferris stared down the camera and sneered "All the old hippies are full of shit." He smirked, "Some guy whose hair is falling out and whose stomach's hanging over his belt and everything he eats makes him fart, he looks at someone like me and he thinks, 'This kid's young and strong and has a full, rich future ahead of him, what's he got to bitch about?' That's just one reason why I need a day off every now and then." Ferris, as originally written, dangles very close to James Spader territory, but Broderick imbues the character with playfulness. In fact, his exhibition of the lovable side of a potentially loathsome role served as his groundwork when, a decade later, he made his all-singing, all-dancing Broadway debut in *How to Succeed in Business Without Really Trying*, where he was basically playing Ferris Bueller smooth-talking his way up the corporate ladder.

The movie was followed by a spin-off sitcom (with Charlie Schlatter in the title role, and Jennifer Aniston as his sis) which came on hard with the TV Bueller taking a chainsaw to a cardboard stand-up of Matthew Broderick, but quickly expired. Once again, Cameron never got a girl . . .

There are those who fail to concur with my assessment of *Pretty in Pink*'s revised ending being more emotionally satisfying than the climax as written. Principal among them would seem to be John Hughes and Howard Deutch because *Some Kind of Wonderful* (1987), their second collaboration, is The Duckman's Revenge. The setup here initially looks to be a reverse gender *Pretty in Pink*. It even begins, like *Pink*, with a literal allusion to the wrong side of the tracks, only this movie's hero is walking down them, seemingly oblivious to the oncoming locomotive. Batting for Molly Ringwald is Keith (Eric Stoltz, with the same hair color and face full of freckles), the artistically inclined high schooler ill at ease among the rich and vicious. His Duckie is Mary Stuart Masterson's pugnacious tomboy drummer, Watts. Less blank than Andrew McCarthy, Lea Thompson is the seemingly unattainable dreamgirl, Amanda Jones. Unable to replicate James Spader's rarefied air of smoothness but hitting the cruelty function with some force, Craig Sheffer is Andrew Loog Oldham . . . actually, Hughes shelves the Stones references at this point, giving Sheffer's villain the much less ludicrous name Hardy Jenns.

Amanda, sick of Hardy's tomcatting ways, agrees to go out on a date with Keith. Hardy, all smiles, tells Keith (whom he has previously treated with considerably less regard than the shit under his shoes) that the best man won and he'd be honored if, after their big date, he and Amanda would swing by the Jenns palace for a party, his parents being in Europe. Keith later finds out that Hardy is planning to perform drastic reconstructive surgery on him. He also suspects that the lovely Amanda is a pawn in Hardy's game. What he hasn't taken into account is that Amanda is a poor girl accepted into high-school high society by dint of her relationship with Hardy. Now that they're splitsville and she's taken up with the socially invisible Keith, she's being frozen out by the vampires she once called friends. Empowered by his notion of Amanda's treachery, Keith resolves to blow her mind, rock her world and take her on the date of all dates. He withdraws his college fund, accumulated over many years and the subject of his father's every waking thought, from the bank, blowing it on preparations for the big night. Watts instructs him on a vital component of the date *di tutti* dates. "This babe has plenty of battle scars . . . you should consider whether or not you feel you can deliver a kiss that kills." She offers herself as a warm body on which to practice but withdraws when she realizes that what she wants and what he thinks he wants are two different things.

Keith's dad (John Ashton) discovers the college money gone and blows several gaskets. Keith was going to be the one in the family who had the chance to make something of himself. "I'm not gonna go to college," bellows Keith, grabbing his moment. "You're only eighteen," wails dad. "Then I'm nineteen, then

I'm twenty, when does my life belong to *me*?" He then explains his reasoning. "In the eyes of most people around here, I'm a nothing. I want to show this girl that I'm as good as anybody else. . . . Didn't you ever have guys at your school that didn't fit in? . . . Well, I'm one of those guys."

As the date begins with Keith showing up outside Amanda's house in a chauffeur(Watts)-driven Jaguar, it looks like he'll get his wish. But he can't contain himself. He starts making bitter references to the fabulous uptown life she must be used to. She can't believe what a passive-aggressive jerk he's turned out to be and the date looks like a disaster. Watts, for her part, is openly hostile. "Break his heart," she tells Amanda, "I break your face." The father of Keith's skinhead friend Duncan (Elias Koteas) is a security guard at a museum. This is their next stop. Walking through the deserted establishment is Keith's chance to display his sensitive side. "This place is my church," he intones piously. "I can come here and what anybody says about me doesn't matter." He leads her down a corridor at the end of which is Keith's portrait of Amanda, rendered in the ever-popular fluffy-kittens-in-a-basket school of painting.

Gearing up to deliver the coup de grâce, he takes her to the Hollywood Bowl, where they are to be the only occupants. She opens her heart to him. "I'd rather be next to somebody for the wrong reasons than alone for the right ones." He loftily retorts, "I'd rather be right." Righteously steamed, she hisses, "You hypocrite. What's hanging in that museum? My soul? No, it's my face. You're using me to pay back every guy with more money and more power than you." He gives her a pair of diamond earrings (having earlier discovered she'd borrowed her jewelry from the friends who subsequently froze her out), telling her, "It's my future. . . . Every cent I've ever earned." No pressure there. But his not-at-all unselfish act touches something deep inside her, showing her the path that now lies ahead of her. "I hate feeling ashamed, I hate where I'm from, I hate watching my friends get everything their hearts desire. I gave in to that hatred and I turned on what I believed in. I didn't have to. You didn't." Rather than allow her this moment of epiphany, Keith intones pompously, "So you won't do it again." And then, with the enormity of the Hollywood Bowl looming in the background, their lips meet. Watts, her heart thumping beneath her stupid chauffeur's uniform, watches from the cheap seats.

But we're not quite home yet. There's still the question of Hardy's party. The usual moronic romping of the upper-class is in full effect as the nervous couple strolls in. Hardy immediately goes in for the kill. "She's deceptively innocent, isn't she?" he leers to Keith. "Did she do you? . . ." Keith lunges at Hardy, who tells him, "She's the trash, you're just a fool." He commands a suddenly gathered clutch of monied muscle to take Keith outside and break his artistic spirit. "Why don't *you* take me outside," says Keith, causing a flicker of confusion to ripple across Hardy's chiseled face. Amanda puts herself between Hardy and Keith. "What do you want?" He sneers at her. "I want you to beg." And just then, Duncan the skinhead arrives with his posse of psychos, streetfighters and gangbangers. The whole tone of the event changes. Hardy is a craven jelly, mumbling entreaties to Duncan to leave. Keith goes up to him, pauses for a second, preparing you for a punch to the jaw, a knee to the groin, even a killer headbutt. Instead, he mutters, "You're over" and Hardy reels back as if he'd just received all three blows. Amanda goes up to him and slaps him two stinging swats. Ouch. Ouch. He tears up! Score one for moral superiority.

Watts is forced to admit admiration for Amanda. "I'm sorry if I misjudged you." She then walks off into the night. Amanda removes her diamond earrings, returning them to Keith. "I'd rather be right," she says. "It's gonna feel good to stand on my own. . . . In your heart, you wanted to give these to somebody else." Keith finally gets it and goes after the wet-eyed Watts, scooping her up in his arms. "Why didn't you tell me?" he asks, a dumb guy to the end. "You never asked," she retorts. He gives her the earrings and says, "You look good wearing my future."

Now there you've got an ending where poor boy gets poor girl, where the rich kid is crushed by the integrity of the underclass and where the object of desire turns out to have a strong spinal cord. I'm sorry, but *Pretty in Pink* kills this in every way. Maybe because he'd followed his characters almost up to college age, maybe because his dialogue was being delivered by an unattractively self-righteous lead character, but *Some Kind of Wonderful* marked the point where John Hughes' fascination with adolescence hit a brick wall. The movie is far from devoid of highlights. Mary Stuart Masterson never puts a foot wrong (and Hughes resists repeating the Ally Sheedy Mistake by prettying her up) and Maddie Corman is a gas as Keith's snarky sister who refers to her sib as "The human Tater Tot." The picture just seems a little tired. The youthful naiveté was missing and the diamond earring motif was no substitute. It's not hollow enough to stand as proof that, yes, "When you get old, your heart dies," but *Some Kind of Wonderful* definitely marks the end of the innocence.

True Romance

4

Love and Affection, Hopeless Devotion and Unrequited Infatuation

You never thought it could happen to you. You—the rabid consumer of adolescent bacchanalia. You—the avid connoisseur of indiscriminate indulgence. You—the furtive video store habitué responsible for turning movies like *First Turn On, Goin' All the Way, H.O.T.S.* and *First Time* into Kleenex classics of a different kind. What was it that made you change your ways? The sudden, shocked realization that you were an encrusted, engorged affront to decent society? A growing disaffection for panty raids and bestiality gags? Or an aching void within you, crying out for something more, something tender, warm and true? Meaningless sex you could get in any multiplex; you were looking for something that spoke to the shudder of vulnerability within you. You—praying for that special someone to look your way and then dying a thousand red-faced mumbling deaths when they do. You—stuck in suspended animation staring at the phone. You want movies as dumb as you are. But, outside of John Hughes' jurisdiction, classic adolescent romances were less than plentiful in the eighties. What

with the grossouts, the hack-'em-ups, the ensemble psy-
chodramas and the deluge of other subgenres, there wasn't
much space for a couple of people to take the first tentative
steps towards discovering each other.

Anyway, most of the stars of the time were so obviously
stuck on themselves, you couldn't conceive of them fixating
on another. What romantic movies there were usually fixated
on the inflexibility of teen cliques and the havoc wreaked by
peer pressure. Sift through the available selection of what'll-
my-cool-friends-think-if-I-go-out-with-a-freak-like-you
movies and you come across two great young love stories. John
Cusack stars in both of them. In adult life, Cusack's been the
choosiest of actors, his reputation growing as he refuses to acknowledge material with even the merest hint of fluff in its
texture. I for one, however, would be elated if he deigned to
participate, now and then, in a boy-meets-girl movie. After
watching him in these two films, who in the diffident, vaguely

troubled, wary, unreadable constituency among us could have failed to find solace in the thought, "If it can happen to him, it can happen to me . . ."

How would you like to have a sexual encounter so intense it could conceivably change your political views?" The opening credits of *The Sure Thing* (1985)—a long, lingering study of honey-limbed Nicollette Sheridan rising like Venus from the Cali surf, lathering herself down with oil and luxuriating on the sand—reel in the viewer hungry for a towel-flicking feast of jiggling cheerleaders and orgiastic excess. Walter "Gib" Gibson's aforementioned line in getting-ta-know-ya repartee clinches the deal. Then Gib (John Cusack) strikes out, something he's been doing with increasing regularity since the halcyon days of junior high. Director Rob Reiner makes clear his intentions very fast, this is something that looks like your run-of-the-mill teen sex comedy, sounds like your run-of-the-mill teen sex comedy but is actually . . . well, I think we all see where Rob's going. Gib wants to be That Guy, that horny wise-ass from all the other movies, but he's not. His friend Lance (Anthony Edwards) is That Guy, the guy with the beer in one hand and the babe in the other, and now that he's about to relocate to college on the West Coast, he's about to be That Guy squared. Gib, on the other hand, is going to school in New England. "The Ivy League stinks, man," commiserates Lance. "All they got there is these ugly intellectual chicks with Band-Aids on their knees from playing the cello." This turns out to be far from the case. Beer flows, bras snap open and booming systems blast Huey Lewis across the grounds. The good times are being had by all, except for Gib, who's floundering in a sea of confusion and despair. He eats pizza out on a park bench while his fat roomie Jimbo makes the sheets sing. His only faint glimmer of hope comes from the prim allure of Alison Bradbury (Daphne Zuniga), a fellow student in the English class run by the loopy Mrs. Taub (Viveca Lindfors). Returning Gib and Alison's respective essays, Taub makes the perceptive point that Gib is wild and uncoordinated while Alison is overly neat and arid. "Loosen up," cackles the prof. "Sleep when you feel like it not when you think you should. Eat food that is bad for you, at least once in awhile. Have conversations with people whose clothes are not color-coordinated. Make love in a hammock."

Gib is playing football with some other students when Alison and a friend pass by. Watching him watch her, one of his teammates says, "The only way she'd go out with you is through pity." Like so many of us who have taken similar sentiments to be words of encouragement, Gib follows her into the swimming pool, tells her he's flunking English and asks for her help, throwing himself into the water to emphasize the gravity of his predicament. She eventually delves into her minutely detailed schedule to find a window for him. Gib enters her room to find her making mumbling noises of affection to her boyfriend, telling him that she also wants to see him in L.A. this Christmas, but doesn't know how she'll get there. Gib, at this stage unable to refrain from acting like a jerk at inopportune moments, treats the study period as a date. He persuades the protesting Alison to join him up on the library roof. His jerkiness momentarily evaporates as he gazes up at the star-filled sky and displays his interest in astronomy, a fascination he's had since he was six. "You'll never believe what I wanted to be when I was six," says Alison, moved by Gib's unexpected sweet side to talk to him like a real person. "I wanted to be a princess." The sight of her, open and vulnerable in the moonlight, extinguishes Dr. Gib and brings Mr. Jerk scrambling back to the surface. He tries to kiss her, she shoves him away and he hits the ground hard. "Did I hurt you?" she inquires. When he gasps "No," she kicks him in the ribs.

Gib is spending another night eating pizza in the hall while Jimbo hits the skins inside. Then he gets a call from the L.A.-exiled Lance. In an act that defies the boundaries of friendship as we understand it, Lance demands that Gib Christmas with him in California. "There's a certain someone I want you to meet." Lance instructs Gib to retrieve the last postcard he sent. Gib finds himself staring at the pouting mouth and doe eyes of Nicollette Sheridan (her character remains nameless). "You're not going to strike out. . . . She loves sex; she's a sure thing, Gib. A sure thing. Now I don't need to explain the deep significance of those words? I told her all about you, and she's dying to meet you, but you've got to get your ass out here by the twenty-second 'cause she's leaving the next day." The breath needed to expel the word *day* has barely left Lance's mouth before Gib has fixed himself up with a ride to Cali.

He's sharing the car with the happy couple of Mary Anne Webster (Lisa Jane Persky) and Gary Cooper—"But not the Gary Cooper that's dead"—(Tim Robbins) and in the back seat . . . guess who? The frost between Gib and Alison hasn't quite spread to the front seat. "You guys know any show tunes?" asks Gary before he and Mary Anne burst into "The Age of Aquarius." Soon, though, the backseat duo's constant bickering has their peppy hosts tight-lipped and downcast. Gib turns away from Alison's wounding disapproval, lapsing into a fantasy of the experience awaiting him. Picturing himself in a *Miami Vice*–style spacious but spare beachfront property, the suave Virtual Gib mouths insincere compliments to his sure thing who silences his babble with the dream retort: "Gib . . . you want it, I want it. You know *I* want it. You don't have to bullshit me to get it. And even if you do bullshit me, you'll still get it."

This reverie is a far cry from Gib's current reality. In a room at the Knotty Pine Motel, Gary and Mary Anne quiver in misery in their bed as Alison and Gib argue over their sleeping arrangements. She refuses to sleep in the same bed with him. He refuses to leave. She yanks the sheets from the bed, stomping off to sleep on the floor. This disagreement is a breeze compared to the next day's twister. Back in the backseat, Gib's mustering his entire arsenal of That Guy behavior. He's a cheeseball-chomping, beer-shotgunning, belching disgrace. When a carful of similarly stupid travelers moons the Gary & Mary Anne–mobile, Gib emits whoops of pleasure. Alison is disgusted. Her disgust disgusts Gib. He labels her repressed, mocking her lack of spontaneity ("There's a time and a place for spontaneity," is her attempt at a defense) with such ferocity, that she is moved to tug off her bra and flash a truck driver. Moments later, Gary, as the owner of the vehicle, is being charged with indecent exposure and reckless driving. No longer in the mood for show tunes, Gary throws the bickering couples' luggage out of the trunk and speeds off, leaving them stranded in the middle of nowhere.

Communication irrevocably breaks down between the two. Unwilling to spend another second in his pork-rind munching presence, she jumps into the first truck to slow down for her. A matter of seconds elapse before she finds out that the annoying immature jerk she left behind is a paragon of virtue next to the seedy leering road rat with whom she's just thrown in her lot. "Gets lonely on the road . . . you look nice," he hisses, before lunging at the shrieking Alison. And just at that second, Gib leaps from the back of the truck where he was hiding, jumps into the front seat, spooks the driver with a boggle-eyed psycho act and drags Alison to safety. He starts to do an I-told-you-so number, castigating her for leaping into a strange vehicle, when she says, "You make it virtually impossible for anyone to be grateful for anything nice you might have done." He acknowledges the insight. She asks why he got on the back of the truck. He shrugs. "I'm the kind of guy who likes to live on the edge."

Alison soon gets to use a variation on the same phrase when she decides to forego a bus journey to L.A. and accompany the suddenly penniless (too many pork rinds) Gib. They wind up in another hotel room and it's a sign of the armistice between the once-warring pair that Alison now lets Gib teach her the rudiments of shotgunning a can of beer. Tying a towel carefully around her neck, he punctures the base of the can and holds it up to her mouth, she splutters and chokes, dropping the beer and convulsing in laughter and gasps. He offers encouragement and leans over her, wiping beer from her mouth. Their eyes meet in one of those smoldering revelatory stares. He breaks his gaze abruptly and she excuses herself. He goes into the bathroom where he overhears her talking to her boyfriend. This is a sharper dose of reality than a cold shower. Jerkiness rises up in him and he surprises Alison by stomping out of the hotel room in a bad mood, winding up in a cowboy bar where he gratefully succumbs to another fantasy. "Come on, Gib, one more time," begs the sure thing. "It was so good . . . confident, creative. I was overwhelmed, you're a true artist." The interlude fades to be replaced by the company of a couple of lachrymose locals with whom Gib gets sauced. He staggers back to the hotel room and collapses on the bed. Where once Alison would have been revolted, now her face relaxes enough to let that tell-tale smile of tolerance play about her mouth, and like an angel of mercy, she arranges the sheets around him.

The next morning, he's desperate to get out of the hotel room, while she's fussing around, sure she's left something behind. Finally, succumbing to his impatience, she exits the room, leaving her wallet behind. The consequences of this are felt later that night when they sit by the roadside with Alison looking miserable and Gib whining incessantly. It starts to rain. They attempt refuge in a tin shack which quickly reveals itself to be roofless. Next door is a locked trailer. Alison produces a credit card from her bag. Gib says it's not the right tool to pick this kind of lock. "I've got a credit card," she yells, pointedly. Her words sink in. Gib is ecstatic. Then her face falls. "My dad told me specifically I can only use it in case of an emergency." Gib nods. "Maybe one'll come up."

Safely ensconced in a hotel, they wine and dine like a happy couple. She even advances him the money to buy her a rose from the waitress. In their room, sleeping in the same bed for the first time as a consensual experience with neither of them drunk, they're giggly and tentative with each other. Gib asks about Jason, Alison's straight-arrow boyfriend. "Does he make you laugh?" Alison considers her answer. "Jason . . . is everything a girl looks for in a guy." She paints a pretty picture of their life together as partners in law living out in a renovated country house in Vermont, raising basset hounds. "I want to be nice and warm and cozy . . . kind of like this." She sighs. "Guess that sounds kind of tame to you." Gib may be lying next to this girl but he's a million miles away from her. He's simultaneously sure of two things: how much he wants her and how much he could never give her what she wants. "No," he replies, "it sounds nice."

Falling into a final sure-thing fantasy, Gib wanders through the beach house looking for the hot body that's all his. He wanders into the bathroom, spotting a familiar shape in the shower stall. He opens the door and is greeted by Alison's smile. He wakes up to find himself cradling her in his arms. She also wakes and he pulls away quickly, flustered. "You were on my side of the bed, nothing happened." A big 18-wheeler is their transportation for the last leg of the journey. While Alison dozes in the back of the truck, the driver asks Gib what's in California. Gib tells the trucker about his sure thing. The vehicle goes over a bump in the road and Alison overhears the trucker repeating in awe the information Gib provided, that he's traveled 3000 miles to sleep with a girl he's never met. "A no questions asked, no strings attached, no guilt involved . . . a sure thing." While the trucker is inspired enough by this news to put the hammer down, Alison is hurt and disgusted. When the big rig drops them off, she's cold as ice to him, bitterly repeating the "no questions asked, no strings attached, no guilt involved" mantra and hurling her rose back at him.

But even though they're no longer together, each feels the presence of the other in uncomfortable ways. When Alison enters Jason's neat-as-a-pin dorm room, she's immediately aware of how unexciting he is. For Gib's part, meeting Lance at a babe-filled campus party, once the stuff of his desolate dreams, now fills him with wariness and reserve. "Tonight's the first night of the rest of your sex life, Walter Gibson," Lance proclaims. "I'm almost nineteen," Gib bawls back, "maybe I'm getting too old for this." Lance is aghast. "What do you want, a goddamn relationship? Every relationship starts with a one-night stand." Meanwhile, Jason is uncomfortable with the preppie in his room who looks like Alison but is shotgunning beer and belching with delight. He's convinced she's been replaced by a doppelganger when Alison hears the sounds of distant revelers and begs Jason to go to the party. "Let's do something pointless, something totally crazy," she says, echoing a Giblike rant.

The fantasy of the sure thing is now made flesh and Gib is treating her like his maiden aunt, smiling and polite but openly uncomfortable. Then Alison and Jason arrive. Gib comes over all studly, dragging the sarong-clad Sheridan onto the dance floor. Alison throws herself at the bewildered Jason. After a quick spat by the punchbowl, they drag their partners in opposite directions. "Jason, let's go to bed," yells Alison. "Careful, Jason, she hogs all the blankets," Gib taunts. "Well, you snore," she calls back shrilly. "Not tonight I won't," he sneers. As they leave the party, Alison is vibrating with fury. "He doesn't even know that girl!" Alone with that girl he doesn't even know, Gib is suddenly subdued. Undeterred by his fluctuating moods, the sure thing reaches for him. Jason asks Alison if she's made love with Gib. She assures him nothing could be further from the truth. "Do you love him?" he asks. This time, she's not so quick to reply.

The next time the two meet is in the first English class of the new semester. Alison cuts Gib dead. Mrs. Taub, however, is transported by an exceptional essay from an unexpected source. She begins to read from "The Sure Thing" by Walter Gibson. "All his young life he had dreamed of a girl like this, five foot six, long silky hair, trim nubile body . . . that really knew how to move . . ." The male component of the class begins to bark and whoop. Alison shakes her head in revulsion. "From across the room he saw her. It was perfect. He knew almost nothing about her, and she didn't know much more about him. It was exactly how it was supposed to be . . . he brought her to his room . . . she leaned over, and whispered in his ear 'do you love me?' Thoughts raced through his mind . . . 'do you love me?'" Gib looks at Alison, she doesn't know what to think. "He knew that she really needed to hear it, but for the first time in his life he knew that these were no longer just words and if he said it, it would be a lie . . . 'do you love me?' she whispered . . . the answer was no." The class erupts in jeers and derision. Alison turns to Gib. "You didn't sleep with her?" Gib faces her. "Still seeing Jason?" She says, "We broke up . . . you didn't sleep with her." And then they kiss on the library roof with the stars shining down on them.

Countless crimes have been committed in the name of unresolved sexual tension. Too many spats between ice-packed princesses and sweaty, bulging punks have ended up as malicious exercises in making the rich girl crawl. The speed with which Gib labels Alison repressed signals a spot of pedestal-toppling in her future. But *The Sure Thing* flies in the face of teen sex romp conventions. Gib's no horny dog. Alison's no prig. At least not after they've spent a little time with their defenses down. Then they're each other's missing pieces, a movie couple you can imagine having a life after the end credits. Though maybe a little unfeeling in the way it casts off the dead skin of Gib and Alison's former partners, this is a film with a lot of heart. Reacting against what she probably predicted as a lifetime's worth of nice-girl roles looming ahead of her, one of Daphne Zuniga's next public outings was as a Mexican hooker in the movie *Last Rites.* The sight of her simulating anal ecstasy as the opening titles played was enough to make you forget how much she adored Old English sheepdogs. As previously stated, John Cusack, in his life as a man, would give a wide berth to any project of a romantic nature, but he saw out the eighties with a captivating performance in a work of enduring sensitivity. . . .

'm going to take out Diane Court" are the first words out of Lloyd Dobler's mouth in Cameron Crowe's *Say Anything* (1989), a movie which manages to be entirely affecting and entertaining at the same time as hitting heights of parent-bashing from which John Hughes would recoil in shocked horror. Crowe's Lloyd, though, is no Hughes hero hiding his hurt under hipster posturing, warding off rejection with his snappy vocabulary. He's a tall, pale, vulnerable but defiantly optimistic kick boxer. He once sat across from Diane Court at a mall, and now on the eve of graduation, the only thing in his life of which he has any certainty is that he wants to take her out. His best friends Corey (Lili Taylor) and D.C. (Amy Reiner) overflow with reasons why this will not happen. "Diane Court doesn't go out with guys like you . . . she's a brain . . . trapped in the body of a game show hostess. . . . Brains stay with brains. The bomb could go off and their mutant genes would form the same cliques. . . . You're a really nice guy and we don't want to see you get hurt." *"I want to get hurt!"* declares Lloyd.

"I have glimpsed our future and all I can say is go back!" This is the lovely, gifted and brilliant Diane Court (Ione Skye) rehearsing her valedictorian address in front of her father Jim (raspmaster John Mahoney) who creases with laughter. All that beauty, all those brains, and she's funny, too. But he's not just her devoted dad, he's her friend. They can tell each other anything, that's the nature of the relationship. "History, oceanography, creative writing, biochemistry. . . .We're going to remember this student who said 'Hey world, check me out!'" That's how Diane Court is introduced to her fellow graduates of Seattle's Lakeside High School, most of whom regard her as an alien being. Her big laugh line bombs but she presses ahead with her speech: "I have all the hope and ambition in the world, but when I think about the future the truth is, I am really scared."

Her fears seem unwarranted. Jim Court tolerantly takes a message from Lloyd, figuring him for just another *schmo,* unworthy of his daughter's attentions. The next message knocks him off his feet. Jumping in his car (and warbling tunelessly but exuberantly along with "Rikki, Don't Lose That Number"), he drives to the nursing home he runs. Practically levitating with pride, he informs Diane that she's won the coveted scholarship, the Reid Fellowship; she'll be studying in England. She slumps to the ground in disbelief. "You stand up straight and admit you're special," demands Jim. "You're the best in the country. . . . One brilliant person who is so special they celebrate you on two continents."

Even though she has no idea who he is, the courteous Diane returns Lloyd's call. He wades through some small talk before taking the plunge and asking her to a postgraduation party. She blows him off, saying she's busy. "So you're . . . monumentally busy?" he asks, and this unexpected retort amuses her and holds her attention. Lloyd, a nervous talker who becomes increasingly whimsical the more he's forced to improvise, promises to give her tips, many tips, important tips on living in England (an Army brat, he was there for two months). Surprising herself, she agrees to go with him, then reaches for the yearbook to check that she hasn't committed to being seen with a pock-marked buffoon.

Jim Court, too, is amused by Lloyd's babbling assurances of his stability and suitability as an escort for his daughter, but—especially after Diane has made a knockout entrance, a vision in white—he's baffled as to what she's doing with him. A wasted party reveler voices Jim's bafflement: "How'd you get Diane Court to go out with you? What are you?" The answer: "I'm Lloyd Dobler." If, as I attested in the previous chapter, the *soirée* in *Weird Science* ranks as one of the all-time worst teen movie party scenes, the raging postgrad kegger in *Say Any-*

thing is one of the best. It has Eric Stoltz dressed as a rooster. It has Lloyd's response to an impromptu bout of career counseling from his guidance teacher (Bebe Neuwirth): "I'm looking for a dare-to-be-great situation." It has the Corey and Joe saga. "I wrote sixty-three songs this year and they're all about Joe, and I'm going to play every single one of them tonight," announces Corey of the guy who broke her heart and left her suicidal. "He likes girls with names like Ashley," she wails. At that exact moment, Joe (Loren Dean) ambles in not with an Ashley but a Mimi, causing Corey to kick up the tempo, slash at her guitar and snarl, "That'll never be me, never be me, never, never, no." By the time she's howling "Joe lies when he cries," the subject of her repertoire is asking to get back together again when Mimi goes to college. This, of course, motivates Corey finally to get over him.

The party is also a belated opportunity for Diane to interact briefly with all the people from whom her intense study schedule shielded her. One girl, Sheila (Kim *Heathers* Walker) asks "Did you really come here with Lloyd Dobler? How did that happen?" Diane says, "He made me laugh," which is both a "Yeah, *right*" moment and an "If only" moment. As dawn breaks (they've spent the last three hours driving around till the drunk kid in the back remembers where he lives), Diane and Lloyd stop off at a 7-Eleven for something to eat. Returning to the car, he points out broken glass on the ground for her to walk round. She tells him, "I've never really gone out with anyone as basic as you." He takes it as a compliment and tells her he wants to see her all the time.

Lloyd's girl buds are nervous because Diane's made the second date a dinner with her dad, his accountant and a couple of his employees. "It's a family audition . . . it's not his crowd, he's got that nervous talking thing. I told him not to speak." The skeptical Corey says, "If you were Diane Court would you honestly fall for Lloyd?" She weighs her words for a second, then her face relaxes into a grin. She says "Yeah" and her "Yeah" is unanimous.

At the Court dinner party, Lloyd is polite and silent and uptight. Then the accountant says, "So, Lloyd, you graduated Lakewood . . . what are your plans for the future?" All eyes are on him. It's a crucial opinion-forming, confidence-building (or killing) moment. The way Lloyd Dobler responds to this deceptively innocuous question is a strong indicator of character. Turning to Jim Court, who is jovially eyeing him like a snake, he responds, "To spend as much time with Diane before she leaves as possible." But Jim's frozen smile demands more. Lloyd tries to articulate a correct response. "A career? . . . I've thought about this quite a bit, sir. I don't want to sell anything, buy anything or process anything as a career. I don't want to sell anything bought or processed or buy anything sold or processed or process anything sold, bought or processed or repair anything sold, bought or processed as a career. I don't want to do that." Talk about sucking the atmosphere out of a room. This really isn't Lloyd's crowd. Jim Court stares at Lloyd like he's a disease. Lloyd has more to impart. "My father's in the army. He wants me to join, but I can't work for that corporation, so what I've been doing lately is kick boxing, which is a new sport . . . as far as career longevity, I don't really know . . ." Shifting under Jim's get-out-of-my-house gaze, Lloyd shrugs. "I can't figure it all out tonight, sir, I'm just gonna hang with your daughter." A few years down the line and a speech like that would have made Lloyd the hit of the party, a living, breathing poster boy for generational malaise. But this is 1988. The adults in the room lapse into embarrassed silence and Jim looks like he's counting the seconds till he can throw Lloyd out before the punk's lack of direction infects his genius daughter. Attention is diverted from the black hole of Lloyd by a knock on the door. It's a surprise visit from the IRS, telling Jim he's under criminal investigation. Here's where things start to go awry for the two men in Diane's life.

"Get ready for greatness," Corey tells Lloyd, after intuiting that he and Diane have gone all the way (in the back of his clunky Malibu to the sappy accompaniment of Peter Gabriel's "In Your Eyes"), then reading the letter he sent her. "I'll always be there for you, all the love in my heart, Lloyd." But Corey reckons without Jim Court's emotional manipulation of his daughter. Using the wide parameters of their liberal relationship, his mounting IRS problems and the gulf separating her specialness from Lloyd's *schmo*hood, he weakens her resolve.

"You owe it to yourself to be on that plane with no attachments. . . . Give him a present, here, let him know you still care; give him this pen." She shakes her head in disbelief. "In a million years I would never give him a pen." At the exact moment when Lloyd makes the big leap and tells Diane he loves her, she breaks up with him. "I feel like a dick, you must think I'm a dick." The distraught and suddenly inarticulate Diane ends up giving him the pen before rushing out of his car in floods of tears.

For Lloyd, the downward spiral is hanging out a Welcome sign. Standing in a phone booth, soaked to the skin in the middle of a Seattle monsoon, Lloyd laments to his sister Constance (Joan Cusack) "I gave her my heart and she gave me a pen," which, in some movies, would have been the cue for a wailing duet called "I Gave You My Heart and You Gave Me a Pen" to well up on the sound track. Taking up residence in the slough of despond, Lloyd drives through the dark lonely night, composing a letter to Corey on a dictaphone. "I hardly remember her; I've wiped her from my mind . . . this is it, the site of our controversial first date. I met her in a mall, I should have known our relationship was doomed." Deciding he knows too many girls, Lloyd takes a detour into Guyville. The advice from the lunkheads and losers hanging around outside the convenience store is direct and to the point. "Find a girl who looks just like her, nail her and then dump her . . . your only mistake is that you didn't dump her first. Diane Court is a show pony, you need a stallion, walk with us and you walk tall. . . ." Lloyd bleeds in front of the boys: "That girl made me trust myself, man. I was walking around, I was feeling satisfied . . . then she cut me loose . . . she won't tell me why." He hurls a bottle against the wall in frustration, causing a spontaneous outburst of white boy freestyling: "Wigging out, he's wigging out . . . Lloyd, Lloyd, null and void."

Back on the road to nowhere, Lloyd resumes his monologue "That was a mistake. The rain on my car is a baptism. . . . My assault on the world begins now. Believe in myself, answer to no one. Iceman. Power Lloyd." Corey and D.C. upbraid him for trying to act like a guy. "The world is full of guys. Be a man, don't be a guy."

The ground beneath Jim Court begins to subside when he's out buying luggage for Diane's flight to England. Taken by the saleslady's sunny smile and pear-shaped ass, he gives her a big grin and starts to strike up friendly conversation. Then she has to tell him his credit card has been rejected. There's a decline code on his account. Next time we see Jim, he's shriveled up in fetal terror, hunched fully clothed in his own bathtub, cowering from the consequences of his actions.

Lloyd launches an offensive on Diane's emotions by standing outside her window, holding aloft a boombox blaring Peter Gabriel's limpid "In Your Eyes." Trying hard to stand by her Dad, she appeals to the human decency of an IRS guy to tell her the truth. He tells her Jim's been under investigation for five years; he's been making a tidy sum, stealing from the geriatric inhabitants of his nursing home. "We have the records. . . . It's going to get worse." Diane succumbs to suspicion and searches her house for incriminating evidence, which she finds in the form of a hidden stash of bills. She goes straight to the nursing home to confront Jim. "I told you everything and you lied to me." Fleeing from the man she thought she could trust, Diane rushes to be with the man she should have trusted but didn't. Lloyd is sparring in the ring—with Don "The Dragon" Wilson!—and Diane's surprise appearance distracts him, giving The Dragon the opportunity to fell him like a tree. Dazed and bloody, Lloyd is still conscious enough to hear Diane's whispers of contrition. "If I hurt you again, I'll die."

Jim is hit with a fine of $125,000 and a nine-month sentence in a minimum security prison. Lloyd turns up in the prison yard, telling the bitter, chain-smoking Jim that Diane came to see him but wouldn't get out of the car. Still protective of Diane's potential, Jim wants to make certain that Lloyd won't be following her all the way to England. Lloyd says, "I've thought about it quite a bit. . . . I should use this time to make plans. I mean, Diane and I can wait for each other." Jim tells Lloyd he made the right decision. "My daughter's a lot different from you. She's very successful, very talented." Letting the beartrap clang shut, Lloyd goes on, "And then I reconsidered. I think what I really want to do with my life . . . I want to be with your daughter." Jim, furious, calls him a distraction. "I'm the distraction that's going to England, sir." Jim is stewing in his orange prison jumpsuit. "You alright, sir?" asks a concerned Lloyd. *"I'm incarcerated, Lloyd!"* he thunders. "I don't deserve to lose my daughter over this. I don't deserve to have you as my go-between, and I can't for the life of me figure out how she could choose to champion mediocrity the way she's learned to around you." Lloyd gives him a letter from Diane which is bulging with expressions of her disappointment and hurt (although he tries to comfort Jim by telling him how an earlier draft concluded with, "I still can't help loving you"). Diane plucks up the courage to come into the prison yard. Jim clings to her, but she pulls away and, as she leaves, gives him a pen. "Write me." Ouch.

Finally, Diane, who's petrified of flying, and Lloyd are on the plane to England, waiting for takeoff. "When you hear that smoking sign go 'ding,' you know everything's going to be okay," he tells her. "Nobody thought we'd do this. Nobody really thinks it'll work," she shudders. "You just described every great success story," retorts Lloyd who, by this time, could pilot the plane with his confidence. As they begin their ascent, Diane and Lloyd fixate on the smoking sign which, after a long moment, goes ding. Then the screen goes black.

If there was ever a film ahead of its time, it was *Hudson Hawk,* but right behind it was *Say Anything.* Wasn't Lloyd Dobler a sweeter-natured precursor of the ragamuffins from the same region who would soon rail against corporate rock whores? Wasn't his "bought, sold or processed" speech a manifesto of befuddled rejection predating the work-shy ethic of the yet-to-be-detected slacker species? Wasn't Diane's "I am really scared" address a blueprint for several million subsequent admissions? And wasn't Corey, with her catalogue of heartsick defiance, an early incarnation of the alt-rock chick? Of course, as ahead of its time as the movie absolutely was in many ways, in its treatment of Jim Court, it was entirely of its era. In fact, it was more so. Other eighties teen movies punished errant parents by humbling them or smashing up their prize cars. *Say Anything* stuck its father in the joint. His stated crime was bilking the aged, but his implicit and far more heinous felonies were smothering his daughter with love and interfering in her romance with a cool dude. Definitely harsh.

My only problem with the movie lies with the casting of its heroine. No disrespect to Ione Skye, but in the context of the film she's supposed to be *extraordinary*, a character to whom two men of completely disparate natures willingly and without question choose to devote their lives. That's a tall order for a mere mortal and Skye doesn't quite rise to the challenge, rarely exuding qualities more exotic than niceness and concern. Is there anyone who could have done the part full justice? Let's see, lovely, brilliant and gifted (uma, uma) . . . a brain trapped in the body of a game show hostess (Uma, Uma) . . . someone so special she's celebrated on two continents (*Uma, Uma*). Nope, can't think of anyone. I draw a further blank trying to think of anyone who could have embodied Lloyd Dobler as unforgettably as John Cusack. Lloyd's character traits—cheerful, devoted, undirected, sensitive, kickboxing—could in the hands of another actor have curdled into a scary, overemoting stalker. Cusack makes him a one of a kind, a guy with a heart of gold, but a guy you don't feel like punching. Trying to salve some of Jim Court's heartache over his daughter's letter full of pain, Lloyd says, "Just knowing a version like that exists, knowing that for a moment, she felt that and wrote 'I still can't help loving you,' that's got to be a good thing, right?" For all that the movie is supposed to be about an ordinary boy and a special girl, nobody who saw *Say Anything* had any doubt that it was the story of an extraordinary guy.

She's cool, he's hot. She's from the Valley, he's not." So read the tag line for Martha Coolidge's *Valley Girl* (1983), an endearing attempt to humanize the much-derided, mallaholic, unintelligible denizens of the San Fernando Valley. Titular heroine Julie (Deborah Foreman who had a smile that was like standing too close to the sun) makes her social circle emit a collective *"Oh m'gad!"* when she dumps her bitchen but brain-free boyfriend Tommy (Michael Bowen) for surly punk Randy (Nicolas Cage), a slice of forbidden fruit from Sunset Boulevard. For a brief moment, it seems that their love will be strong enough to bridge the Great Divide between her PVC and his leather. Then the rest of the Vals close ranks, threatening to ostracize her if she's not back with her own kind by the time of the prom. "Like, he's got the bod, but his brains are, like, totally bad news," moans Julie of Tommy. Nevertheless, she caves in to peer pressure, breaking the sensitive Randy's heart. Gag me with a spoon. However, Randy makes a *Pretty in Pink*–style nick-of-time appearance at Julie's prom. Then he un*P.I.P*–like decks Tommy, dragging Julie off if not into the sunset then onto Sunset Boulevard. This one dated so fast it was a period piece by the time it came out on video, but it still remains hilarious (the pencil-sharpener earrings, the glasses-on-ropes) and intermittently touching.

Often pegged as The Man Who Would Be Matthew Broderick, Jon Cryer actually stepped into a pair of shoes vacated by Broderick when he starred in *No Small Affair* (1984). The movie was begun in 1981, with Broderick and Sally Field in the lead but shut down after 10 days filming due to exhaustion on the part of director Martin Ritt. When shooting resumed three years later (with Jerry *Street Smart* Schatzberg at the helm), the Cry*meister* was the Head Babyface in Charge, radiating adorable innocence as Charles Cummings, a socially maladroit 16 year old who compensates for his failure at interacting with the world by throwing himself into photography. He comes across and becomes consumed by that most rarely glimpsed of items, a picture of Demi Moore fully clothed. He tracks her character, Laura Victor, to the bar where she sings and is set emotionally aflame by the searing soul power of her performance (or at least the performance of the singer to whose lyrics Demi moves her lips in sync). Stranded in dues-paying purgatory, Laura's career is going nowhere. Charles, now a man with a mission, launches an insane one-man campaign to alert the world to Laura's star potential. He places his photo of her on billboards, bus shelters, taxi cabs and lamp posts. Pretty soon, people are asking, "Who's that girl?" On the strength of his enterprise, she gets a record deal and flies off to L.A. But before she goes, she pays back his devotion by gently deflowering him. Like his alter ego Broderick, Cryer's cutie-pie looks were both his fortune and his fate, forever placing him under the Yellow Pages listing Nice Guys R Us. Of all the Mr. Congeniality roles in his past and in his future, he never was and never will be more appealing than he was in *No Small Affair*. He makes Demi Moore seem sort of likable and even pulls off a nightmare of a scene where his well-meaning brother buys him a hooker to ease his painful passage into manhood. Standing naked but clutching an oversize pillow, he stares mute and embarrassed at the ground before shyly asking the pro, "Can I have a hug?" Now, *that's* cute . . .

You may never know who I am but that hasn't stopped you from giving me the greatest gift I've ever known." Such is the substance of the love letter that causes all the trouble in *Secret Admirer* (1985), The sentiments expressed belong, in theory at least, to Michael Ryan (C. Thomas Howell), who is enraptured by the creamy blondness of airhead narcissist Deborah Anne Fimple (Kelly Preston). She doesn't know he's alive so he writes her a letter straight from his heart and persuades his long-suffering platonic pal Toni (Lori Loughlin) to act as go-between. Toni does what anyone in similar circumstances would do. She steams open the letter and is amused and dismayed by Michael's inept syntax and clumsy attempts at sincerity. Gazing at a picture of him, she puts pen to paper and lets her own, long-suppressed, nonplatonic feelings flow onto the page. The touching note is a megaton success, working its way into Deborah's heart. Even though Michael is a nothing and a nobody to her, the fact that he was capable of expressing himself in such exquisite terms gives his existence new meaning to her. "You're a poet," she says.

Then the letter becomes the catalyst for confusion and disaster. First, Deborah's hard-ass cop dad (Fred Ward) finds it and thinks his wife's playing around, then Deborah's teacher mom (Leigh Taylor-Young) finds it, looks up in the middle of class to meet the gaze of Michael's dad (Cliff DeYoung) and blushingly figures him to be her secret admirer. Deborah's dad becomes a raging cuckold, recruiting Michael's mom (Dee Wallace Stone) to spy on their philandering partners. Meanwhile, Michael is finding the luscious Deborah to be far more appealing as a distant subject of worship than a flesh and blood soul mate. Her play-by-play recaps of her shopping day leave him mute, nodding and disillusioned. In bed the situation is worse. "What do you want me to do?" he asks. "Do it right!" she snaps.

The Ryan and Fimple marriages, on the verge of extinction, are saved at the last minute when a furious Michael snatches the letter from his arguing parents, yelling at them to leave his things alone. Deborah goes to see Michael, bearing copies of the letters she received, unable to believe the poet who penned such pearls could have turned out to be so callow and cruel. Michael stares at the unfamiliar writing. Then he realizes: his overlooked platonic pal Toni was the author. And he loves her! But it's too late. She's taking off for a year on a floating school. He tracks her to the harbor, bawling "I love you" at the top of his lungs and diving into the water to follow her. She throws caution to the wind, hurls herself off the boat and meets him halfway for a big kiss-up in the brine.

Secret Admirer is thinner than the paper on which the love letter is scribbled, but it's an engaging piece of piffle. The two femme leads are zesty comediennes—Lori Loughlin, particularly, plays a far pluckier best pal than a lunkhead like Michael deserves. C. Thomas Howell brings his usual brand of magic to the proceedings, i.e., he manages to stand upright and doesn't spit food at any of the other actors when he delivers his dialogue.

It's Saturday night. All across the country, carefree kids are drinking, dancing and engaging in acts of debauchery. Everyone's having the best night of their lives. All except Ronald Miller and his company of geeks. At least that's what Ronald (Patrick Dempsey) thinks at the start of *Can't Buy Me Love* (1987) as he spends another weekend playing cards with a bunch of misfits blinking behind bottle glasses, buck teeth and braces. This is the geek's dilemma: *these* are my friends, I'm one of *them,* but the alternative is despised solitude. Taking the $1000 he painstakingly saved after a million mornings mowing suburban lawns, Ronald goes to the mall to splurge on the telescope of his dreams. He's just about to hand over the cash, when he sees Cyndi Mancini (Amanda Peterson), a pe-tite blonde who is the focus of much awed popularity. Ronald claps eyes on Cyndi at the exact time she is undergoing an ex-perience completely alien to her: a crisis. She's stained her mother's murderously expensive white suede ensemble and the cleaning bill is too steep for her. She crumples in despair. Ronald does what any of us would do. He steps in with his $1000, offering to pay for the cleaning if she will pose as his girlfriend for a month. She is appalled, but rather than attempt to convince her mother that the notorious White Suede Bandit had struck again, she accedes to Ronald's ridiculous request, stipulating that their contract is only valid during school hours and excludes any physical contact.

Being seen in her exalted company (and dudded up in New Wave threads, Ray-Bans and a moussed 'do) gives him accep-tance by association. The hulking jocks who previously tossed him and his craven kind into lockers and threw shit at their houses now tolerate him as an amusing distraction. Cyndi's girlfriends, all of whom look like *Hustler* centerfolds (a wry comment, I'd like to think, on how the popular crowd must seem to a dweeb like Ronald, but probably just a bad casting call), are quick to convey their availability to him. He's a hip and happening guy; he's gone, as a stunned spectator com-ments, "from zero to hero." He's also increased his standing in Cyndi's eyes. Where once she viewed him with contempt as a geek pimp, now she basks in his admiration, empathy and openness. Lonely now that her football-star boyfriend has gone to college, she finds Ronald's company preferable to the sluts and sportos that make up her much-envied cool clique. She even feels free enough to show him the book of poems she scrawls in secret. On the last day of their contract, Ronald takes Cyndi to his Special Place, a resting ground for vintage airplanes. They've both shared secret parts of themselves with the other and what started as a sordid business deal has now become something much more real. "You'll have to help me here, I don't really know too much about this. How do we do this?" says Ronald. Cyndi, charmed by his open vulnerability and nervousness about the relationship into which they're about to enter, starts to say "We just take it slowly." Not listening, he goes on, "I've never broken up with anyone before." Awwww. Unbelievably, the sucker's yearning for popularity runs so deep he is oblivious to Cyndi's feelings for him. Next day they stage a loud public breakup and Ronald Miller is now hip, happening and, most important, unencumbered, free to run with the big dogs and jump on Cyndi's bitch buddies. Life is sweet.

At this stage, *Can't Buy Me Love* could go in one of two directions. It could either develop into a "Be careful what you wish for, you might get it" scenario or it could point the finger of impending retribution at Ronald Miller. The latter route is quickly chosen. The first indication of his impending shame comes when the jocks persuade him to take part in a shit-throwing raid on what turns out to be the house of Kenny (Courtney Gains), one of his former geek friends. When the two exbuds come face to face, Ronald gets a stricken glimpse of what he's become. Everybody else gets the same glimpse at a New Year's Eve party. Cyndi's football-hero boyfriend gets wind of her affair with this insect Miller. He gives her a hard time. She gets drunk and reveals to a houseful of the hot and happening that Ronald is a traitor in their midst. He paid her to make him popular, and like fools, they admitted him to their inner circle. Within seconds, jocks who had drunk beer with him and babes who had blown him unite in consigning Ronald to instant oblivion. As he stumbles home, the enormity of his fate is brought home to him as he passes a house where a bunch of his former geek friends are happily toasting the New Year. A stranger to both camps, stateless and unwanted, Ronald realizes despised solitude has, in fact, become his destiny and quite rightly bursts into tears.

He makes many painful and humiliating attempts to rekindle the relationship he had with Cyndi, but to no avail. His old friend Kenny is scarcely more welcoming. "You threw shit at my house," he yells when Ronald tries to engage him in conversation. But when one of the jocks gives Kenny some schoolyard hassle, Ronald comes into his own. He places himself firmly between geek and aggressor and delivers a stirring "What happened to us?" speech, reminding the jock how they all used to play together as kids before they became consumed by the notion of identity. His words strike a universal chord and he is accepted back into the geek fold. As for Cyndi, she's not sure they can ever be friends again, but just at the last moment, just when she's about to hit the mall with her hip friends and he's consigned to another million mornings mowing suburban lawns till he can afford the telescope of his dreams, she leaves the girls behind, jumps on the back of his mower and—yes!—they mow off into the sunset.

You'd have to be a fucking idiot to find anything remotely profound in *Can't Buy Me Love* and luckily, I am. With almost every conceivable thing going against it—its unsavory premise (however dorky Ronald is, he's still making another human being his paid companion), its questionable performances (Patrick Dempsey had a marked propensity to act like he was in a musical) and the fact that half the budget went to securing the rights to The Beatles' title tune—the film touches on some truths about the iniquities of the schoolyard caste system and the desperation growing inside some of the dispossessed. Something about the film always catches me unawares and has me welling up. Maybe it's because I always thought that the Molly Ringwald character should have ended up with Anthony Michael Hall rather than Judd Nelson at the end of *The Breakfast Club,* and in this movie, she does.

Brats Out of Hell

5

The Rapid Rise and Long, Slow Fall of the Brat Pack

If the librarian at Lone Star Junior High in Fresno had any notion of the ultimate consequences of her actions, perhaps she might not have been so enthusiastic in her petitioning of Francis Ford Coppola. However, her missive so powerfully conveyed the deep affection that the students at her school felt for S. E. Hinton's novel of midsixties teen alienation, *The Outsiders,* and was so rigid in its conviction that he was the only auteur visionary enough to bring the book to filmic life, that Coppola was inspired to take on the task.

None of which is intended for a second to suggest that his subsequent movie of *The Outsiders* (1983)—which bears a dedication to Lone Star Junior High—was anything less than a completely involving wallow in wounded innocence. It totally captures the "us against them" fervor that 16-year-old Susie Hinton poured into her story, putting even the most boorish viewer firmly on the side of its assembly of trembling-lipped angelic underdogs. Ravishing to look at, its Cinemascope framing and super-saturated close-ups render

the cast iconic and gorgeous. What might have given the Lone Star librarian a moment's pause, though, is the realization that she was, in effect, laying the foundations for a platform that would introduce an entire stud farm of fresh young acting talent into the national consciousness. Many of *The Outsiders'* ensemble had debuted in earlier movies or TV shows, but their collective participation in a movie so drenched with emotion and a sense of separatism (there are no adult characters and only one female, Diane Lane, of any importance) meant that they were suddenly perceived as a fully formed new generation of stars, fluent in the argot and the angst of the new generation of cinemagoers. Separately and in factions, these leaders of the new school enjoyed a speedy trajectory through soundstages, bedroom walls, nightclub back rooms and tabloid front pages. Some of them approximated the shambling humility and unformed aspirations of the gauche guy or gal next door. Others played at being reckless rule breakers, thrusting young heartthrobs whose leather biker boots shone with the slavishly applied saliva of prostrated studio heads.

The fact that some of the actors who appeared in teen ensemble movies would carouse offscreen in the same groupings led to the coining and exhaustive utilization of a term that evoked shudders and nausea in both those to whom the moniker applied and the others for whom it was inappropriate.

"We take a bad rap," declared Rob Lowe, addressing a Sacramento rally of screaming teenagers during his brief stint as a political agitator. "We're the yuppie generation. Man, I hate that, I hate that almost as much as I hate the Brat Pack. Well, I'm here to tell you, I'm no Brat Packer and you're not yuppies." He was half right. His audience crossed economic boundaries but their perception of him was as an oversexed, overindulged, irresponsible purveyor of teenage fantasies, a suave swinger who kept movie sets waiting while he cavorted on a waterbed with a bunch of cheerleaders, a taser gun and a cowboy boot full of coke. In other words, a charter member of The Brat Pack. For some young actors who came to prominence in the eighties, inclusion under the Brat umbrella was a heinous example of character assassination.

Natural selection gradually separated the performers whose potential stood a chance of being realized from the lightweights whose appeal dwindled with every inch they grew. Tom Cruise put a million miles of road between himself and the descending mantle of Brathood by plotting a career curve that savvily aligned him with credible veterans (Newman, Hoffman, Duvall, Scorsese, Stone), a ploy that emphasized his ambition and made his youthful vitality seem like an attribute rather than an affliction. Matt Dillon, an actor so moody he even played a character called Moody (in *My Bodyguard*), had his intense Irish brooding, his lethal cheekbones and his aura of menace and mystery to sustain him through even the most sluggish and inane of projects. Nicolas Cage, who came ascloseasthis to getting the role of John Bender in *The Breakfast Club,* had several sleevefulls of tricks. Just when you thought you had him pegged as your favorite Martian, he became the guy next door, then the hero, then the heavy, then the heartbreaker. Sean Penn cultivated a Brawling Poet persona. Robert Downey, Jr. is that enviable but unsatisfying entity, a performer of perpetual potential. The stars of C. Thomas Howell and Ralph Macchio rose and fell in tandem with those of the Brats, but somehow they lack the essential obnoxiousness to make them eligible for inclusion among that number. Demi Moore acted like a star till people believed she was one. Patrick Swayze, whose resume boasts *The Outsiders* and *Red Dawn,* was already in his late twenties and Timothy Hutton's career went off the boil after *Taps* and *Ordinary People* (I'm not part of that loony *Turk 182!* fringe), which leaves . . .

The Usual Suspects

Who we talk about when we talk about The Brat Pack:

EMILIO ESTEVEZ

This scion of the Sheen dynasty refused to freeload off the name of his famous father. The proud use of his original family name was a proclamation to the world that he was no spoilt second-generation Hollywood son and heir, coasting through his career on favors and unearned goodwill (his brother Carlos' decision to change his name to Charlie was another sort of statement). Estevez was the Renaissance Man of the Brats. By the time he turned 25 he had penned a screenplay (an adaptation of S. E Hinton's *That Was Then . . . This Is Now*) and written, directed and starred in a movie, *Wisdom*. His work ethic and amiability made him the only one of this group to carry on a consistent, if moderately successful screen career into the nineties. What I'm trying to say here is, if the Brats were The Beatles, he would be George.

ANTHONY MICHAEL HALL

Has an opening credit ever filled an audience with such shivers of anticipation as *Sixteen Candles'* "and Anthony Michael Hall as 'The Geek'"? His unforgettable turn as Rusty Griswold in *National Lampoon's Vacation* had already confirmed the pint-sized, preternaturally confident Hall (whose given name is Michael Anthony Hall) as the perfect conduit for John Hughes' scattergun dialogue. However, his Geek was an astonishing amalgam of every conceivable irritating adolescent trait and his flawless performance marked Hall out as the premier comedic talent in teen movies. For his role in *The Breakfast Club,* he made the switch from stupid to serious, the same switch that comic actors the stature of Steve Martin, Billy Crystal and Bill Murray have never managed to pull off. Then the growth hormones kicked in. *Weird Science* was released only a matter of months after *The Breakfast Club* but all the *schtick* that once seemed so adorable was suddenly a whole lot less cute. And what was up with that old-black-man voice he kept lapsing into?

ROB LOWE

So pretty, he looked like he was carved out of soap. So clean, he looked like you could eat off him. And, as it turned out, many people did. Reluctant to ruin such flawless features, he rarely allowed any kind of reaction or emotion to cross his face. After the scandal-magnet of the videotape capturing him in flagrante with a youthful admirer, his line-free brow was eternally furrowed.

ANDREW MCCARTHY

The passive guy. Helplessly sucked down by the undertow of female desire, his bewildered fragility made him irresistible to Jacqueline Bisset in *Class,* Mary Stuart Masterson in *Heaven Help Us* and Molly Ringwald in *Pretty in Pink* and *Fresh Horses.* What inspired such licentious, lubricious behavior? A pair of panicked eyes that bulged out like those of a deer caught in headlights and a mouth stuck in the permanent pucker of a cat's asshole.

JUDD NELSON

Judd's mother used to be a Democratic representative to the Florida State legislature. His father was an attorney. These are professions that require one to be voluble, articulate and opinionated. It's fair, I think, to suggest that those qualities rubbed off on young Judd. For those of us whose first experience of him was his force-of-nature, scenery-chomping turn in *The Breakfast Club,* it came as a shock to realize that *he was always like that!* Swaggering on screen with one hand full of bluster and the other packed with bombast, his entire career seemed to be an endless hysterical rehearsal for a one-man show titled *I, Iconoclast.*

MOLLY RINGWALD

The eighties were full of Girls On The Verge. Girls virtually vibrating with beauty, brains, personality and pep. There was Jami Gertz (the Teri Hatcher of her day), Virginia Madsen, Kelly Preston, Jenny Wright and many more. What made Molly Ringwald so special? That was the question posed by her movies. "What do you think about Samantha Baker?" asked *Sixteen Candles'* lunkhead Jake (Michael Schoeffling) of his chin-up partner. "You really don't think she's got something?" enquired *Pretty in Pink*'s insecure Blane (Andrew McCarthy) of his preppie pal. Even in *The Breakfast Club,* raging bull John Bender (Judd Nelson) was driven to impossible heights of abuse by the demolition job Ringwald's princess was doing on his roughneck heart. She was the girl next door but she somehow sort of *wasn't.* The red hair was a mitigating factor in infusing Ringwald's ordinariness with a hint of the exotic. That intangible quality, coupled with her formidable battery of pained reactions, briefly made her America's eighties Everygirl.

ALLY SHEEDY

Ally Sheedy should have had Jennifer Jason Leigh's career. If this book was a sitcom, I'd be pausing right about now for the laugh track to kick in. Stupid as it is, I stand stubbornly by the statement. Alexandra Elizabeth Sheedy just *stank* of presence: weird, uncomfortable presence, but presence just the same. Obviously, her soaring performance—her *Gypsy,* her *Evita,* her *Mommie Dearest*—was as *The Breakfast Club*'s dandruff-flecked wacko, but go back to her earlier work and she's still stinking. Even though she's not playing more than standard girlfriend roles in *Bad Boys, War Games* and *Oxford Blues,* she's still simmering with untapped sexuality; it's in the way she raises her pointy chin, the taunt in her eyes and the lazy drawl of her voice. (Or it could be me.) If she hadn't tidied up her hair, if she hadn't played a succession of supporting roles, if she'd found a director who saw the weirdness within, maybe she'd have had a glittering career of junkies, hookers and emotional trainwrecks ahead of her. Our loss.

Bonfire of the Vanities

Popularity is a pit bull. It can ensure fame and respect come your way or it can turn on you like a . . . uh . . . wild dog. The transition of public figures from pinups to punchlines is often brutally swift. For the Brat Pack, the turning point came in the summer of 1985. What was it that caused the world to look on this group with such open derision?

Was it that sudden fame had made them unbearable? Was it the drunken skirmishes outside lurid nightspots? Was it the flaunting of ill-gotten riches? Was it the speeding tickets? Was it that they all started wearing glasses and pretending they knew who the President was? These were all contributing factors but the main reason for the Brats' collapse can be summed up in three words: *St. Elmo's Fire.*

Sanity, restraint and coherence exit via the ejector seat in this multi-storyline smash-up chronicling the floundering of a gaggle of self-satisfied Georgetown grads. The least toilet-trained of this group of big babies is Rob Lowe's Billy Hixx, a deadbeat dad and itinerant sax honker (when we see him perform in a painfully elongated musical sequence, he's like an asthmatic Clarence Clemons). Billy's distaff counterpart is Jules (Demi Moore), a frazzled fast-track party slut whose knuckles drag under the weight of two armsful of bangles and whose nostrils are about to evaporate under the pressure of the buckets of blow she's vacuuming up. Always on call to rescue Jules from being gang-banged by Arabs or bail Billy out of jail is Alec Newberry (Judd Nelson), the college political firebrand who's suddenly done a postgraduation volte-face, throwing in his lot with a Republican senator. "We could get a longer sofa,"

is his rationale to girlfriend Leslie Hunter (Ally Sheedy, her witchy weirdness diluted by shorn hair, lacy blouses and pearls). Pining away for Leslie is Kevin Dolenz (Andrew McCarthy), a bitter, blocked hack attempting to maintain an air of slit-eyed, nicotine-clouded cynicism while beavering away on an op-ed piece about The Meaning of Life. Sharing Kevin's unrequited obsessive nature is his roomie Kirby Kager (Emilio Estevez), a law student smitten by a chance encounter with Dale Biberman (Andie MacDowell), a doctor with whom he once had a date. Last, and definitely least, there's Wendy (Mare Winningham), the frumpy virginal doormat in love with and endlessly tolerant of Billy. The conscience of the group, Wendy disdains their heartless pursuit of materialism, choosing to help the needy by slaving for the Department of Human Resources. "You get yourself some hot clothes and get yourself a man and you won't be worrying about all this shit," advises a welfare recipient she attempts to aid.

How do you even begin to pick a highlight from *St. Elmo's* embarrassment of riches? The blatant and strenuous attempt by the movie's quartet of boy Brats to outdiva one another makes nominating an outstanding performance almost impossible. Emilio Estevez initially seems to be the least impressive of the four. But discount at your peril his stalking of dishy doctor Andie MacDowell, whom he has earlier described as "the only evidence of God that I can find on this entire planet with the exception of the mystical force that removes one of my socks from the dryer every time I do the laundry." Riding his bike in the pouring rain to a delightful uptown dinner party, he presses his soaked nose to the windowpane, sucking in every inch of her coltish beauty. Unable to restrain himself, he crashes the do, squelches in and approaches MacDowell. She turns and drawls, "How are yew?" His agonized reply: "I'm obsessed, thank you very much." Figuring she's the kind of gal who's turned on by a high roller, he uses the house of the Korean lobbyist for whom he's working to throw a loud, lurid party in her honor. When she fails to show, he tracks her all the way up to the ski lodge where she's, of course, weekending with a concerned medic. She tries to let him down gently, saying she's flattered, whereupon he grabs her and lays a big deep sucking kiss on her. This has the effect of transferring his infatuation. She's left shivering in the snow, her womanhood awakened. He speeds off whooping and punching the air in triumph. Good going, dude.

Andrew McCarthy is called upon to participate in one of the most stupefying scenes in contemporary popular culture when he—not the most spontaneous of performers, I think it's fair to say—has to screech along in an unshackled castrato to Aretha Franklin's "Respect," all the while pounding on a pair of bongos and bouncing around on a bed in a state of electrified abandon. It's only just compensation that his piece on The Meaning of Life finally sees print. On the front page of *The New York Times*.

For Rob Lowe, the movie was a chance to show that he was more than the poreless, porcelain doll of the aggregate. Here, he was the irresponsible, immature, promiscuous bad boy, stunning in skinny tie and shades, the catch phrase "It was out of hand" always dangling from his lips. Though his overpowering pulchritude makes his costars seem like a mound of dog turds (and the guys don't come off looking too good, either), he only has one scene where he's fully *in the zone.* Seeking to revenge herself on the husband who's treating her like side salad, Billy's wife Felicia (Jenny Wright, so good in *Near Dark*), turns up at the bar where he's wheezing into his axe with a hunk on her arm. "Get your hands off my wife, man," yells Billy, jumping off the stage and initiating a big brawl that spills out into the street. ". . . you ever have boys, do me a favor and have them neutered straight away . . . they knock up some bitch and they're fucked, FUCKED FOR LIFE!" declares Billy. "I hate you, you little bitch." Felicia's date knocks Billy on his ass. She sees the blood, gasps "Billy" and, seconds later, they're devouring each other.

But *St. Elmo's'* garlands go to The Juddster. In *The Breakfast Club,* he was the movie's unacknowledged center, here he's openly and often referred to as the group's leader. It is not a position he takes lightly. When he's not doing that combination eye-popping, nostril-flaring, hair-flicking thing, he's striking noble poses like Greta Garbo in *Queen Christina.* His biggest, maddest, *Juddest* hit is Alec's epochal breakup scene with Ally Sheedy's Leslie. He wants to marry her, but she can't commit and has an inkling that he can't keep it in his pants. She calls him on it, he throws her out and she, on the rebound, ends up in bed with Andrew McCarthy's lovestruck scribbler. Which is, of course, where a contrite Alec finds her. She turns up a couple of days later to remove her belongings from the massive loft where once they happily cohabited. She hoped to find him gone, but in he stomps, thunderous and clutching a pigskin. "You can't have the Pretenders' first album. You can have all the Billy Joel, except *The Stranger.* NO SPRINGSTEEN IS LEAVING THIS HOUSE!! You ran out on this relationship, you take the consequences." When he accuses her of fucking McCarthy's Kevin, she rightly retorts "You fucked many." Astounded, he protests, "Nameless, faceless many." She goes to another room and he sits alone, wounded, desolate and posing up a storm. Finally, he can take no more. "*Wasted*

Love!" he bellows like he was announcing a song title, then hurls the pigskin across the huge loft. "God, I just wish I could get it back!"

Small wonder, faced with such an onslaught, that the ladies of *St. Elmo's* were trampled underfoot. But it turns out to be Demi Moore's addled fuck toy Jules, that paradigm of her decade (who blithely rationalized sleeping with her boss with the retort, "This is the eighties. Bop him for a few years, get his job when he gets his hand caught in the vault, become a legend, do a black mink ad, get caught in a massive sex scandal and retire in disgrace, then write a huge best-seller and become a fabulous host of my own talk show") who gives the movie its big heartfelt climax. Her lush life turns out to have been a lie, her credit line has been cut off, the furniture in her big pink apartment (with its wall-filling mural of Billy Idol) has been repossessed, she is fired from her job. Huddled in a shivering foetal position in her locked apartment with the windows open and the winter wind sending her curtains billowing in the familiar MTV fashion, Moore is a picture of existential emptiness and despair.

This, the movie tells us, is where the empty-headed pursuit of money, power, sex, drugs and pink furniture gets you. Her friends all attempt to break into the apartment (apart from Alec, who tries to drop Kevin off a fire escape), but it takes fellow fuck-up Billy to talk Jules back from the edge. "This isn't real. . . . It's St. Elmo's Fire," he says, not by way of disassociating himself from the calamity in which he's stranded but in reference to the seafaring legend of fire in the sky. "They made it up because they thought they needed it to keep them going when times got tough." Billy looks away from Jules and straight at us. "We're all going through this," he assures those in the audience left catatonic by their canceled credit. "Hey, this is our time on the edge." Grateful for his unexpected empathy (he's earlier attempted to put the moves on her), she breathes, "I never thought I'd be so tired at twenty-two."

His job done, Billy departs for New York and a new life (but not before tenderly devirginizing Wendy). The remaining members of the group (Alec, Kevin and Leslie have resolved to remain friends till she makes up her mind between them) pause outside St. Elmo's bar, the scene of so many of their youthful reveries. Should they go in for a brewski? They've all got work in the morning and make arrangements to meet for brunch that Sunday. But not at St. Elmo's. "Why don't we go to Houlihan's? It's not so noisy, not so many kids."

For all that it was reviled on its release and for all that it might seem to be an artifact entirely specific to the eighties, *St. Elmo's Fire* is, I contend, another movie that's way ahead of its time. With its affectations, ludicrous plotlines and thudding performances, this film is the cornerstone from which *Melrose Place* and MTV's *The Real World* eventually grew. The tantrums and tirades thrown by these series' ensembles of posturing, humorless, attention-craving early twenties idiots are distant, tinny echoes of the original inanities delivered by Nelson, Lowe, McCarthy, et al. Totally quotable, endlessly watchable, lovely to look at—writer/director Joel Schumacher delivers innumerable Washington fall and winter tableaux—and gruesome to listen to (David Foster's saccharine score is smeared obtrusively over every scene), *St. Elmo's* met a swift and brutal end at the hands of both critics and ticket buyers, dashing the hopes of many . . . of several . . . of me for a *thirtysomething*-style sequel. In order to distance themselves from the debacle which had the effect of compartmentalizing the Brats as self-infatuated camera-hoggers only comfortable among their own kind, the component parts of the group split into separate entities, venturing forth under their own steam.

My Brilliant Career
The Solo Flights of the Brats

Molly Ringwald wasn't coming off any bloated Brat Pack project. *Pretty in Pink* had cemented her star status. She'd been on the cover of *Time*. She'd been sought out for projects as diverse as a remake of *Breakfast at Tiffany's* and *Blue Velvet* (her mother read the script and rejected it before her daughter saw it). Then Warren Beatty stepped in, courting her for a project penned by his longtime collaborator James Toback. *The Pick-Up Artist* (1987) was the story of a sidewalk sweet-talker who finally meets the right woman. Of course, after one night, she wants nothing more to do with him. Robert Downey, Jr. at his most pantingly eager to please is the eponymous pick-up dude, Jack Jericho. Ringwald is ice-cool museum guide, Randy Jensen. Her reluctance to get involved with Downey stems not from the fact that he sweats, shakes and gesticulates enough to make Chris Farley look like James Spader, but that she's the daughter of a gambler (Dennis Hopper) in trouble with the Mob. The film has a heavyweight cast on board (Hopper, Harvey Keitel, Danny Aiello), but Ringwald seems divorced from the proceedings. She cuts back on the flushing and lip chewing without substituting anything in their place. Warren Beatty had his name removed from the finished product, which is dominated by the manic Downey of whom Ringwald would later comment, "Drinking didn't seem to be his drug of choice."

Downshifting from his comic tour de force in *Sixteen Candles* to his weepy search for self-esteem in *The Breakfast Club* established Anthony Michael Hall as a guy with more than one string to his bow. Moodswinging from the supposed zaniness of *Weird Science* to the supposed suspense of *Out of Bounds* (1986) proved to be the tyke's undoing. In this film by Richard Tuggle (director of Clint Eastwood's pervo *Tightrope*), Hall benches all his natural attributes, his teen wise-ass persona, his shy-guy sensitivity and his Swiss-watch timing.

In their place is the blank stare of a taciturn Iowa farmboy, atrophying in the boredom of his loveless family home. Upping sticks to spend some time in L.A. with his adored brother and sis-in-law, Hall's almost-mute Daryl picks up the wrong dufflebag at L.A.X., leaving the airport with a sackful of heroin. A hilarious comedy of confusion fails to ensue. Instead, bad hombres slaughter his West Coast relatives. The LAPD characteristically want to set him up for the crime.

Daryl goes on the lam, hooking up with New Wave bubblehead Dizz (Jenny Wright), who gels his do, fits him out in checkerboard shirts, flip-up shades and baggy pants, all the better to blend in with the decaying glamour of L.A. street culture.

Thus disguised, he can swim in the sleazy stream that runs from Melrose to Silverlake to Venice Beach, evading the cops and chasing the narcotic nogoodniks. As delineated, *Out Of Bounds* contained the ingredients for a sizzling fish-out-of-water culture-clash smash. Instead, it's a big fizzle. Hall switches *like that* from a heartland naif to a punked-up streetfighter, showing little enthusiasm for either role.

Ally Sheedy is a self-centered, coked-out, credit-card immolating Hollywood kid. In this movie, I mean. She may have lost that youthful foxiness but she had enough savvy to take a poke at her public perception in the cute *Maid to Order* (1987). Winding up in jail for speeding and cocaine possession, Sheedy's Jessie Montgomery is bailed out by her long-suffering widowed father (Tom Skerritt) who wishes on a star that he had no daughter. Enter braying fairy godmother Beverly D'Angelo who makes the wish a reality. Rejected by Skerritt who treats her like an unfamiliar interloper, Jessie has no one to turn to. Fairy godmother D'Angelo finds her alone and dejected on a park bench, waves her wand and gets her a job as a maid in the house of screeching Malibu arrivistes Valerie Perrine and Dick Shawn. Jessie gets a fresh perspective on the values and behavior of the wealthy and thoughtless. She also has an opportunity to revel in the simplicity and sass of the folks below stairs. After a few scrapes involving her unfamiliarity with washing machines, irons and stoves, she worms her way into the hearts of the staff, especially the taciturn secret songwriter barely played by Michael Ontkean. I know it's faint praise but *Maid to Order* is easily the equal of any of the more successful Touchstone comedies of the time. Best scene: a skinny-dipping Sheedy is gallantly offered a towel by Ontkean. He turns away as she gets out of the pool, then sneaks a look to see her walking away with the towel wrapped around her head. She still had it.

Andrew McCarthy also took the cutie-pie route with *Mannequin* (1987), a broad and sappy fantasy that successfully exploited his sole asset: that look of bewilderment. He gets plenty of opportunities to gawk and drop his jaw, playing a department store stock clerk befriended by a mannequin (Kim Cattrall) who comes to life only when they're together. For audiences, the astonishment was generated not by the bland coupling of warm flesh and cold plastic but the over-the-top-and-into-orbit hamming of Meshach Taylor as McCarthy's flaming window-dresser colleague and, of all people, James Spader, simpering and hissing as the store's evil, effete manager. Starship's Abba-esque theme tune made this a big international hit but now it's not so much dated as violently unwatchable.

Speaking of violently unwatchable, what of Judd Nelson's first solo steps? Glad you asked. The movie was *Blue City* (1986), and what a movie it was. Ally Sheedy is on hand as love interest, but here, finally, after taking the strain in two seminal group movies, you get your pure, primo 100% uncut Judd. His prodigal-son character, Billy Turner, doesn't let the dust settle for a second after his unexpected return to Florida's Blue City. He stomps into a bar bouncing a basketball, flicking his hair and flaring his nostrils. Naturally, his presence ignites a fight. He's thrown in jail and bawls for the cops to call his old man, the Mayor. It turns out he *is,* in fact the Mayor's son, but Hizzoner is recently deceased. Released, Billy goes on a rampage. He wants to get to the bottom of his dad's death. He wants answers, Goddammit! He goes back and forward between police chief Paul Winfield, crime boss Scott Paulin and his stepmother Anita Morris, figuring that if he harrasses and bellows at them long and loud enough they'll let slip their complicity in Mayor Turner's offing.

Aiding him in his reign of terror are perky desk sergeant Sheedy and her brother, played by David Caruso. They hold up a local mob-operated dog track at gunpoint, throwing steaks to the mutts; they knock over gambling dens, intimidate and challenge corrupt cops. Billy even harangues his buxom

stepmom, following her around the supermarket, punctuating his accusations by throwing frozen turkeys into her shopping cart. "You are the sorriest excuses for outlaws I've ever seen," comments police chief Winfield, accurately. Billy, though, does not let his ineptitude stand in the way of dragging his father's killer to justice. "I'm going to stick to him like a cheap suit in the rain," he snarls. You think you've seen Judd Nelson act obnoxious? If you haven't seen *Blue City*, you haven't seen anything! He's such a prick in this movie that, bereaved son though he may be, you're practically begging for one of the city's legions of felons and fascist cops to beat him to death. An equal opportunity offender is first—and last—time director Michelle Manning who, when she can't think of any other way to advance the plot, throws in montages of Nelson moodily riding around on his motorcycle.

In retrospect, *Wisdom* (1987) was perhaps not the most appropriate title Emilio Estevez could have chosen for his writer-director-actor triple whammy. He displayed little of

Brats Out of Hell

the title quality in his conception and execution of this tortuous tale of a *schlub* made ineligible for the job market because a minor felony put a stain on his otherwise spotless record. Seething at the injustice of Reaganomics, Estevez's John Wisdom hits on the idea of utilizing his leisure time to make a stand for the property owners and farmers who are being crushed by the banks. The idea of becoming a contemporary Robin Hood gets him hot and soon he and his extremely accommodating girlfriend (Demi Moore) are crisscrossing the country, holding up banks and destroying mortgage records. Their exploits make them folk heroes and media hot items. Of course, this kind of behavior can't be allowed to continue unchecked. The Man brings all his forces of oppression to bear on Johnny Wisdom who is captured at gunpoint, cuffed and incarcerated. And that's when he wakes up! His whole great egalitarian notion was all a dream! Suffice it to say that not only was *Wisdom* the last movie to bear Estevez's name as writer or director until 1996, but his then-girlfriend Demi Moore left him soon after for Bruce Willis.

The best thing that could happen to you would be an industrial accident." So says Jim Belushi to Rob Lowe in *About Last Night . . .* , in an attempt to convince him that his prettiness is a liability. But before entering into that movie, Lowe had made concerted efforts to fuck up the glacial perfection of his features in *Youngblood* (1986), a hockey pic which saw him getting bashed into barriers, pounded into the ice, smashed by elbows and socked by full-on fists. "Rocky plays hockey," scoffed cynics on hearing that Lowe was playing a farmboy (stung by accusations of being privileged LA powderpuffs, the Brats felt the need to align themselves with the honest folk who tilled the soil) who joins a minor-league Canadian team. But, Van Damme's *Die Hard* on ice flop notwithstanding, you can't go far wrong with a hockey movie, and this one totally zips along. It even packs a rip-roaring climax with Lowe's Dean Youngblood, having gone back to the farm beaten and bloodied, returning to the rink, throbbing with resolve and smashing pucks into the back of the net.

All Grown Up
The Brats Play House

"Sunrise, sunset . . . quickly go the years . . ." It seemed like only seconds ago we were sharing teen traumas with Brats, now suddenly we were picking out baby clothes and combing flea markets for that perfect antique lamp.

About Last Night . . . (1986) pitted the idylls of yuppie couplehood against the cold sweat of commitment. Bed-hopping babes Danny (Rob Lowe) and Debbie (Demi Moore) stop changing partners and warily test the waters of monogamy while their best buds, Bernie the boor (James Belushi) and Joan the shrew (Elizabeth Perkins), openly root for the relationship to fail. Adapted from a black-hearted David Mamet one-act play, *Sexual Perversity in Chicago,* the movie stayed faithful to its source material in as much as it was still set in Chicago. If you remained unconvinced on the previous occasions I played the ahead-of-its-time hand, you're not going to budge on this one. But, for a prehistoric peek at the adorable, acerbic, dizzy, muddleheaded, antics of the relationship-phobic inhabitants of *Friends* (and its various, less-accomplished knock-offs), look no further than *About Last Night . . .* Although they boast yuppie accoutrements, the central quartet are going nowhere in low-paid, unglamorous professions, they're confined to cramped living quarters and they comport themselves with an ironic but wistful regard to their carefree school days. Putative star Rob Lowe is consistently and visibly outclassed by his costars (he flinches away from rollicking Jim Belushi like he's scared the big lug's going to hurl a sucker punch at him) but his limited access to his emotions makes him occasionally effective at conveying the ambivalence of a guy who lets slip the words "I love you," then wishes he'd slit his throat.

There's good news and bad news about *For Keeps* (1988), penned by the *About Last Night . . .* screenwriting duo of ex-SNL dweeb Tim Kazurinsky and Denise DeClue. The good news is that Molly Ringwald is pretty in pink again. The bad news is that it's pink maternity smocks. The minute you're introduced to Ringwald's Darcy, you know she's doomed. She pulls down straight As, she edits the school paper, she's got her pick of colleges vying for her favors, and she's got Stan (Randall Batinkoff), a fresh-faced dreamboat who is her soulmate in overachievement. Up to now, they've restricted themselves to chaste cuddling, but on a camping trip under the stars, they finally and irrevocably Go All The Way. She starts feeling queasy in the mornings and suddenly two bright futures go down the toilet.

Her bitter mom (Miriam Flynn), abandoned by her husband years previously, reacts in horror to the grim future she envisions for her prematurely pregnant daughter. Stan's strict Catholic parents want the eventual child put up for adoption. Even Stan reveals himself to be less than a model of sensitivity when he says, "You can always put it up for abortion . . . uh, adoption." Darcy goes through what should have been her last triumphant school year waddling under the weight of her swelling belly. "I love it when the smart kids act stupid," sneer bitchy high-school girls as she stomps by. Her water breaks at the school prom. After she gives birth to baby Esme, her relationship with her clingy mom collapses (*For Keeps* is unique in the Ringwald resumé because it breaks with her tradition of counseling or being cheered up by father figures, ranging from Paul Dooley in *Sixteen Candles,* the indulgent dad who drove her to school in *The Breakfast Club,* Harry Dean Stanton in *Pretty in Pink* and Dennis Hopper in *The Pick-Up Artist.* She even had a small role as Cordelia in the Jean-Luc Godard version of *King Lear*). She and Stan refuse all parental assistance, stubbornly subsisting in a tiny, drafty hellhole.

This couple who seemed most likely to couple now seem like Peg and Al Bundy. She's buckling under the weight of postnatal depression and also feeling guilty that Stan had to give up his place in the architecture program at Cal Tech to support them. For his part, Stan has actually become a miserable shoe salesman, alternately propositioned and mocked by his customers. The guilt and misery eventually causes them to separate until Darcy finds out that Cal Tech has accommodations for married students and their offspring. This inspires a

tearful reunion with Ringwald running down an empty street, clutching her daughter and screaming "STAAAN! STAAAN!"

For Keeps, though it confirmed that Ringwald's appeal was tied to her ability to portray a flustered young girl, holds up better than most of the Oh-my-God-it's-a-baby! movies around at the time including, ironically, the one directed by another of Molly's father figures, John Hughes. His first step outside the teenage arena he'd made his own was *She's Having A Baby* (1988), an autobiographical and extremely unlovable account of his days as a conflicted father-to-be. Kevin Bacon fills Hughes' shoes and conveys the young man's fear of parenthood, suburbia and conformity via an interminable parade of those cute fantasy sequences then prevalent on *thirtysomething.* While Bacon wrestles with temptation and the dilemma of giving up the empty world of advertising for the life of the mind he subsequently chose, his adoring wife (Elizabeth McGovern) has next to no lines and has little to do but bear the

prosthetic bulge. The movie's few noncomatose moments come courtesy of Alec Baldwin as Bacon's rascally best friend who besmirches his bud's married bliss by bringing a rock-video slut into their happy home and encouraging her to demonstrate the tricks of her trade.

As adult life provided progressively fewer outlets for the Brats to strut their particular stuff, the incorrigible Judd Nelson happened upon a grown-up role that was tailor-made for his brand of histrionics. In *From the Hip* (1987), directed by Bob (*Porky's*) Clark, he turned the Judd amps up to 11 and shook the foundations of sanity as Robin "Stormy" Weathers, a law student who gets into a prestigious and venerable Boston law firm, then pulls every showboating, attention-grabbing trick in his humungous book to get to argue a case in court. Unequaled in the field of overemoting to a captive audience in an enclosed space, Weathers soon becomes a smash on the court circuit. But is this master showman sufficiently skilled to dazzle a jury into acquitting an obviously guilty party? Here's where the movie examines its protagonist's moral mettle by giving him a high-profile case defending an English professor (John Hurt) accused of molesting and murdering a young girl. Weathers, infatuated with his own abilities, takes the case, confident he can get the prof off. Mad tactics like seizing the murder weapon—a hammer—and whacking the shit out of the courtroom with it, then yanking a vibrator out of the prosecutor's briefcase and waving it in his face, start to tip the scales of justice his way.

Gradually, though, the scent of doubt hanging over his snooty client's innocence blooms into a world of compost. "You are really bloated with self importance," Nelson tells Hurt, "I'm sick of seeing you strut around like some ridiculous peacock." Instead of invoking the Pot Kettle Black clause, Hurt assumes breeding and intellect will trump raging nostrils and popping eyeballs. *Big* mistake. In order to manipulate the client into sticking his own foot into the beartrap, he objects loudly when the prosecutor paints Hurt as a sex offender. "He's sexually inadequate," booms the great defender, "A weak man. A scared man. Impotent. IMPOTENT!" The accusations, the overacting, the nostrils, the eyes—Hurt can take no more, he leaps from the witness stand, grabs the hammer and suddenly the glove fits and nobody wants to acquit.

Pick any below-par *Matlock* and the chances are good it'll be better written than this, though it won't have the numbskull energy. Nelson, clearly convinced this movie is his *And Justice for All,* gets so worked up he almost ruptures a kidney. His scenes with the sly, understated, languid Hurt are hilarious to watch. One bellowing and stabbing the air, the other acting. Condolences to Elizabeth Perkins, saddled with the role as the movie's moral center, a sweet, nice, loving, nurturing nursery-school teacher who convinces her man to do the right thing.

The Downward Spiral
When Good Brats Do Bad Things

The world of letters had its own Brats. Chief among these chroniclers of eighties excess and ennui was Bret Easton Ellis, whose novel *Less Than Zero* (1987) painted a grim picture of numb adolescent Angelenos, drifting untouched through a haze of sex, drugs, decay and death. A required accessory rather than a rattling good read, the book still screamed *movie:* the white powder, the blue water, the dark glasses. A skillfully rendered film adaptation could stick a dagger into the empty heart of the decadent Hollywood lifestyle tacitly condoned by the Brats. The resultant movie excises the novel's amoral recountings of underage couplings and same-sex encounters, showing us the sunny cesspool through the panicked eyes of Clay (Andrew McCarthy), a privileged insider, coming home from college for Christmas and shocked to the core by the way his friends have degenerated. His buddy Julian (Robert Downey Jr.) is a junkie and a hustler, his onetime girlfriend Blair (Jami Gertz) is a beautiful blank slate. Turning a vision of hopelessness into the story of how one guy attempts to straighten out his messed-up friends isn't one of the great Hollywood rewrite crimes, but it definitely rates as a missed opportunity.

"Finally, a Rob Lowe movie everyone wants to see," quipped every stand-up comic and talk-show host after Rob Lowe was caught on tape with his pants down, his dick out and a teenage admirer on the other end of it. While Lowe went on the offensive, chiding the prurient interest of the media and emitting dire prognostications of our future as Tabloid Nation, the saturation publicity didn't hurt the fact that during the time of the unfortunate incident, he was making a movie in which he played a character wicked and venal enough to videotape a bout of intercourse with an underage partner. *Bad Influence* (1990), directed by Curtis Hanson, featured both Lowe and James Spader playing against type. Smartly capitalizing on the fact that most of us secretly harbored feelings that Lowe's outer yumminess covered an evil interior, he poured relish into his depiction of Alex, one of those versatile predator-voyeur-psycho types. Spader, normally the repository of unruffled sadism (he'd rattled off another yawning scumbag in *Less Than Zero*) plays Michael, a timid innocent whose heavily repressed dark side is brought to the surface by the demonic Alex. This is fine and dandy when the pair indulge in harmless pranks like knocking over a 7-Eleven. Alex seems like a friend in need when he frees Michael from the smothering clutches of his straight-laced fiancée, Ruth (mad-eyed Marcia Cross) by using their engagement party as a suitable occasion to air footage of her soon-to-be-spouse being straddled by a ravenous babe. Soon, though, Alex's idea of fun veers towards the homicidal. Realizing that he's volunteered for the sidekick role in a crime duo, Michael has to make a stand against the sinister figure who taught him how to walk and talk. An otherwise standard Psycho Within flick, the best thing about *Bad Influence* is its lip-smacking portrayal of L.A. decadence. Every nightclub is a glittering Gomorrah, filled with dead-eyed sinners writhing to some plodding electro backbeat.

Molly Ringwald as dirt-dumb, chain-smoking small-town bad girl? Say it ain't so. Unfortunately, it was and it was called *Fresh Horses* (1988). Andrew McCarthy frets up a storm as the college kid whose marriage plans are wrecked by his inexplicable moth-to-flame attraction to Ring-wald's earthy slut. So inert, it's like staring at stills.

No Brat was more suited to making the transition from hero to villain than Judd Nelson. Not for him though, surprisingly, the moustache-twirling, insanely cackling and hilarious postslaughter quip that came to characterize every bad guy who followed in the footsteps of Alan Rickman's *Die Hard* Eurolouse. Perverse to the end, Nelson, who'd played his leading-man roles like a drooling nutjob, imbued the serial killer he played in *Relentless* (1989) with a regretful calm. More in tune with the m.o. of the Judd we knew of old was the fact that his psycho was driven to kill by the pressure of being the son of a decorated police hero. The eighties may have been almost over, but Judd Nelson was still blaming his old man.

Wired

6

Arcade Rats, Science Fair Freaks, Time Travelers, Hackers and Teenage Geniuses

In 1995, Hollywood forgot its past and was condemned to eat it. This was the year when evidence was hefty enough to suggest that before he or she was sufficiently confident to deal with solid food, the average American child had flamed the neighborhood bedwetters and downloaded a book depository's worth of Jennifer Aniston gifs. The timing could not have been better for a slew of cyberspace-based movies, but like skeet shot from the sky, down they plummeted: *Hackers, Johnny Mnemonic, Strange Days* and *Virtuosity*. If the powers behind those executive decisions had paused and taken stock of a period a decade earlier when similar thinking lead to similar stiffs, much embarrassment could have been spared. Back in August of 1985, Hollywood put so much stock in the fact that the only time a breed of teenager left the PC in their bedroom was to blast aliens in the local arcade that, in the space of two weeks, they unleashed three teen science movies. The fact that *Weird Science, Real Genius* and *My Science Project* went gurgling down the toilet (although only the first mentioned left any lingering

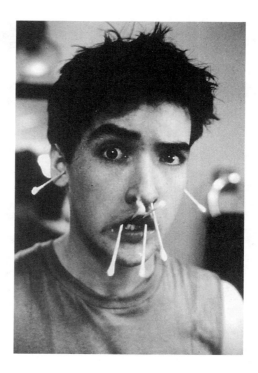

odor) points up the essential dilemma Hollywood has always, and will continue to face when dealing with science-minded teens. You might assume that this demographic, long characterized as socially inept, would rush, flattered, to patronize any onscreen depiction of their avenue of interest. In point of fact, they're aching for the chance to disdain the product aimed their way, bursting for the opportunity to go into tortuous detail about the many ways Hollywood got it wrong. Of course, if you satisfy this crowd, you'll have their scary, anal devotion for life and beyond. For every *Tron* and *The Black Hole* that becomes an object of ridicule, there's a *Star Wars* and a *Blade Runner* that becomes a religion. In fact, of the decade's mountain of youth-skewing movies, the teen science cycle, though brief, contains the biggest box-office hit. That would be *Back to the Future* but it wasn't the defining I Am Geek, Hear Me Roar experience. That honor goes to a movie that both thrilled the mainstream and validated the cognoscenti. That movie is *WarGames* (1983).

With a latter-day output that includes snores like *Point of No Return, Nick of Time, The Hard Way, Another Stakeout* and *Drop Zone,* director John Badham exhibits all the symptoms of a guy who hates his job. *WarGames,* though, dates from the period when he was wide awake. This slick peacenik movie nails its colors to the mast with a precredits sequence showing a random test in a nuclear missile base. As one of the two men entrusted with initiating the launch of the rockets refuses to turn the fateful key, it is established that the fate of the world is too important to be left in human hands. To this end, NORAD boffin John McKittrick (Dabney Coleman) supervises the installation of a massive lump of metal called W.O.P.R. (War Operation Plan & Response), whose sole function is to devise attack scenarios, calculate acceptable losses and remove human frailty from the picture. Crusty Chief of Staff General Jack Barringer (Barry Corbin) is unimpressed by the big computer, taking its introduction as a personal affront to him and his men.

Meanwhile, somewhere in Seattle, nascent hacker David Lightman (Matthew Broderick, as fresh as a newly hatched chick) is so aroused by a catalogue detailing a new range of games from a company called Protovision that he attempts to tap into their system to score a sneak preview. He gets a printout of a games list that includes titles like Biochemical Attack and Global Thermonuclear War. For a seasoned arcade warrior like himself, these titles are caviar. Searching for a password to allow him access into the system so he can start blasting, he explores the first game on the list, Falken's Maze. This was the work of noted scientist Stephen Falken, who specialized in refining computers to the point where they could learn from their mistakes; in effect, think for themselves. Researching the life of Falken, David finds that his son and wife were killed in a car crash and that he died soon after. This sad fact thrills David, who keys in the name of Falken's son, Joshua. That's the password! He's in! In fact, he's in the big W.O.P.R. computer. "Shall we play a game?" it purrs through a voice box. The machine thinks David is its creator, Falken. "How about Global Thermonuclear War?" suggests David, who thinks he's talking to a state-of-the-art computer game. "Wouldn't you prefer a good game of chess?" asks the computer.

David is insistent and the game begins. He picks the Soviet side, sentencing Las Vegas and Seattle to be reduced to rubble by his first strike. In the NORAD Combat HQ a Missile Warning is announced. As David and his gal pal Jennifer (Ally Sheedy) giggle and slurp Tab, the defense base is crawling with frantic military men, declaring a state of Def Con 3 and readying a missile response. Suddenly, David's rarely glimpsed dad bawls at him to come downstairs and pick up the garbage. He switches off the computer, and over at NORAD, as unexpectedly as it appeared, the threat to the West vanishes. The next night, a newscast spreads the horror story of the three-minute nuclear alert. "I'm screwed," whimpers David. "Throw the number away and act normal," advises Jennifer. Then Joshua (W.O.P.R.'s informal name) calls *him*. Trepidation oozing from every pore, he asks the machine its primary goal. "To win the game," it replies. He unplugs the phone, hugs it to his chest and pretends to ignore the time ticking away to the culmination of the game he started. The Feds track David down and haul him in for questioning, figuring him to fit the profile of a Commie convert. Almost evangelical in his own belief in David's rottenness is Professor McKittrick. "No way a high-school punk could put a dime in a telephone and break into our system. He's working for someone." Stuck in McKittrick's office, David appeals to Joshua. "Is this a game or is this real?" The computer replies blithely, "What's the difference?" It then, handily, goes on to tell David that he's a hard guy to track down. The list of addresses Joshua failed to reach him at includes a classified contact spot in Oregon. David grabs on to the fact that Falken's still alive.

The Feds catch him messing with McKittrick's computer and lock him in an infirmary room where he demonstrates some of the ingenuity that would go on to remove much of the stigma from being a computer nerd and make an icon of Mac-Gyver. A simple pair of scissors, a cunningly concealed personal stereo. Everyday items but in the hands of David Lightman, they become the tools he uses to record and play back the security lock signal, springing him from captivity.

Once he's out, he sends an ever bigger scare into the bladder of corporate communications, demonstrating deftly how to cheat a payphone with a ring-pull cap. David, joined by Jennifer, heads towards Oregon, secret home of the now pseudonymous Falken, while Joshua continues building toward the final countdown.

The death machine's creator turns out to be something of a letdown. Stephen Falken (John Wood) is fey and morbid, ignoring the entreaties of David and Jennifer by drawing a condescending analogy between the upcoming end of civilization and the demise of the dinosaurs. "Nature knows when to give up. I could never get Joshua to learn to give up. Did you ever play tic-tac-toe? It's always a tie, the game is pointless." Back in the war room, they believe you can win a nuclear war, that there can be acceptable losses. Extinction is part of the natural order." Jennifer blurts out, "I'm only seventeen, I'm not ready to die," but Falken is unmoved. "This is unreal, you don't care about death because you're already dead," accuses David. Their touching faith finally penetrates the darkness inside him and he joins them in the mad rush to NORAD HQ where they've just reached a state of Def Con One. Falken pleads with Barringer to have sense. "You are listening to a machine. Do the world a favor and don't act like one." The general calls off his response. Even though the computer map shows destruction across the country, contacts at various air bases report that they are alive and well. It was all a fantasy dreamed up by a nutty machine! Backslapping and hugging sweep through the base. After spending most of the movie overestimating Joshua, the collected humans now make the mistake of taking the computer for granted. While the forces of war and science congratulate each other, Joshua whizzes through selections of digits looking for the correct code that will launch the missiles. The good times are over as soon as they began.

Barringer orders the bombers back to fail-safe. David's last-gasp solution is to engage Joshua in a game. His various suggestions are denied. Then he proposes tic-tac-toe. The computer is flummoxed by the fact that the first game ends in a draw. David has Joshua play itself. As the machine continues to hurtle through numbers looking for the missile launch code, it simultaneously goes through all the possible options in a game of tic-tac-toe. It hits the launch code. The missile engines ignite. Then it runs out of game options. It learns that neither of its games can be won. "A strange game," it intones, "the only winning move is not to play. How about a nice game of chess?"

Excuse me while I change my soaking shorts. *WarGames* is a real cake-and-eat-it movie. Its honorable intentions are endlessly undercut by its blatant irresponsibility. "They're just machines, don't you see?" it implores us in one breath, then continues, "but look at the cool shit you can do with them." While none of its adult characters come off smelling of roses, it takes the unusual step of portraying its military men in a more humane light than its scientists. And as for Matthew Broderick's performance as David Lightman, every computer shut-in across the country probably walked with a spring in their step after seeing one of their number portrayed as a cool, resourceful brainbox who could not only infiltrate the toughest systems but snare a sturdy girlfriend (Ally Sheedy's Jennifer complemented David's cerebral tendencies by being an aerobicized, bike-riding picture of Outdoor Girl desirability). These were qualities that he would display again, though this time with less interest in the fate of mankind, when he took on the role of Ferris Bueller.

If *WarGames* depicted government as a body outpaced and intimidated by the very technology whose existence it authorized, Martha Coolidge's *Real Genius* (1985) took the opposite tack. Its dweebs were the innocent lackeys of a shadowy cabal of warmongers who exploited their aptitude to construct the perfect killing machine. This is why little Mitch Taylor (Gabe Jarret, the spitting image of Sarah Jessica Parker) is brought to Pacific Tech (modeled almost exactly on Cal Tech) to join the crack physics team of TV science guy Jerry Hathaway (William always-the-asshole Atherton). "Compared to you, most people have the intellect of a carrot. We're different. Better," Hathaway tells Mitch. So Mitch becomes another one of Hathaway's lab rats, beavering away on a laser project that, unbeknownst to them, was sold to the government as a weapon with such a powerful yet limited range of fire that it could be shot from space and would strike and vaporize any individual target.

Hathaway is happily diverting much of the funding from the project into the construction of a palatial home, but when the word comes down that a working model of the weapon is needed in four rather than the original eighteen months, he puts intolerable pressure on his prodigies. Luckily for the snivelling Mitch, he has a bosom buddy in the shape of campus physics legend Chris Knight (Val Kilmer). "I used to be you and lately I've been missing me, so I asked Hathaway if I could room with me," drawls Chris, who has evolved from a grind into a leisure-loving wise-ass put-on artist ("I didn't want you to think I was all brain, no penis," he tells a prospective employer). When Chris, Mitch and their colleagues discover the true nature of the project they've sweated blood over, they conspire to sabotage a test firing. Replotting the weapon's coordinates, they direct the beam through the window of Hathaway's dream home, which now has a ton of unpopped popcorn as its centerpiece. Stranded among the furious military men, Hathaway has to sit and steam while unleashed popcorn smashes through the windows, doors and roof of his house.

This socko ending included, *Real Genius* has much to commend it. Michelle Meyrink is a hoot as the hyperkinetic girl genius, Jordan, and Jon Gries as the eternal burnout student Laszlo, and Robert Prescott as the evil asswipe Kent both perform with aplomb. But Val Kilmer is big-time Not Funny, shooting for a Bill Murray–style hepcat and missing by miles. And then there's the uncomfortable question of Gabe Jarret. Not since the big-nosed kid from *The Last American Virgin* has such a *real*-looking individual stumbled through a piece of escapist entertainment. Jarret's frozen grin and moist-eyed gaze of worship is appropriate when he's an intimidated rookie, but when he's supposed to be acting in a loosened-up capacity and he's still standing like someone just opened an umbrella up his ass, he's become more of a threat to our safety than any laserbeam.

The *Manhattan Project* (1986)—or *Manhattan Project: The Deadly Game* as it was cumbersomely retitled—was a direct attempt to mate the tension of *WarGames* with the science-geeks-versus-the-government stance of *Real Genius.* In the movie, penned and directed by Woody Allen's writing partner, Marshall Brickman, Professor John Mathewson (John Lithgow) comes up with a new process for diffusing liquid plutonium. The usual shady cabal of shadowy figures are so impressed with his work that they send him off to spearhead plutonium production in a secret nuclear weapons plant in Ithaca, New York.

Mathewson has a deep-seated yearning for local Realtor Elizabeth Stevens (Jill Eikenberry) and tries to woo her by making friends with her smart-ass son Paul (Christopher Collet). Paul is suspicious of the weirdo putting the moves on his newly separated mom (typecasting for Collet, who was suspicious of the weirdo putting the moves on his mom in *First Born*) but Mathewson, playing on the kid's science-buff nature, invites him to his lab, drawing a veil over the true nature of his work. However, on the outside of the plant, Paul spots a five-leaf clover and this hideous mutation raises his suspicions that something is Very Wrong. When he tells his gal pal Jenny (Cynthia Nixon), she urges him to do something, to summon up the spirit of Anne Frank. "She's in my English class," she says, after seeing his blank face.

Paul, showing that David Lightman/MacGyver–style ingenuity, breaks into the plant, steals a jar of plutonium and decides to make his own atomic bomb. The reasons for this are kind of hazy. It may be so that Jenny has an angle to write an outraged article about the nuclear menace hidden in Ithaca. It may be because Paul is turned on by the idea of constructing "the world's first privately built nuclear device," or it may be because he wants to win the science fair. This is where he and Jenny take the finished 50-kiloton bomb. It's also where the FBI swoop down on Paul. In the middle of their interrogation, a bunch of science-fair nerds, who hail Paul as their god, spring him from the clutches of the Feds. This is the film's single funny sequence; smothering the agents in hydrogen and destabilizing the electric system, the nerds evolve into sinister, sniggering gremlins. Paul and Jenny return to Ithaca, using the threat of the bomb to force Mathewson into admitting the secret plant exists. Will he set off the device? Will the army shoot him? The sweaty tension that made *WarGames'* final act so effective is entirely bungled here. Paul's barely sure of his motives so why should we care?

In the *Weird Science/Real Genius/My Science Project* race for the teen-genius nomination, the last movie was completely shut out. The most mindless of the three, its scatter-as-many-dumb-gags-explosions-and-effects-as-we-can-to-cover-up-the-fact-we-don't-have-a-story approach to its subject matter threw up a constant stream of rueful chuckles. With the pressures of coming up with a bright idea for his high-school science project weighing heavy on his mind, Michael Harlan (John Stockwell) digs through a military junkyard, appropriating enough carelessly tossed-away circuit boards and generators to construct a superpowered device that, when switched on, kicks the door of the space/time continuum wide open. Bob Roberts (Dennis Hopper), the hippie science teacher, gets sucked into the void. In exchange, Cleopatra, squads of goose-stepping Nazis, a neanderthal man, a bunch of gladiators and, for a slam-bang finale, Godzilla are plucked from their own time zones and tossed into the maelstrom of Michael's school. If you mated *My Science Project* (1985) with *Bill & Ted's Excellent Adventure,* jettisoning along the way the former's pallid leads (Stockwell and Fisher Stevens as his murderously annoying buddy, Vince) and the latter's unhurried pace, you'd have a mad, monstrous beast of a movie. Still, no complaints about the finale, which returns Bob Roberts from the outer limits, driving a VW and proclaiming hoarsely, "The future is a groove!"

Sure, his Porsche is parked in a place so exclusive that even breathing near it in a manner that could be interpreted as suspicious is sufficient provocation for a squad of security operatives to stomp on the skull of the offender till his eyebrows spring out. But let's take a moment to show some sympathy for the plight of the Hollywood executive. The power to green light a project is both a blessing and a curse.

Because *you just don't know.* You pass on some puerile pitch. Someone else says yes and it makes a mint. That's why a trap-door failed to open beneath the feet of the hypothetical maniac who, between bong hits, blurted out the following premise: "It's *Mad Max*. It's *Starlight Express*. It's young. It's wild. It's the future. There's no water. The government keeps the people in chains. But these kids, these crazy, beautiful kids, they save the day. And they're on skates, see, so the dark forces of oppression can't catch them, and did I mention they're hot-shit hockey players, too? Oh yeah and, there's this magic sphere that unites the kids, tells them they can make it. It's got heart. It's got magic. It's got kids on skates playing hockey in the future! *Solarbabies*." Or something like that. Mel Brooks gave the go-ahead for this exact movie to be made under the aegis of his production company, Brooksfilms and, in doing so, gave himself a cast-iron defense against anyone who might say his name hadn't been associated with a funny film in years. Jason Patric and gorgeous, hapless Jami Gertz must have figured with the skates and the story they'd signed up for another *Lost Boys* exercise in high-speed, high camp. But, even though they and their colleagues (including James LeGros and Lukas Haas) are called upon to carry themselves like a chorus line in a Broadway stinker that'll never see a second night, the agony in their eyes is all too apparent. Shockingly, *Solarbabies* (1986) was written by Walon Green, best known for scripting *The Wild Bunch* with Sam Peckinpah, which gives a whole bunch of credence to the auteur theory.

Imagine if you were but a towheaded tot and one or both of your parents sat you down and made a speech that went as follows, "Your life will be a long string of disappointments. You will end up locked in a loveless sham with someone whose presence will fill you with dread and loathing. Your dreams will crumble to nothing and you will waste your days doing a job you hate and working for people you fear." If he'd included exactly such a paragraph of dialogue, director Joe Dante couldn't have done a more consummate job of pissing on the goodwill of his audience than he did in *Explorers* (1985).

There's magic in the air as three young boys, dreamer Ben

(Ethan Hawke), nerd genius Wolfgang (River Phoenix) and surly punk Steve (Bobby Fite) construct their own spacecraft. When the kids share the same dream and they wake up possessing the knowledge necessary to equip their homemade craft with the capacity for interplanetary travel, you know that someone is calling to them . . . Out There. You're ready to abandon yourself to that Spielbergian leap into wonder. Then they make it to the outer reaches of the galaxy and meet the life-forms that reached out to touch them. The aliens are big, stupid squishy lumps of Jell-O mold who receive all their stimuli via trashy American TV and whose only mode of communication is through endless pop-culture references (yeah I know, but at least I never promised you a voyage filled with wonder). The aliens are kids. Green, distended and squishy, but kids, nonetheless. Kids dumbed down by their exposure to mindless entertainment. Sucker us in, then slap us about the face, why don't you? Dante tries to sugar the pill with a no-place-like-home conclusion, but the damage has been done. *Explorers* joins *Gremlins* and his segment of *The Twilight Zone* movie to provide conclusive proof that Joe Dante is a grim brother whose speciality is making *die kinder* feel sick and miserable.

SpaceCamp (1986) is the ultimate *"Don't touch that!"* movie. A group of bright sparks are taking a learning course at NASA. They're inside a rocket for a flight simulation program. One of the kids touches a button after they've been explicitly advised to keep their hands to themselves, and before you can say, "Houston, we have a problem . . ." that big tin can has loosed its moorings. Luckily, Kate Capshaw's on board (maybe the only time the preceding five words have been used to start a sentence) and is a fully trained astronaut. She's got her hands full with a crew of wailing, complaining homesick geniuses including Lea Thompson, Kelly Preston, Leaf—now Joaquin—Phoenix (a very chubby little kid) and an actor called Larry B. Scott who had the misfortune to portray the sole black face in many a teen movie (he also had *Solarbabies* and *Revenge of the Nerds* on his resume). *SpaceCamp* has substantially the same plot as *Apollo 13,* and while it's not in any way a better film, or better acted, or better written or better directed—in fact, comparisons with *The Astronuts* are probably more appropriate—its crew of whiners, none of whom have a noble bone in their bodies, make it more fun.

He takes out the trash. He never talks back. He gets straight As. He's a star in Little League. He's too good to be true. He's *D.A.R.Y.L.* (1985), or Data Analyzing Robot Youth Lifeform, as he's known to the dangerous minds at the defense center who constructed him from old bits of string, hair dryers and egg cartons. This potentially lethal weapon (played by Barret Oliver) is stolen from the government and left to fend for himself. He's quickly adopted by doting parents Michael McKean and Mary Beth Hurt and sucked into the bosom of suburbia. Though his strange affinity for electrical appliances (one touch and he credits dad's ATM account with thousands of dollars) and ability to knock a baseball into the next town draw bemused glances, he's accepted as a local prodigy, then the Feds track him down. But Daryl doesn't want to be a Pinocchio assassin any more. He wants to scrape his knee and drink too much and skip school like a real live kid. I kind of wish this insipid movie had been a hit because it would have had an excellent setup for a teen *T2* sequel with the good robot versus the evil cyborg that can morph from school bully into pet dog into hot, panting neighborhood slut (another excellent idea and here I am just throwing it out there to the wolves).

A 12-year-old kid (Joey Cramer) disappears from his Fort Lauderdale home. After a long fruitless search, his parents come to terms with the fact that he's never coming back. Eight years later he returns, not a day older than he was when he vanished.

According to *Flight of the Navigator* (1986), he's spent the previous years whizzing about the galaxy in a spacecraft overseen by a wacky robotic flight commander (voiced by Paul Reubens under the pseudonym Paul Mall) well-versed in Earth pop culture. Now back home, he has to deal with the parents who had accepted his death and a younger brother who now towers over him. When the inevitable shady government scientists descend on him, brandishing ink-blot tests and anal probes, they discover he has mental access to the topography of a million hitherto undiscovered star systems. They want to know what he knows. He starts to buckle under the pressure. Naturally, the alien spacecraft springs him from confinement and takes him back in time to the minute before he was abducted. You got your goofy space adventure side to *Flight of the Navigator.* You got your serious, somber missing-presumed-dead son returns home to find his world has changed side to *Flight of the Navigator.* You can be either of these movies but my strong feeling on the matter is, you can't be both.

Even though *Tron* failed to drum up much custom from those constituents joined at the wrists to their joysticks, *The Last Starfighter* (1984) continued to stroke the arcade rats. Lance Guest plays the trailer-park kid whose only respite from his grim reality is the time of day when he can blast the shit out of some space invaders. His record high score brings him to the attention of a giant lizard (Robert *The Music Man* Preston under a ton of prosthetics) who claims to be a headhunter for the Star League of Planets. The league is in dire need of hot-shot fighter pilots to defend the universe from space invaders almost exactly like the ones Lance has been zapping on screen. Coming up with a dumb premise and then executing it in a way that best exploits the central conceit, no matter how limited, may not seem to be a momentous achievement. But, as the past entries prove, so many movies try to be more than their basic theme and end up shortchanging the audience. For the reason that it achieves its limited aims—dude shoots aliens—*The Last Starfighter* deserves respect.

Finally, the movie that kicked off the eighties teen science cycle. Just as The Fonz found his greatest big-screen success playing against type in *Night Shift,* so Chachi shook off his Bad Boy image, playing the geek in *Zapped!* (1982). Scott Baio's Barney starts the movie nagged and derided by his shrill and unpleasant parents, who disapprove of all the hours he spends in the lab working on pointless experiments. Little do they know, he's cultivating some primo hemp, and for reasons apparently unconnected with sheer cruelty, teaching mice to scuba dive into a vat of alcohol. While he's engaged in this activity, baseball coach Scatman Crothers accidentally knocks a beaker of some mysterious liquid into a jar containing another. The two compounds when combined produce a mysterious telekinetic effect which means that the mice can attract cheese by the power of thought, and more important, Barney can pop blouse buttons. He alternately does this and frets about doing it up until the school prom when he does it to such an extent that he loses his powers.

Zapped! is *Carrie* played for laughs, except that there's no movie, just a succession of lame stunts. Barney continually plays second banana to his stud bud Payton (Willie Aames; yup, we're witnessing a virtual prequel to the decidedly non-telekinetic *Charles in Charge*) and his bossy girlfriend, Roberta (Felice Schachter). Best bit: under the influence of Barney's primo hemp, Coach Scatman Crothers hallucinates meeting Einstein, then being chased by his wife who is riding a chariot and firing salamis at him.

Boys to Men

7

Hoodlums, Heartthrobs, Yuppies, Preppies, Sportos and Streetfighters

'm the bad guy? How did that happen?" wondered Michael Douglas's embodiment of angry, white maledom in *Falling Down* a split second before he was erased from a world that no longer tolerated his brutish ways. Always the most intuitive of A-list actors, Michael Douglas knew that for his stock character, the flawed white guy, the jig was up. Nobody had the time to listen to him whine, to lend a shoulder to his neuroses, provide constant reassurances of his potency, excuse his thoughtless behavior or indulge his delusions of grandeur. Suddenly, testosterone was second in line only to acid rain as the chief despoiler of our natural resources. Suddenly, accusations were rife that being a man meant belonging to a club whose entrance requirements included aggression, abuse, lying, cheating and cowardice, and whose motto was *Trap, Dominate, Fuck, Destroy.* (I fully accepted the accusations, I just couldn't get past the bastard at the door.) All of which makes a retrospective appreciation of male-targeted teen fare a task one takes on with mixed emotions. Because the eighties was Disney-

land for guys. A whole galaxy of reprehensible behavior is on show in these movies. Dumb guys, deadly guys, bullies, buffoons, betrayers, predators, punks and thugs. And they're all celebrated; their alienation is the result of an adult world unworthy of them, their hooliganism is a stirring example of youthful high spirits, their stupidity excused by naiveté or, in one notorious example, patriotism. The fulfillment of male fantasies is, of course, still a major function of the movies but today its tempered with self-awareness; the Action Dudes know that we know they're impossibly over-developed slabs of lunkhead beef, the comics break themselves up with their doody-obsessed Big Kid *schtick*. Back in the days when the multiplex was a boy's town, the audience was sincerely invited to share the hero's pain, exult in his triumphs, sympathize with his sulks and burn with his desires. Now that the parameters of our tolerance for masculine misbehavior have narrowed, how do these movies that expected us to invest our emotions in the well-being of white guys hold up?

That's why they call it high school...

Fast Times At Ridgemont High

From the man who brought you "Mr. Mom" & "National Lampoon's Vacation"

It's the time of your life that may last a lifetime.

Samantha Baker is turning sixteen and she's fallen in love for the first time. It should be the best time of her life.

But...her family is so preoccupied with her sister's wedding they totally forget her birthday, the boy she loves doesn't know she exists and the class clown is putting the make on her.

And...she still has to go to school, ride the bus, put up with an annoying younger brother, a hopelessly vain older sister, four delirious grandparents and a whacked-out foreign exchange student.

Well, hang in there, Samantha. The day's not over yet. You may still get one wish.

Sixteen Candles

Turning sixteen isn't easy, when you've fallen in love... for the first time.

A JOHN HUGHES FILM • A CHANNEL PRODUCTIONS PRESENTATION
SIXTEEN CANDLES Starring MOLLY RINGWALD PAUL DOOLEY JUSTIN HENRY ANTHONY MICHAEL HALL
Music by IRA NEWBORN Director of Photography BOBBY BYRNE Executive Producer NED TANEN Produced by HILTON GREEN
Written and Directed by JOHN HUGHES Soundtrack available on MCA Records and Cassettes A Universal Picture ©1984 Universal City Studios, Inc.

the laughter.
the lovers.
the friends.
the fights.
the talk.
the hurt.
the jealousy.
the passion.
the pressure.

the real world.

A JOHN HUGHES PRODUCTION

PARAMOUNT PICTURES Presents MOLLY RINGWALD HARRY DEAN STANTON
"PRETTY IN PINK" JON CRYER ANNIE POTTS JAMES SPADER and ANDREW McCARTHY
Edited by RICHARD MARKS Music Score Composed by MICHAEL GORE Executive Producers JOHN HUGHES and MICHAEL CHINICH
Written by JOHN HUGHES Produced by LAUREN SHULER Directed by HOWARD DEUTCH A PARAMOUNT PICTURE

PG-13 PARENTS STRONGLY CAUTIONED
Some Material May Be Inappropriate for Children Under 13

COPYRIGHT © 1986 BY PARAMOUNT PICTURES CORPORATION.
ALL RIGHTS RESERVED.

DOLBY STEREO
IN SELECTED THEATRES

Original Soundtrack Album Available on A&M Records,
Cassettes and Compact Discs

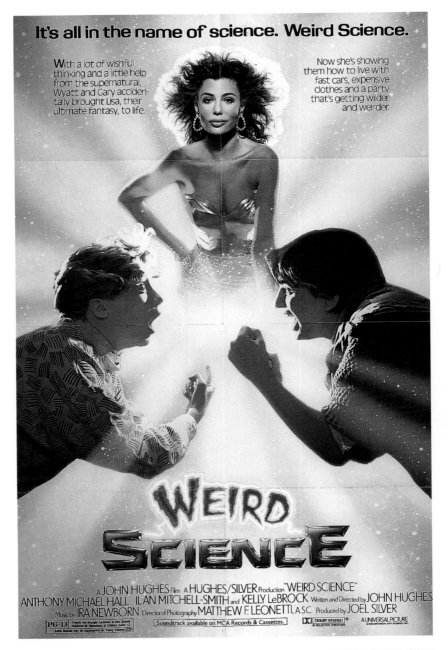

... and dorks created woman...

Weird Science

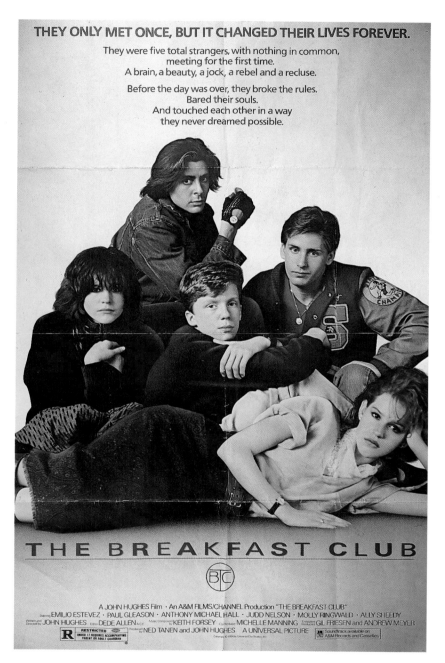

THEY ONLY MET ONCE, BUT IT CHANGED THEIR LIVES FOREVER.

They were five total strangers, with nothing in common, meeting for the first time.
A brain, a beauty, a jock, a rebel and a recluse.

Before the day was over, they broke the rules.
Bared their souls.
And touched each other in a way they never dreamed possible.

THE BREAKFAST CLUB

A JOHN HUGHES Film · An A&M FILMS/CHANNEL Production "THE BREAKFAST CLUB"
starring EMILIO ESTEVEZ · PAUL GLEASON · ANTHONY MICHAEL HALL · JUDD NELSON · MOLLY RINGWALD · ALLY SHEEDY
Written and Directed by JOHN HUGHES Editor DEDE ALLEN A.C.E. Music Composed by KEITH FORSEY Co-producer MICHELLE MANNING Executive Producers GIL FRIESEN and ANDREW MEYER
Produced by NED TANEN and JOHN HUGHES A UNIVERSAL PICTURE Soundtrack available on A&M Records and Cassettes

The agony and the ecstasy

The Breakfast Club

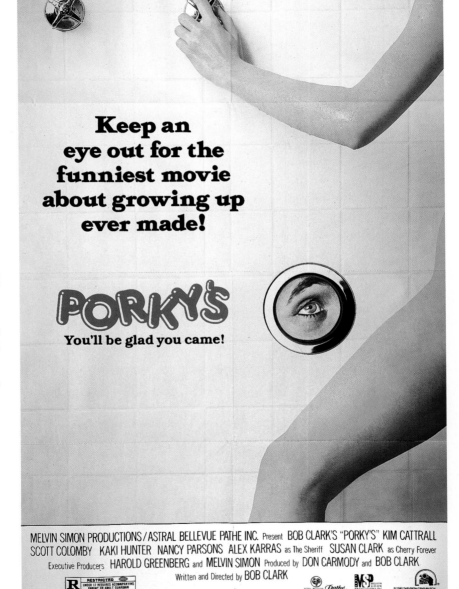

Keep an
eye out for the
funniest movie
about growing up
ever made!

PORKY'S

You'll be glad you came!

MELVIN SIMON PRODUCTIONS / ASTRAL BELLEVUE PATHE INC. Present BOB CLARK'S "PORKY'S" KIM CATTRALL
SCOTT COLOMBY KAKI HUNTER NANCY PARSONS ALEX KARRAS as The Sheriff SUSAN CLARK as Cherry Forever
Executive Producers HAROLD GREENBERG and MELVIN SIMON Produced by DON CARMODY and BOB CLARK
Written and Directed by BOB CLARK

R RESTRICTED
UNDER 17 REQUIRES ACCOMPANYING
PARENT OR ADULT GUARDIAN

LEISURE RULES

MATTHEW BRODERICK

FERRIS BUELLER'S DAY OFF

One man's struggle to take it easy.

A JOHN HUGHES FILM

PARAMOUNT PICTURES PRESENTS FERRIS BUELLER'S DAY OFF
MIA SARA   ALAN RUCK MUSIC SCORE BY IRA NEWBORN EDITED BY PAUL HIRSCH EXECUTIVE PRODUCER MICHAEL CHINICH
PRODUCED BY JOHN HUGHES AND TOM JACOBSON WRITTEN AND DIRECTED BY JOHN HUGHES
A PARAMOUNT PICTURE

PG-13 PARENTS STRONGLY CAUTIONED
Some Material May Be Inappropriate for Children Under 13

COPYRIGHT © 1986 BY PARAMOUNT PICTURES CORPORATION. ALL RIGHTS RESERVED.

Cry Freedom!

Ferris Bueller's Day Off

et's start at the top. What film is more Boy and more eighties than *Risky Business* (1983)? As I stated in the introduction, most of the movies of the era fly in the face of the prevalent—and still prevailing—perceptions of the decade. Though the eighties are commonly held to be about Greed, Power and Excess, the most successful of the teen films cautioned against avarice, attempted to bridge social divides and sided with the underdog, except this one. It started off like another glossy, frisky, suburban teen sex farce but *Risky Business* soon turned out to have a heart of glass. The guy we're rooting for, Joel Goodsen (Tom Cruise), isn't just a good son, he's a paragon of virtue, a grade-A student so focused on his future even his hormonally instigated fantasies of naked girls soaking in the shower are interrupted by nightmares about being three hours late for his SATs. His adrenaline is set racing at the prospect of being named a Future Enterpriser in a scheme set up by his high school to find the capitalist tools of tomorrow. With priorities so far out of whack, is it any wonder his parents prize their lad almost as much as they enjoy the many material possessions littering their lovely home? It is with considerable reluctance that the Goodsens take off for the weekend, leaving the spoils of their labor in the care of Joel, but if parents didn't disappear for weekends teen movies would be marketed as family fare.

So out of the picture they go and the stage is set for the scene that constitutes the sole reason *Risky Business* is fondly recalled as a big-hearted festival of fun. Mom and Dad are history, out comes the Chivas and Coke, Seger blasts from the speakers and Joel, in his jockeys, redefines unshackled white suburbanite liberation with his air guitar, his pelvic thrusts and his couch humping. "Just take those old records off the shelf . . ." Joel's thin veneer of civilization may have melted away but even in his pants-free primal state, he's still buttoned down next to his unsightly friend, Miles (Curtis Armstrong, the Most Exalted Potentate of Grossout). Miles, a motivational speaker specializing in mischief, sees it as his mission to makes sure Joel uses his time sans parents as unwisely as possible. "Joel, you wanna know something? Every now and then, say 'what the fuck.' 'What the fuck' gives you freedom. Free-

Boys to Men

dom brings opportunity. Opportunity makes your future." So saying, he dials a hooker and leaves a message on her machine, giving Joel's name and address. The black transvestite who shows up takes one look at the trembling, tight-lipped Joel and, every inch a pro, says "I know what you need." Enter Rebecca DeMornay's Hitchcockian frosty blond sex specialist, Lana. "Are you ready for me . . . Ralph?" she murmurs, putting mocking emphasis on Joel's hastily assumed nom de plume. Accompanied by the Arctic blasts of Tangerine Dream's score, Lana gives of herself so unselfishly that Joel and we believe that he has touched that one spot that she keeps at a far remove from the johns. But when morning comes and Joel finds, to his consternation, that he lacks enough ready cash to meet her $300 fee, she's all ice and all business, refusing to leave the house until he meets his part of the arrangement.

Flustered, he rushes off to the bank to cash in a savings

bond. But when he returns, not only is Lana gone but also conspicuous by its absence is his mother's beloved Steuben glass egg. He goes in frantic search of the hooker and the bauble and winds up rescuing Lana from her vicious pimp, Guido (Joe Pantoliano). Saving her requires a car chase that climaxes with Joel's dad's revered Porsche ending up at the bottom of Lake Michigan (situated in the same city that houses the wreck of Cameron Frye's father's beloved Ferrari). First the egg, now the car, and it gets worse! By the time Joel gets home, Guido and associates have stripped the Goodsen spread of furniture, holding it as ransom till he's repaid the loss of Lana's earning power.

His parents are due back in a day, and the interviewer from Princeton is about to drop in on Joel to find out what he's made of. He doesn't leave town and begin a new life under the name Ralph. He doesn't even swallow a handful of pills. He exploits the weakness that got him into this pickle. Lana recruits a bunch of cheerful colleagues, and they turn Joel's empty home into a suburban bordello. Suddenly, he's a cool dude, glancing knowingly over the top of his Ray-Bans, the fate of a hundred high school virgins in his hands. His savoir faire and acumen even steamrollers the doubts of the Princeton guy, who finds he's doing an interview in a house of ill repute.

Guido returns the precious Goodsen belongings but, malicious to the end, tosses the Steuben egg at Joel. Does he, in *Ferris Bueller* fashion, decide to take a step back and let that egg—*that damned egg!*—splinter into a million pieces thus ending his subjugation at the hands of material possessions? No, he hurls himself across the lawn in agonized slow motion, attempting to catch it before it hits the ground. Even though he has good hands, there remains just the merest shadow of a hint of a scratch and that's what Mrs. Goodsen zeroes straight in on. She expresses grave disappointment, but just as all seems to be lost, Joel's dad breaks the good news: his son's going to Princeton. As he accepts his Future Enterpriser award, Joel makes mental plans to continue his profession in college. "I deal in human fulfillment. I grossed over eight thousand dollars in one night. Time of your life, huh kid?"

Years before Gordon Gekko got to give his historic "Greed Is Good" address, Joel Goodsen was laying out the terms of the times: financial reward is everything, the upper-middle class lifestyle must be preserved and maintained at all times, a capitalist is just a prostitute in a different kind of business suit. Brrr . . . And writer/director Paul Brickman keeps the movie consistently chilly. Lots of space, lots of darkness, lots of neon, Tangerine Dream's electropulse and the frostbite that is Rebecca De Mornay. Brickman never took the *American Graffiti* step of outlining his characters' futures, but if I might be so bold, I'd say that Joel ends up bankrolling a Republican presidential candidate's campaign and that he's either bought Lana's silence or had her shut up permanently.

Food riots in Poland. El Salvador fails. Greens control Germany and demand end to nuclear arms in Europe. Mexican revolt. The U.S. stands alone." If ice water ran through *Risky Business'* veins, *Red Dawn's* blood was boiling. In his capacity as writer and director—his resume includes *Conan the Barbarian, Apocalypse Now, Big Wednesday* and *Jeremiah Johnson*—John Milius has been absolutely unabashed in his mythologizing of Man. Man the killer with a code; Man the noble savage, smeared in his own feces, clad in the pelt of a mountain lion he killed, fucked and skinned with his bare hands; Man the warlord, claiming fresh territory as his own, trampling and raping all who bar his way.

In *Red Dawn* (1984), Milius tapped into the festering right-wing paranoia of the early eighties and used it to fuel a freakish teenage tough-guy fantasy. His scenario, which doubtless caused sleepless nights in many a bunker, was that a coalition of Russian and Cuban forces were rolling slowly but inexorably across the southern and northwest borders, surprising and quickly conquering the heartland. Then, they come to Calumet, Colorado. *Big* mistake. Sure, it looks grim at the outset. A fresh-faced history class is attempting to pay attention (as the teacher delivers a lecture on Genghis Khan) while outside, the sky goes black as a mass of pinko paratroopers drop in to crush the town under their heels. In a matter of moments, it seems, Lenin posters line the streets and dissenting locals cool their heels in internment camps. But not everyone is un-prepared for the attack. A band of teenagers led by the barely civilized Jed (Patrick Swayze) stock up on Spam, grab a cache of munitions and head for the woods, with the last words of slain countryman Harry Dean Stanton ringing in their ears: "Avenge me, boys." Thus the boys (Swayze, C. Thomas How-ell, Charlie Sheen, Darren Dalton, Doug Toby, Brad Savage) plus two female recruits (Lea Thompson, Jennifer Grey) be-come a crack vigilante unit, known and feared as . . . the Wolverines (the name of their high school football team)! Using booby traps, improvised ingenuity and the element of surprise—methods not dissimilar to the ones Macaulay Culkin employed to prevent Joe Pesci and Daniel Stern from ransack-ing his home—the Wolverines turn the tide in favor of the tat-tered remains of Old Glory.

Red Dawn was much maligned on its release, but for the wrong reasons. This was around the time that Rambo was set-tling old scores, that Reagan made his "Begin bombing Russia" joke on an (oops!) open mike, that Chuck Norris' *Invasion U.S.A.* was on big screens and Kris Kristofferson's *Amerika* was on TV. Milius' movie was the only one that portrayed its heroes as scared and crippled with self-doubt. They even got caught up in questioning the morality of their vigilante action. Ambivalence was also on show in the enemy camp. A Cuban commander (Ron *Superfly* O' Neal) was depicted expressing more admiration for the crazy kids that were blowing up his tanks than his creepy Russian colleagues.

Call *Red Dawn* a dud action movie if you want (even with a hand on the pump, Lea Thompson was still perky). Deride it for ludicrous Man-mythologizing scenes like the one in which Jed makes a Viking of whimpering Robert (C. Thomas Howell) by killing a deer and forcing him to drink the blood ("Kinda makes you feel different inside," observes Bob). But as far as irresponsible bug-eyed red-baiting movies of the eighties went, it may have been the least retarded. And, as far as Boy movies went, there were many worse offenders.

Bad Boys

You know him: The leather. The swagger. The thin skin. The misunderstood, brooding loner with the loud bike, the oily hair and the dark secret. Nice girls shudder away from him but nurse forbidden desires for his rough touch. Other guys sneer at him, but fear his rage and envy his instant access to the wildness within. Everybody loves the bad boy.

In a decade bursting at the seams with young actors who appeared to covet nothing more than the chance to play tortured loose cannons, very few were actually able to summon up the necessary *cojones* to do a good Bad Boy. The doyen of hoodlums with heart was Matt Dillon, an actor so rebellious he even played a character called Rebel (in the movie *Rebel*). Talk about your impeccable credentials: Dillon was the bad influence in Jonathan Kaplan's little-seen *Over the Edge,* a movie about a bunch of disaffected California kids left to rot in an airless upwardly mobile ghetto. When Dillon's Richie, the kid who leads the others into drink, drugs and crime, gets shot by an overzealous cop, the other teens go on the rampage. Originally planned for release in 1979, Orion Pictures (who scheduled it as their debut movie) yanked it from their schedule after a few test screenings, fearing it would incite copycat violence. Hysterical as that reaction sounds, *Over the Edge*'s climactic scene, of the kids locking the parents who all but abandoned them in a classroom, then smashing the shit out of the school, packs a hell of a kick. You sort of want to break things after you see it. Or at least barge into things and pretend you didn't see them there.

Dillon went on to play someone approaching the Good Boy/Bad Boy crossroads in *Tex* (1982), the first film in his S. E. Hinton troika. His titular Tex is a 15-year-old Oklahoma farmboy, growing up without parental influence (his father is on the rodeo circuit). He takes a little drink, gets involved in a little horseplay, pays lip service to the notion of petty crime, but, ultimately, comes out okay. This slight film, directed by Tim (*River's Edge*) Hunter is made special by Dillon's amazing ability to make a slack jaw and a glazed expression suggest hidden depths and inner turmoil.

Along with *Tex* cohort Emilio Estevez, Matt Dillon was one of the massed ranks of Bad Boys hurtin' and brawlin' and weepin' their way through Francis Ford Coppola's fairy-tale adaptation of S.E. Hinton's *The Outsiders* (1983). Dillon, Estevez, C. Thomas Howell, Tom Cruise, Patrick Swayze, Rob Lowe and Ralph Macchio were the Greasers, a band of dirt-poor, ill-educated, no-account Tulsan teens. They may have sported oilslicks on their head and cows on their backs, but these Greasers were angels with dirty faces, pure of heart and loyal to a fault. As Coppola empties vats of treacle, canonizing his cast and bathing his central characters, Ponyboy (C. Thomas Howell) and Johnny (Ralph Macchio) in angelic hues, only Dillon's devilish Dallas strikes the right Bad Boy chord. "If he was here, I'd probably . . . fall in love with him or something," shuddered Diane Lane's Cherry Vallance.

Lane was suckered by Dillon's seductive slack jaw once again in Coppola's second Hinton adaptation, *Rumble Fish*. "You're smart, Rusty James," she told his character, "just not word smart." The story of a nascent bad boy and his worshipful relationship with his legendary elder brother, The Motorcycle Boy (Mickey Rourke), *Rumble Fish* (1983) is dazzling to behold for about fifteen minutes. After that, its black-and-white impressionism (interrupted only by the deep red of those metaphorical fish) and post–rigor mortis performances made it indispensable solely in the noggins of advertising executives and video directors who suddenly had a fresh concept to pilfer.

A fourth Hinton adaptation, 1986's *That Was Then, This Is Now,* both starred and featured a script by renaissance man Emilio Estevez. His character Mark enjoys the hoodlum lifestyle, rumbling and hustling with best bud Bryon (Craig Sheffer). Then two blows shatter the fabric of their friendship. First, their laconic mentor Charlie (Morgan Freeman) is wasted in a shootout. Then Bryon takes up with nice girl Cathy (Kim Delaney) and wants to change his no-good ways. Mark, smarting at being tossed aside, lashes out at those around them, he descends into massive sulks and plaintive cries for attention, like getting Cathy's little brother hooked on drugs. You really notice the absence of Coppola's melodramatic hand on this one. Director Christopher Cain's showiest moment is when he shoots one of Mark's miserable monologues about how he never had nothin' or no one with the raindrops on the nearby window pane reflected on his face. *Like the sea of uncried tears welling within him!*

Snatching Matt Dillon's Bad Boy baton was Sean Penn. Here was a guy who lived the role long after the cameras had stopped turning. He was involved in numerous public rumpuses, he did short periods of hard time and few women seemed able to resist his puppy-dog psychosis. Sean Penn was such a Bad Boy he even starred in a movie called *Bad Boys* (1983). In it, he played Mick O' Brien, a criminal-minded young citizen whose purse-snatching, car-jacking lifestyle is abruptly terminated after he gets involved in a shoot-out, the end result of which is the accidental death of the young brother of Hispanic gang leader Paco Moreno (Esai Morales). Mick gets banged up in a juvenile correctional facility seething with murderers, rapists, junkies and gangbangers. In order to immediately establish himself as top dog in juvie hall, he wraps a bunch of Coke cans in a blanket, walks right up to the reigning inmate and smashes his head open.

Mick may have communicated the fact that he's one tough fuck but his time is ticking away fast. On the outside, Paco Moreno has sworn vengeance for the death of his brother. To this end, he rapes Mick's devoted girlfriend, J.C. (Ally Sheedy in her big-screen debut) and commits enough blatant offenses to get himself confined behind bars. The tension mounts till finally the prisoners—desperate for entertainment and obviously incarcerated in the days before a decent basic cable package went hand in hand with a sentence—barricade the screws in their offices, turning the prison into a battleground for the Ultimate Fighting Championship between Mick and Paco. Not until Rowdy Roddy Piper interrupted *They Live* to stage a protracted demonstration of his wrestling prowess would a modern movie contain such a lengthy scrap. After what seems like several days of kicking, punching, gouging and scratching, Mick straddles Paco's barely conscious body, holds a knife above his head and prepares to slam it down into the body of his enemy. As the knife hangs in the air, the other prisoners chant *"Kill! Kill! Kill!"* The blade descends, the chant stops and Mick looks spent. It takes a moment for the camera to pull back and reveal the knife embedded in the ground.

For the first and, to date, only time in his scene-stealing history, Sean Penn was consistently upstaged in this movie by his wacky, pint-size sitcom smart-ass cellmate Horowitz (played by Eric Gurry, who previously performed almost the exact same role in the Al Pacino movie *Author!, Author!,* which was written by Beastie Dad Israel Horovitz). Going Mick's Coke-cans-in-blanket assault one better, Horowitz wreaks havoc on a psycho called Viking (Clancy Brown) by wiring a radio to explode and leaving it in the thug's vicinity. It's hard to tell which is more unbearable; Viking's screams of agony following the destruction of half his head, or Horowitz's cackles of delight.

Aidan Quinn, who has a battery of nice guys, good eggs and repressed rebels to his credit, donned leathers and jump started a Harley in *Reckless* (1984), the *Naked Gun* of eighties Bad Boy flicks. Everyone's got it in for his miserable Johnny Rourke, including his drunken dad, the fascist coach who won't put him in. Sometimes it gets to be so much that the only thing he can do to release the tension is ride way up to the top of a hill, look down on the stinking, grey town and its little people with their little lives, suck down a brew and revel in his own charisma. In this last-mentioned activity, he is not alone. The regulation rich girl suffocating inside her pampered existence and dying for a hunk on a hog to drag her away from dullsville is on hand and she's played by Daryl Hannah. "I'm fucking perfect and I'm sick of it," she spits at Johnny, giving him an open invitation to cover her with axle grease. Among their more brazen exploits is breaking into the high school and scattering the personnel files around as they run wild through the corridors, laughing, kissing and shrieking to the accompaniment of Kim Wilde's call to arms, "Kids

In America." *Reckless* was written by Chris Columbus who went on to direct the *Home Alone* movies.

Penelope Spheeris, known in the nineties as the director of, among others, *The Little Rascals, The Beverly Hillbillies* and *Wayne's World,* spent the previous decade avidly chronicling the exploits of misfits and rejects on the edge of society. *The Boys Next Door* (1985) was a white-trash-on-a-killing-spree bloodbath featuring two Cali kids, Roy (Maxwell Caulfield) and Bo (Charlie Sheen) celebrating their graduation from high school and upcoming entry into the real world by driving around splattering strangers. Society is implicitly fingered as the true culprit.

Class of 1984 (1982) takes no such pains to absolve it's eponymous antagonists. "Unfortunately, this film is partially based on true events," warns the opening announcement. Music teacher Andrew Norris (Perry King of TV's *Riptide*) turns up for his first day at Abraham Lincoln High School to find that a gang of homicidal punks have the institution in the grip of their cut-off leather gloves. They intimidate, beat and torture at will, deal drugs and run a vice ring. Norris immediately bumps heads with the leader of the gang, a suave maniac called Stegman (Timothy Van Patten of . . . for 100 points . . . too slow, TV's *The Master*), who is given to leering pronouncements like "I am the future. Life is pain. Pain is everything." Though Stegman is a prodigious enough talent to bring water to the eyes of Norris with his self-composed sonata, he's also psychotic enough to slice up the bunnies in the biology class run by Terry Corrigan (Roddy MacDowall of . . . I'm going with *Tales of the Gold Monkey*). When the punks rape Norris' pregnant wife, he snaps. At a school concert recital while the orchestra is sawing its way through the 1812 Overture, he wastes them, one by one, with Stegman plummeting to his death in front of a packed auditorium just as the band hits the rousing climax. That's the second-best bit. The best is when school wimp Arthur (Michael J. Fox of TV's . . . too easy) is found hanging from the flagpole.

James Spader, an actor normally content to stand and sneer from the sidelines, was pressed into Bad Boy mode on two occasions. In *The New Kids* (1985), he was the effete, drawling, platinum-coiffed, pit bull caressing, Tennessee Williams–like head of a crew of inbred, mouth-breathing troublemakers out to rub dirt in the pretty faces of new kids in town, Lori Loughlin and the never-heard-from-before-or-since Shannon Presby. In *Tuff Turf* (1985), he's a rich kid hit by hard times. His relocation to the grubby side of the tracks is eased by the fact that the hot moll of the local thuglord throws herself at him. Spader's what-the-hell-am-I-doing-here performance in the first movie is enthralling, but the second film has the edge. Not only does it require him to break sweat and engage in physical contact, but at one lunatic juncture, he has to crash a swank party and sing a heartfelt ballad. And you thought the Academy's snubbing of *Hoop Dreams* was a sin . . .

Jock Itch

If the hacking up of nubile coeds in slashers can be traced to the payback fantasies of vengeful nerds, the criminalization of the athlete in eighties' movies has its genesis in the same resentment. Here's one of the great anomalies of the decade: what could be more inspiring, desirable and downright American than the prospect of young men and women engaged in the act of healthy competition? The same sporting life that regularly reduces guys like Bob Costas to blubbering wrecks was, in the cinema of teen, seen as a breeding ground for nazis, morons, sadists, rapists and enemies of freedom. How many million movies have you seen where the heavy, the tormentor of the hero, the abuser of women, the force of oppression, was the dumb jock? Emilio Estevez's *Breakfast Club* sporto had to be deprogrammed via doobage before he could confront and discard the boorish, bullying side of himself. In *Heathers,* Christian Slater shrugs off the slaying of two football stars, reasoning that he's rid the world of date rape and AIDS jokes. While movies like *Field of Dreams* and *Bull Durham* acted as

Valentines to sport, the same marquee that trumpeted their presence also announced countless horror films and comedies that screamed "I have seen the enemy and he's wearing the number nine jersey!" Sure, you don't have to dirty your cuticles digging for high-profile, pro-sport teen flicks but when you come across them, be aware that they're espousing a minority view.

In the 1990s any lithe and limber slice of beef who can kick over his head stands a better than average chance of winding up with his own straight-to-cable "Feet of Fury" revengefest. But back in the heady years of teen stroking, the martial arts arena was the personal province of one man. Surname: Macchio—brutal, musclebound, remorseless. First name: Ralph—timid, whimpering, puny. Put them together: enter *The Karate Kid* (1984). Director John G. Avildsen had, with *Rocky,* displayed some proficiency in telling the story of an Italian-American underdog rising to face impossible odds. Dropping back a generation and switching contact sports, he followed Daniel (Macchio), a New Jersey kid relocated to the seemingly welcoming climes of Southern California. While the physically unprepossessing new kid has enough reserves of nervous personality to win a date with a pretty classmate (Elisabeth Shue), his presence makes enough enemies to inspire an attack by students who are also members of the local karate club. They don't just kick sand into his face; after they've beaten him to a bloody pulp, they rev up their motorbikes and send torrents of sand spraying into his wounds. But help is at hand. Before the karate nazis (all spookily clad in those Halloween skeleton suits) can attempt some Seagal-style eye gouging, a portly diminutive figure steps out of the shadows, and with a few deft kicks and wrist-snaps, sends the gang scampering away in disarray.

Daniel's savior is the local maintenance man, Mr. Miyagi (Noriyuki "The Artist Formerly Known as Pat" Morita). A fount of specious Oriental mysticism, Miyagi becomes Daniel-san's *sensei,* teaching him when to walk away and when to take on an opponent. Of course, Daniel doesn't immediately realize he's being granted access to ancient wisdom; he thinks he's being used as cheap labor to paint Miyagi's fence and wax his car. Hostilities between Daniel and the disciples of the embittered Vietnam vet, Kreese (Martin Kove), who runs his karate school with such a heavy hand he makes R. Lee Ermey look like Stuart Smalley, reach a peak at a martial arts face-off. Kreese instructs his star pupil to cripple Daniel, and this thug who, in the opening attack was cheerfully gearing up to ride his motorbike across Daniel's head, starts to snivel like a baby. This has the effect of transferring the mantle of ultimate evil to the corrupt adult. The hapless student hacks away at Daniel's ankle, causing him to collapse in agony. At the climactic moment, Daniel spreads his arms, raises his leg and strikes the legendary crane stance which enables him to put the other guy on the mat. Emotionally, we the audience are right down there on the ground, writhing with the loser, such is the pummelingly professional job done by Avildsen, Macchio, Morita and Kove. I haven't been packed in ice, I've seen a few movies in my time, but there were times during the final fight I actually found myself worrying that Daniel might not make it.

Responsible for filling far more dojos than any Van Damme rampage, *The Karate Kid* went on to inspire three sequels. None was anywhere near as entertaining, but *Part II* (1986) is worth mentioning being as it started *the exact second* the first one left off, with Kreese attempting to mete out a sound thrashing to Mr. Miyagi and having both his chopping hands shattered in the process. (An attempt to sire a distaff spin-off in 1994's *Next Karate Kid* ended in humiliation and despair. Rather than focusing on a rampaging riot grrrl hellbent on kicking her way to self-esteem, excellently-named femme lead Hilary Swank was forced to essay the role of an ornithologically-inclined problem child who barely has *one decent fight* in the entire movie!)

D o you ever wake up sweating in the middle of one of those dark nights of the soul when you realize how little your life actually amounts to and how much time you've devoted to staring blankly at things like Rob Lowe's rowing movie? In *Oxford Blues* (1984), he's a Vegas car valet who fakes his way onto the acceptance list for the venerable British university in order to meet and mate with his dream girl, aristo-wench Lady Victoria (Amanda Pays). Cue culture shock with Lowe's Nicky D'Angelo navigating his big red car through leafy glades and past tea shops, punching the air in triumph. Oblivious to the disdainful looks and exquisitely constructed put-downs that greet his unwanted appearance in the gleaming spires, he puts some of that brash Yank know-how to good effect, gate-crashing a boatrace and rowing, clad in leather jacket, to a second-place finish. This gets him the attention of Lady Victoria and the enmity of her boyfriend, Colin Gilchrist-Bishop (Julian Sands, working that sneer of cold command), who is, of course, Oxford's long-established rowing god. Under the tutelage of college professor Routlege (Alan Howard, doing a dissipated swinger thing) and rowing team cox Rona (Ally Sheedy), Nick becomes a little less of a self-centered hey-everybody-look-at-me-I'm-American attention grabber and more of a team player. In the end, Nick and Colin put aside their differences and in a resolutely unrousing climax, row together against Harvard. *Oxford Blues* is a bomb, of course, but it's almost worth your indulgence for the scene where the nonverbal Lowe is moved to interrupt a debate titled Should Columbus Have Stayed in Spain? with a spirited defense of the U.S.A.

Full of gasping, spluttering young men falling open-mouthed into thick puddles of mud and slithering ungracefully around rain-soaked playing fields, *All The Right Moves* (1983) is about as unglamorous as a teen sports movie starring Tom Cruise can be. Cruise plays a high-school football star desperate to get out of his dying Pennsylvania mill town to make some sort of life for himself. Lea Thompson as his girlfriend and Craig T. Nelson, taking on the role of coach for the first—but sadly not the last—time, see their futures bound up with his. *Johnny Be Good* (1988) takes the same setup and makes a pig-brained calamity of it. Johnny Walker (skinny little Anthony Michael Hall, now a hulking, barely recognizable wall of flesh) has such a good arm that scouts from rival colleges lose their minds in his presence, offering him women, money, cars and drugs up the wazoo if he'll sign with their schools. He takes a hedonistic tour of various colleges before being humbled by his family into realizing that he was in danger of becoming a sell-out and signing up with the one institution who put on the plate only the prospect of a solid education.

Once you get past the shock of Hall's appearance (he looks like he's been bench-pressing buses), there are many other indignities to contend with: Paul Gleason (*The Breakfast Club*'s Vernon) as Johnny's sleazy Coach, Uma Thurman, making an unhappy major movie debut as the love interest, Jim McMahon, shown filming an Adidas spot that is included in its entirety, and Judas Priest's version of the title tune. The only light relief comes from Robert Downey Jr., who looks to be improvising his entire part. The movie grinds to a halt as he launches into a bout of babbling free association. You find yourself letting out a weary sigh when the plot starts up again.

'm eighteen. I haven't done anything. I made this deal with myself, this is the year I make my mark." This messianic burst of introductory resolve heralds what sort of movie? A spiritual awakening? A loss of virginity? A rite of passage? *Vision Quest* (1985) fancies itself as all of those but what it actually is is a wrestling movie. Louden Swain (Matthew Modine) is a high-school grappler obsessively attempting to drop his body weight so he can get down to 168 pounds and become eligible to take on the legendary, unbeatable Chute.

At the height of his my-body-is-a-temple insanity, distraction shows up in the deadpan form of Carla (Linda Fiorentino), a would-be artist en route to California whose car breaks down and who ends up staying at the house of Louden and his old man (Ronny Cox). Sexual tension? By the bucketful. Louden's concentration goes all to hell and pretty soon, he's furtively picking her panties out of the laundry basket and ecstatically inhaling their warmth. Driven insane by the mistaken belief she's boffing his English teacher, he throws himself at her and is whacked away. Finally, she accedes to his innocent babbling (confirming that a tender, romantically inclined Linda Fiorentino is not radically different from an icy, contemptuous Linda Fiorentino).

After a literal roll in the hay with Carla, Louden is amazed that he ever got himself so worked up by a stupid wrestling match. This meandering movie's one piece of tension is finally introduced. Has Louden lost his edge? Will he step in the ring with Chute? The answers to both questions are in the affirmative. He regains his hunger to choke Chute when Carla takes off unannounced for Cali (she comes back for the big fight, of course) and after a colleague has delivered a tragic monologue about sitting in a hotel room watching a football match on Mexican TV, where the sight of Pele scoring a goal caused him to blubber like a child. Matthew Modine was a good choice to play Louden. Even when he's squeezing the last breath out of Chute, he still seems like a sensitive guy.

Action Men

Concurrent with the rise of the teen flick was the ascension of the Big Dumb Action Movie into the status of international language. Few young actors packed sufficient musculature to kick ass convincingly (and Anthony Michael Hall looked too weird and bloated), but there were a few notable attempts to mate Hollywood's then-reigning Genres of Shame.

Not only is Anthony Edwards one of the few actors to become famous after his hair fell out, but he is also one of the only performers to have starred in a paint-gun action movie. *Gotcha!* (1985) confirmed the worst fears of every parent who worked their fingers to the bone so their child would have the college education they missed out on. The kids at UCLA do nothing but run around shooting guns loaded with dye pellets at each other and screaming "Gotcha!" when they score a splattery hit.

After a stressful semester of dodging the dreaded dye, Jonathan (Edwards) and roomie Manolo (Nick Corri) take off for Paris. Jonathan hasn't had time to digest a baguette before he's been propositioned and relieved of his virginity by sultry stranger Sacha (Linda Fiorentino, deadpan and contemptuous). Enamored of her husky Czech accent and skillful manip-

ulation of his *schwantz,* and oblivious to the fact that she virtually has the words *Hi, I'm a spy* tattooed on her tongue, he follows her to East Berlin where, she claims, she's doing some absolutely straightforward courier business. Of course, she's using the sap to transport secret microfilm across the border. The notion that a babe like Sacha would snuggle up to such a drip stretches the credulity of the East Germans, and the pair are pursued back to UCLA. This is where the months spent messing up the dorms with the pellet gun come in handy. The commies are no match for the wrath of a few good splattergun-toting students. All that remains is for a contrite Sacha to reveal herself as Cheryl Brewster from Pittsburgh and Jonathan to play an I-feel-so-used scene. Maybe one day that nice Dr. Greene will shake his head sadly and lecture some poor victim on the danger of playing Gotcha! Or watching it . . .

Target (1985) is *True Lies* with Matt Dillon as Jamie Lee Curtis. When Matt's glammy mom goes on vacation, he dreads having to spend time trapped alone with his drop-dead dull dad (Gene Hackman). Then mom gets herself kidnapped and dad turns out to be a spy who's as handy with his fists as he is with a piece. Matt's slack jaw gets a major workout in this cool-dad fantasy.

Young Guns (1988), the Brat Pack on horseback movie now best remembered for inspiring the Warren G hit "Regulate," had a few things going for it: a nifty rock-video title sequence, a slo-mo peyote freakout, Emilio Estevez going gun crazy as Billy the Kid. Mostly, though, the gun-toting ensemble of regulators (Estevez, Charlie Sheen, Kiefer Sutherland, Dermot Mulroney, Casey Siemaszko) seemed like such contemporary figures, it was at times hard to remember you weren't watching a time-travel romp. A similar-in-all-respects sequel followed.

Nice Guys

Ren McCormick wasn't looking for trouble. He may have been the big city kid newly arrived in this small, God-fearing town, but he just wanted to cut loose, Footloose (1984). A nice guy who just wants to fit in, Ren (Kevin Bacon) nevertheless stirs up a wasp's nest among the other teens. Some of them want to be cool like him, some of them want to stomp him into the ground. Preacher's daughter Ariel (Lori Singer) who is supposed to be willful and mercurial but is portrayed as being *out of her mind,* is hot for his body. Her father, the very Reverend Shaw Moore (John Lithgow) disapproves of Ren's presence, especially when the punk has the temerity to demand the right to stage a senior prom. No dancing in this town! After much soul-searching and anguish, the kids shake their booty (outside the city limits) and Ren cuts loose under a shower of silver glitter. Let's hear it for the boy!

If you'd corralled a bunch of kids into a cinema in 1955 and shown them a test screening of *Footloose,* chances are the response sheets would have been returned bearing the phrase "Squaresville, daddio." But, like the similarly dilapidated *Dirty Dancing, Footloose* seemed to have been constructed with a sinister tracking device that bypassed audience cynicism and aimed straight at deep-rooted sentimentality. Luckily, later flops like *Sing!* and *Rooftops* proved that the device had some design malfunctions.

The same bland quality that made Andrew McCarthy the Hootie of the Brat Pack worked to his advantage in *Heaven Help Us* (1985). In this story of the rigors of a Catholic education, his new kid in school, Michael Dunn, doesn't do much more than look wary and bewildered but he acts as a center of calm, anchoring the movie's ensemble of goofballs. Gobbling up the scenery around him are Matt Dillon's little brother Kevin as the school bully Rooney (who has a real rousing moment when he hauls off and slugs the school's fearsome disciplinarian priest, Brother Constance), Malcolm Danare as the corpulent egghead, Caesar, and that odd little guy Stephen Geoffreys as Williams, the kid who beats off 5.6 times a day. Best bit: Wallace Shawn's Brother Abruzzi opening a mixer with a speech on lust. "It's the beast that wants to spit you into the eternal fires of hell, where for all eternity your flesh will be ripped from your body by serpents with razor-sharp teeth." And take it easy on the punch . . .

The combination of Ralph Macchio and a curmudgeonly old ethnic geezer worked like a charm in *The Karate Kid*. In Walter Hill's *Crossroads* (1986), Macchio's eager innocent was a classical guitar prodigy nursing a burning ambition to make his name on the lucrative blues circuit. To this end, he hooks up with grizzled old bluesman Willie Brown (Joe Seneca) a onetime sideman to the legendary Robert Johnson. Macchio's character Eugene hopes Willie will teach him Johnson's famous unrecorded 30th song. To prove himself worthy of such an honor, Willie drags Eugene across the Mississippi Delta country, wheezing out epigrams like "Where I come from, you don't play no harp, you don't get no pussy," landing him in fights and sticking him with his bar tab so the kid can, you know, *feel* the blues.

It turns out Willie isn't just fucking with Eugene for the pleasure of watching a white boy squirm. His delta odyssey has a purpose and what a nutball purpose it is. It transpires Willie sold his soul to the devil—or Scratch as he's known round these parts—many years ago, and now that he's in the twilight of his years, the deal seems like one of his less-inspired decisions. Once they reach the crossroads between Hell and Earth, Eugene faces off against Scratch's disciple, a demonic back-combed axe hero (played by guitar bore Steve Vai, then of Whitesnake) in a battle for Willie's soul.

Blues purists may have suffered perforated ulcers over the notion that the struggle for the legacy of the blues was being fought by two white kids but there's no denying the fascination of the spectacle. Big Hair lets loose a finger-blurring assault of arpeggios and feedback. Eugene (or at least the musician whose fingers Macchio attempts to stay in synch with) counters with a chooglin' 12-bar. And, in the end, his integrity triumphs over hairspray, padded crotches, effects pedals and Satan worship. *Crossroads* was an unlikely big studio release under any circumstances, but as a teen-aimed movie in the middle of the eighties, it ranks as a quixotic act worthy of our bemused admiration.

Bridging the great divide between Moody Rebel and Nice Guy was a kinder, gentler Matt Dillon in *The Flamingo Kid* (1984). Set in 1963, this, the best of Garry Marshall's amiable eighties extended sitcoms, finds Brooklyn boy Jeffrey (Dillon) moving on up beyond the block and into a summer job as a *cabana* boy in the swank El Flamingo Beach Club. There he's taken under the grimy wing of shifty car dealer Phil Brody (Richard Crenna). Seduced by the sand, the sea and the tan, toned availability of Brody's hardbodied daughter (played by Janet Jones, who was in even more awesome shape in the otherwise lamentable *American Anthem*), Jeffrey sees the borough he once thought of as home now transformed into a sucking pit, one that's already mired his plumber Pop (Hector Elizondo), but one that's not going to keep him from landing his share of the good life. Who ends up with ultimate possession of Jeffrey's soul? The poor but honest plumber or the corrupt car dealer? Hmm. Tough one. Best running gag: the noises Jeffrey makes while he's eating.

Girls on Film

8

Heathers, Whores, Babysitters, Bitches, Sorority Sisters and Sluts

What's that sound? Late at night you hear it, high, mournful and sustained, like a pack of lost dogs baying at the moon, crying for home. But it's not dogs, not wolves, not coyotes, not cows. It's the Actress's Lament: "Noooooo rooooooles," they're moaning. Always the supportive wife or the willing girlfriend, the nutty ex or the victim who motivates the hero into ass-kicking action, never the motor that drives the story. "Nooooooo rooooooooles." And if women of substance and stature are sitting *shivah* for their careers, imagine the purgatorial existence of the striving young actress in the eighties. These were the days, lest we forget, when Mr. Short Horny 14 Year Old held Hollywood in his hairy palm. Desperate to appease and arouse this raging satyr, the industry made regular sacrifices of young, firm female flesh. Sometimes, in the T&A category, it was perky bikini filler. In splatter, it was cold, prone and full of holes. If they weren't on hand to quell any suspicion that the hero was gay, the function of girls in teen movies (except for those helmed by John Hughes) was to display

good-natured tolerance in the face of stalking, voyeurism and fumbled attempts at seduction. On the other side of the screen, the female sector of the audience lavished fickle moments of devotion on innumerable pimplefree sub-Brats. The girls in these films were either receptacles or they were about to be knocked off pedestals. Concerted efforts to contrive features that subverted male wish-fulfillment fantasies were doomed from the outset. The femme-helmed splatter misfire *Slumber Party Massacre,* directed by Amy Jones and written with supposedly satirical intent by Rita Mae Brown, chopped coed meat just as methodically as any other substandard cleaver-wielder. But the fact that women were creating and choreographing the garroting and impaling of empty-headed, bikini-clad sorority sisters failed either to shame or shed any fresh light on the dubious genre. The outcome was similar when the teen sex comedy was replayed through female eyes.

"All you need is a bikini and a diaphragm," declares Laurie (Lynn-Holly Johnson, the bad tempered, blind figure skater from *Ice Castles*) at the outset of *Where the Boys Are '84.* The quartet of Spring Break–crazed students (the others are played by spiketop sexpot Lisa Hartman, Wendy Schaal and Lorna daughter-of-Judy-sister-of-Liza Luft) descending on Fort Lauderdale acted as demented and rapacious as the swinging dicks that ogled and belched through a million male-dominated raunchfests. But, due to an irrevocable cinematic double standard, the girls on the beach could not enjoy quite the same kind of dirty good time as the baboons on the balcony, who squirted happily in their shorts every time a thing in a thong jiggled past. Horny Laurie may have been hot for "a bonehead with the most incredible bod," but deep down she really wanted to find true love. And when she thought she'd stumbled over Mr. Right, he turned out, as a punishment for her earlier lusty pronouncement, to be a male hooker.

Just as recasting actresses like Sharon Stone, Bridget Fonda and Lori Petty as Action Babes would prove fruitless in the nineties, so altering the chromosomes of existing teen formulas was, a decade earlier, a box-office no-no. The grossout and the splatter were too firmly entrenched in the business of pressing male buttons to capture the imaginations or customs of girls. However, as the eighties drew to a close, the previously neglected gender would have its revenge in the shape of a movie that banged the last nail in the coffin of the teen era.

Veronica Sawyer: "Why can't we talk to different kinds of people?"
Heather Chandler: "Fuck me gently with a chainsaw. Do I look like Mother Teresa?"
—from *Heathers,* written by Daniel Waters

If nineties prime time's most beloved Virtual Companions had been in business in the eighties, it would have been an altogether less adorable affair. "I'll Be There for You," their signature tune would have crooned and then carried on, "Stabbing you in the back, spreading rumors about you and making your life a living hell." War movies had Nazis. Spy movies had Commies. Cowboys had Indians. Eighties teen movies had *friends.* Hip, cool, powerful friends. Icy, perfectly accessorized arbiters of taste who decided with the arch of an eyebrow or the curl of a scarlet lip who would be allowed to continue breathing the precious air of the inner circle and who would be plunged into social oblivion. Wielding their power of exclusion like a psycho with a kitchen knife, friends caused eating disorders, soiled sheets, nervous breakdowns and capsized relationships. Their reign of terror was quiveringly depicted in movies like *Valley Girl, Pretty in Pink, Some Kind of Wonderful* and *Can't Buy Me Love.* In all those films, the moral superiority of the downtrodden prevailed over the vicious manipulation of the wealthy oppressors. And then there was *Heathers* (1989), whose visionary screenwriter, Daniel Waters, took as his inspiration the abuse of power among the popular and whose solution to their smirking sadism involved absolutely no moral superiority whatsoever. Black of heart, glossy of hair and tart of tongue, *Heathers* is more quotable than the Old Testament and crueler than an off-duty call girl's candid conversation.

Westerburg High in Springfield, Ohio is dominated by three witches: evil-eyed she-wolf Heather Chandler (Kim Walker), her ass-kissing second-in-command Heather McNamara (Lisanne Falk) and bulimic Heather Duke (Shannen Doherty). Perfectly coiffed and coutured, they patrol the playgrounds and dining halls of their fiefdom, striking fear into the hearts of the lower orders with a withering putdown or a roll of the eye. Their numbers are swelled by the reluctant addition of someone who has the spotless, crease-free look of a Heather but is actually a Veronica (Winona Ryder). Troubled by the duality of her popularity-by-proxy and her internal qualms about being associated with the wicked queens, Veronica finds herself, by day, going along with whatever soul-crushing prank Heather Chandler has dreamed up, then, by night, repenting and venting into a frenzied journal. Thus, she is forced to forge a "hot and horny yet realistically low-key note," in the handwriting of a jock to fool school blob Martha Dumptruck (Carrie Lynn) into thinking he has the hots for her. "Come on," commands Heather, "it'll be very. . . . The note'll give her shower-nozzle masturbation fantasies for weeks." Martha Dumptruck is summarily hoodwinked and mocked by the slobbish object of her affection. Heather exults, "They all want me as a friend or a fuck. I'm worshipped at Westerburg and I'm only a junior."

Veronica's salvation lurks in the shape of J.D. (Christian Slater), the new kid in school with the laconic drawl, the permanently arched eyebrows and the gun he pulls on two dumb jocks when they try and intimidate him. "I don't really like my friends," Veronica confides to J.D., after Heather Chandler has made her snub childhood friend Betty Finn in order to attend a college dance. "They're people I work with and our job is being popular and shit." She opens up even more to her diary. "Betty Finn was a true friend and I sold her out for a bunch of Swatch dogs and diet Coke heads. Killing Heather would be like offing the Wicked Witch of the West . . . East . . . West. God, I sound like a fucking psycho. Tomorrow, I'll be kissing her aerobicized ass but tonight let me dream of a world without Heather, a world where I am free."

For Veronica, J.D.'s Bad Boy influence soon becomes as intoxicating as Heather Chandler's gift of popularity. Soon, he has her convinced to play an innocent little prank on her mentor/tormentor. Sneakily ensconced in the Chandler kitchen, the mischievous pair attempts to concoct a cocktail that will make Heather puke. First, they try to hawk up some phlegm in order to garnish the drink with spit. Both come up dry (for all the murder and teen-suicide jokes that abound throughout the film, this spit scene is the only one ever excised when *Heathers* is shown on TV). J.D. plumps for some lethal Hull Clean Liquid Drainer. "That'll kill her," chides Veronica, but he sneaks the poison into the drink without her noticing. J.D., remarkably, convinces Heather to down the brew by surmising it might be too intense for her to handle. She rises to the bait, swallows, gasps "Corn nuts" and collapses through a glass coffee table. "I'm gonna have to send my SAT scores to San Quentin instead of Stanford," panics Veronica. But J.D. makes Heather's death look like a suicide, even faking a note: "I died knowing no one knew the real me." This has the effect of making a martyr out of the previously hated and feared Heather. "I blame not Heather," intones the priest at her funeral, "but rather a society that tells its youth that the answer can be found in the MTV video games. We must pray that the other teenagers of Springfield know the name of that righteous dude who can solve their problems. It's Jesus Christ and he's in the book." Amen. "Technically, I did not kill Heather Chandler," prays Veronica over the coffin, "but, hey, who am I trying to kid? I just want my high school to be a nice place."

But it isn't. It's full of slugs like Ram and Kurt, the two dumb jocks who filled their shorts when J.D. pulled a gun on them. Heather McNamara persuades Veronica to accompany her on a double date with them. It inevitably ends in a bout of cow tipping, but Kurt spreads rumors that the evening came to a satisfactory climax, with Veronica providing both of them with oral accommodation ("He said that he and Ram had a nice little sword-fight in your mouth last night," says bleeding heart Peter Dawson). J.D. invites Veronica to avenge this slander by luring the two goons into the woods where he will shoot them with a rare form of bullet that breaks the skin but inflicts no lasting damage. Once unconscious, he plans to frame them as participants in a gay death pact. He's already composed a note: "Ram and I died the day we realized we could never reveal our forbidden love to an uncaring and un-understanding world. The joy we shared in each other's arms was greater than any touchdown, yet we were forced to live the lives of sexist, beer-guzzling jock assholes." He also takes pleasure in assembling a tableau of homosexual artifacts: a copy of *Stud Puppy,* a candy dish, Joan Crawford postcard, mascara and mineral water. Veronica expresses puzzlement over the last choice. J.D. says, "This is Ohio. If you don't have a brewski in your hand, you might as well be wearing a dress." Totally under the spell of her hot, if fiendish, new boyfriend, she acts as bait luring both jocks into the woods where J.D. shoots them both. Dead. She finds herself at another teenage funeral. At this one, Kurt's dad stands over the casket, bawling, "I love my dead, gay son."

Teen suicide becomes media topic *du jour.* The hapless Martha Dumptruck attempts to kill herself in a failed effort to court popularity. Teachers and classmates search for meaning in the suicides of Heather, Ram and Kurt. The hit single "Teen Suicide (Don't Do It)" by Big Fun receives heavy rotation (coincidentally, a British teenybop group called Big Fun was enjoying their momentary burst of success at exactly the time the movie was released in the U.K.).

Depressed by the posthumous acclaim bestowed on her un-witting and undeserving victims, Veronica moans to her mother, "All we want is to be treated like human beings." Mrs. Sawyer, up to this point a chirpy automaton, responds with probably the most stirring retort ever delivered by an adult character in a teen movie. "Treated like human beings? Is that what you said, little Ms. voice-of-a-generation? How do you think adults act with other adults? Do you think it's just like a game of doubles tennis? When teenagers complain that they want to be treated like human beings, it's usually because they *are* being treated like human beings." Wow. Mrs. Sawyer's light blinks off after that diatribe, but it's still a killer. So, Veronica decides, is J.D. She breaks up with him, suddenly seeing him as less of a hunk and more of a homicidal maniac. Taking her defection to heart, he plans to blow up the entire school when they're gathered in the gym for the big basketball game. *Heathers* doesn't exactly fizzle out at this point but the climax is definitely problematic. The boiler-room gun battle between Veronica and J.D. and the ticking-clock race to defuse the bomb before it blows the school sky high are played in such a straight action-movie way that you expect Veronica to deliver a sneering "School's out" after she blows off J.D.'s fin-ger. Instead, she says, "Know what I'd like, babe? Cool guys like you out of my life." And he obliges, setting off the bomb that's strapped to his chest.

In the movie's closing moments, Veronica squashes the pos-sibility of a revival of the Heather dictatorship by confiscating the scrunchee of power from Heather Duke and publicly align-ing herself with the now wheelchair-bound Martha Dump-truck. Would a climax as black as the preceding content have worked better? Scenarist Waters banged out several variations, including endings where Veronica blew up the school, where she was shot through the chest by a not-quite-dead Heather Duke and where students of all social classes were finally united in a mixer in Heaven.

Winona Ryder called the movie "one of the greatest pieces of literature I have ever read," a point she went on to prove by starring in several literary adaptations that weren't anywhere near as entertaining, insightful or audacious as *Heathers*. Daniel Waters' script is ablaze with imagination, his lexicon of freshly-minted teen colloquialisms is thrilling and his plotting is crap (the scene where J.D. explains the origin of "Ich Luge" bullets and how they don't kill the victims is painful to behold). The rhythmic spring of his dialogue is not dissimilar to that of John Hughes, which is ironic because it was Waters' mingled fascination and revulsion with the way that kids were coddled and catered to in, among others, the Hughes movies that inspired him to pen a script that laughed loudly in the face of teen traumas.

Highly praised though her later work has been, Winona Ryder has never come close to bringing to a character the complexity she brought to Veronica Sawyer (and she's certainly never let herself be smeared with dried blood and gunpowder). Christian Slater brings *exactly* what he brought to *Heathers* to every other film he's been in, but to less satisfying effect. As for Shannen Doherty, at that point known solely as Wilford Brimley's tomboy granddaughter on *Our House,* that stroke of casting surpasses visionary and touches on sinister (legend has it she stormed out of an early screening in tears, bawling "Nobody told me it was a comedy!"). It isn't a perfect movie, but it's kind of a masterpiece. And, released in 1989, when the flood of teen movies had slowed to a trickle, it stands as an unanswerable Last Word. Any adolescent-based movie that followed it would have had to have been sharp as a Samurai sword to avoid incineration by comparison (the only film of consequence to wash up in its wake was *Say Anything*). *Heathers,* in fact, killed the genre that inspired it stone dead.

Way-ass back in time, at the beginning of the eighties, indications were strong that we were about to be knee-deep in Girl movies. There was *Foxes* (1980), Adrian Lyne's hilariously overblown expose of little Hollywood girls Growing Up Too Fast. Abandoned by indulgent parents, these Spandex-clad nymphettes get their education in bedrooms, barrooms and backstage areas. A feather-haired Jodie Foster is, of course, the sensible, social glue bonding the movie's quartet of titular temptresses together. Cherie Currie, ex-frontbabe of The

Runaways, is the hot hedonist, pumped full of drugs and happy to sell her soul for an Access All Areas laminate. Future daytime talk show host Marilyn Kagan is the bighearted fat girl struggling to keep up as her buds speed along the fast track (she winds up finding true love with Randy Quaid), and the never-heard-from-before-or-since Kandice Stroh is the head-turning flirt. *Foxes* has many moments of madness—Currie's molestation by a pair of married swingers, a guest appearance by glam-metal hags, Angel—but nothing tops Sally Kellerman's crackpot tirade against these rotten, ungrateful kids: "You're like miniature forty year olds. And you're mean. And you make me hate my hips!"

Making the *Foxes* hate *their* hips were the barely formed bitches in *Little Darlings* (1980). Summer camp class warfare between pugnacious urchin Angel (Kristy McNicol) and well-groomed princess Ferris (Tatum O'Neal) is resolved, not by a catfight or a breakdown, but a loss-of-virginity contest.

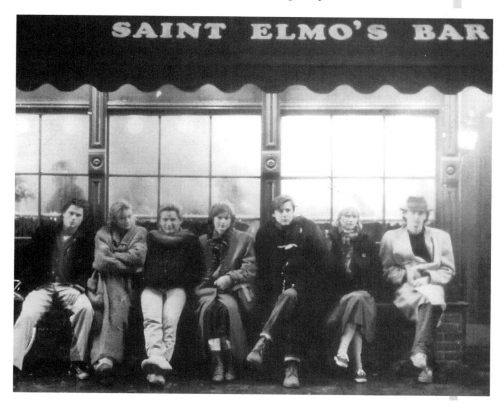

Rich and poor girls set aside their petty differences in *Times Square* (1980). Heavily promoted as the new wave *Saturday Night Fever*, Allan Moyle's feverishly ill-conceived movie paints a picture of Manhattan's human sewer as a neon theme park filled with electricity, with vitality, with *Life!* And it's that life that pampered Robin Johnson, daughter of the city commissioner, is sheltered from, until she falls into the clutches of foul-mouthed street queen Trini Alvarado. Robin's commish dad is involved in one of those evil redevelopment programs threatening to rid 42nd Street of its heart, its soul and its streams of squishy semen. But once Trini has taken her new friend for a fun evening of stealing ambulances and hurling TV sets out of windows, she knows her heart belongs among the bright lights and the peep shows. Local DJ Johnny La Guardia (Tim Curry) hears of the duo's late-night exploits and turns them into folk heroes, labeling them The Sleez Sisters and whipping the city into a frenzy with tales of their anarchic antics. The movie sputters to a close with the girls giving a screechy rendition of their notion of punk rock atop a Times Square marquee, while underneath freaks, straights, mohawks, tourists and hookers gyrate, united by the beat and the magic of the big city. The passing of the years, the getting of wisdom and the lowering of expectations; none of them have dimmed this film's proficiency in inducing the plaintive reaction, "Huh?"

And, of course, there was Brooke. She may have been a big bore with her declarations of eternal chastity and her adoring appearances on the arms of Bob Hope and George Burns, but Brooke Shields had a brief reign as America's make-out queen. Though it was her Calvins commercials that compelled Mr. Short Horny 14 Year Old to spend that extra hour in the bathroom, her movie output had two high spots. *The Blue Lagoon* (1980) was both a riot of titillation and a mush-minded Babies Playing House fantasy, with its stranded boy and girl speedily shrugging off the constraints of civilization and building their own desert island love nest. (It inspired a very pale imitation in *Paradise* (1982) with Phoebe Cates and Willie Aames.) If that movie centered around the notion of an adult-free idyll, *Endless Love* (1981) was a long, sobbing scream of *"It's not fair!"* directed at the narrow-minded parents who attempted to keep Brooke away from the only boy who ever made her feel like a natural woman (it's said director Franco Zeffirelli achieved the elusive natural-woman effect by squeezing Brooke's big toe during the sex scenes). This early burst of activity was never equaled. Girl movies, some splendid, some rancid, peppered the rest of the decade, but their appearances were always sporadic.

eaving Las Vegas may have given Elisabeth Shue a burst of belated recognition but, in my own private academy, she was already basking in commendations for her incandescent showing in *Adventures in Babysitting* (1987). "I was never that sweet," she now says, trying to put some distance between the girl-next-door tag that kept her mired in lightweight work for years. Deny it though she might, Shue is a beacon of niceness (she's probably doomed a whole new generation of actresses to playing hookers-with-hearts-of-gold), and her presence saves this film from sinking into a swamp of shoddy stereotypes. This first movie to be directed by Chris Columbus (who, as a screenwriter already had *Gremlins* and *Young Sherlock Holmes* to his credit—or shame) was intended as a teenage, suburban *After Hours,* dragging a gaggle of whitebread tykes out of the safety of their comfortable environs and into the mean streets of Chicago.

Shue's Chris Parker is a stood-up senior who is not only blown off by her big date but has to accept as a booby prize a night babysitting the two Anderson kids, 15-year-old Brad (Keith Coogan), who nurses a mother of a crush on her, and 9-year-old Sara (Maia Brewton), who carries an even more disturbing torch for the Mighty Thor. Chris gets a call from a friend whose attempt to run away from home went awry, marooning her in the bus station. Bundling up the Anderson kids and the unwelcome addition of Brad's horndog buddy Daryl (Anthony Rapp), Chris heads for the big bad city. Here come the complications: they blow a tire, Chris realizes she's left her purse in the 'burbs, they get a lift from a one-armed man who drives past his house to find his wife cheating on him. With

Girls on Film

me so far? Then they sneak into a car that's being hotwired by a crook and wind up in the headquarters of a national car-theft ring. They sneak out, but not before Daryl has stolen a copy of *Playboy* that has vital financial information hidden in it (well, where else would you leave vital financial information?). The crooks give chase. The kids stumble into a blues club where sweaty legend Albert Collins is rocking out. He insists the sub-urban interlopers pay their dues. Chris leads her charges in a squeaky improvised rendition of "Babysitter Blues" to massed applause. They evade their pursuers, stranding them on a per-ilous rooftop.

Chris gets the kids home before their parents show up. *Adventures in Babysitting* crams a ton of fun into its breathless pace, but it also wraps its cast in cotton wool. These kids don't seem like they come from the suburbs; the big city and its at-tendant grouches, nuts, cops, drunks and array of black faces perplexes them so much, they come off like they've just been hatched from pods. At one point the car thief (Calvin Levels), whose latest acquisition the kids stowed away in, looks at the shiny, milk-fed faces of the Anderson brats and pleads with his bosses to give them a break. "They're just kids," he says, the subtext being they don't belong in this jungle, not like *us*. Throughout scenes like these, Elisabeth Shue remains the epitome of grace, resilience and—yes!—likability. For all those attributes, the Best Babysitter Award goes to . . .

I've seen *Citizen Kane*. I've seen *Raging Bull, Gone With The Wind, Intolerance, Lawrence of Arabia, Death in Venice* and *The Searchers*. They're all classics and if you add together the number of times I've watched all of them combined, it still wouldn't come close to the number of times I've seen *Just One of the Guys* (1985). Maybe it's just me, but it feels like some-one's started a cable station solely devoted to showing this stu-pid movie. First thing in the morning, last thing at night, afternoons, evenings, weekends: *it's always on!* (Of course, it could also be argued that I watch too much TV.)

Pert, popular, possessed of good grades and a studly boyfriend, Terry (Joyce Hiser) has everything she wants, ex-cept the chance to kickstart her career in journalism. She failed to win an internship on the local paper because, her professor claims, her essay was a snooze. She's convinced she was overlooked because she's a babe. So she does what anyone in the same circumstances would do; she sticks some balled-up socks down her panties and goes back to school passing for a boy. Even though Terry's been initiated into the mysteries of crotch alignment and urinal etiquette by her hormonally strafed idiot brother Buddy (Billy Jacoby in an I'm-an-asshole performance that'll make your teeth ache) she still flounces through the school gates looking like the perfect candidate for a thrashing at the hands of local roughnecks. Instead, a gathering of girls take in the sight of Terry, her new wave two-tone jacket, her hip eyewear and her skinny frame. Their awed response: "He looks like a cross between Elvis Costello and the Karate Kid." One girl (Sherilyn Fenn) is warm for his form to the degree that she doesn't even mind that his/her crotch is stuffed with socks. "How small can it be?" she says, cheerfully. But Terry has fallen for Rick (Clayton Rohner), a sardonic loner who thought he'd found a weird kindred spirit in the Costello Kid.

Misunderstandings pile up, reaching a climax at the school prom when a tuxedo-clad Terry has to tell her bemused boyfriend she loves someone else. Rick, the object of her affections, tries to let her down gently. "I'm not gay," she tells him, "I'm a girl." "Right," he retorts, "and I'm Cyndi Lauper." Finally, she pulls open her shirt to reveal her excellent breasts, giving him the opportunity to play the Jessica Lange/Sally Field "I-feel-so-used" scene. In the end, of course, Terry gets to write a scalding "Dude Like Me" investigative piece and Rick manages to deal with her in babed-up state. This ain't no *Yentl*. Despite swishing up a storm in boy clothing, Terry never stirs up any sexual confusion in Rick. She never attracts any unwarranted attention and almost every opportunity to mine girl-in-a-guy's-world scenarios for discomfort is avoided. It's puerile and irritating, but . . . *it's always on. . . .*

It's Christmas in L.A. and a comet passes overhead, turning onlookers into either piles of dust or flesh-eating zombies. That's the situation waiting for sisters Regina (Catherine

Mary Stewart) and Samantha (Kelli Maroney) when they wake up in *Night of the Comet* (1984). As their day wears on, they not only have to face the end of the world as they knew it (Reggie escaped the comet because she was shacked up with a projectionist in a steel-lined booth and Sam ran away from her stepmother, spending the night in a tool shed), but they also have to engage in a shoot-out with zombie stock boys when shopping at the deserted mall. As if that wasn't enough, out in the desert, a team of weary scientists are preparing to pick them up to use them as lab rats. With truck driver Hector (Robert Beltran) in tow, they prove equal to every challenge. Writer/director Thom Eberhardt (also responsible for the fitfully amusing Keanu Reeves Whoops-I-sold-my-date-to-a-pimp movie, *The Night Before*), has a low budget and limited resources, but in video-arcade addict Reggie and pep-squad member Sam, he's got two fabulous characters and he uses them to make magic. Whether they're discussing firepower ("The Mac-10 was practically designed for housewives," says Reggie, dismissively) or fighting over Hector ("My sister who has swiped every guy I ever had my eye on has now swiped the only guy in the whole freaked-out world," laments Sam), these girls light up the screen. I sought out the counsel of many respected cinema theoreticians for their perspective on *Night of the Comet* and the response was unanimous: *Cool fucking movie.*

A highlight of *Night of the Comet* is when the two sisters happily go on the rampage in the empty mall. As they try on clothes and dance in the aisles, Cyndi Lauper's "Girls Just Want to Have Fun" plays on the soundtrack. Lauper wouldn't, however, give her assent for her version of the song to be used in another teen movie. This one was called *Girls Just Want to Have Fun* (1985). That is correct; she would not allow the song to be used in the movie it inspired. Lauper herself does not appear in the film, but just as a note-for-note cover of her hit blares through the film, so her presence is conjured up by Helen Hunt playing Lynne Stone, a wacky, garish, Day-Glo free spirit who liberates the wild woman lurking inside good girl Janey Glenn (Sarah Jessica Parker). Janey wants, more than life itself, to throw down on DTV, the local after-school dance party, but her major dad vetoes such seditious behavior. The faux-Lauper madcap gets her friend hooked up with a hot, throbbing dance partner, Jessie (Lee Montgomery). Snooty rival Natalie (Holly Gagnier) is driven by jealousy and insecurity to sabotage Janey and Jessie's chances. As retribution, the good-girl-turned-sassy recruits a posse of psychotic punks to smash up the princess' debutante ball. Finally, Janey and Jessie dance up a storm as her old dad watches on TV, wiping away a proud tear. My feeling is this: you can't go far wrong with a dance movie, and even though Sarah Jessica Parker is no hoofer (her partner Lee Montgomery, who, to be fair, is no actor, does most of the work), the stupidity of the plot is pretty much nullified by the flailing and writhing. Weirdly, Cyndi Lauper would go on to make occasional guest appearances on *Mad About You,* the sitcom that stars Helen Hunt. She wouldn't let her song appear in the movie it inspired, but she wound up acting opposite someone who played a role she inspired in that movie.

usanna Hoffs, the Bangle with the googly eyes, starred in *The Allnighter* (1987) a campus farce directed by her mom. Something about this film is a little *off.* The actors—Joan Cusack, Michelle Pfeiffer's little sister DeDee, Pam Grier, Michael Ontkean among them—hurry through their lines and barely acknowledge each other. It's a lot like watching a rehearsal. But, just as you start to slump and drool, along comes a scene so astounding it snaps you back into full consciousness. It's not the one you're thinking, either. It's not the queasy mother-directs-daughter's-big-love-scene ("Let go. Scream. Surrender to his hugeness.") It's much, much worse. Hoffs' character, a brain we're begged to believe, is desperate to get laid by *somebody* before her commencement from her SoCal Frisbee college. Michael Ontkean, barely playing a washed-up sixties rock star, is on the campus. She resolves to throw herself at him and prepares by painting her face like Bozo, stuffing tissues down her bra and strutting her stuff in front of the mirror in time to "Respect" by Aretha Franklin. First Andrew McCarthy in *St. Elmo's Fire,* then Susanna Hoffs in *The Allnighter.* Two dumb movies sunk to new levels of humiliation by a single song. Such is the power of "Respect."

Justine Bateman doesn't sing That Song in *Satisfaction* (1988), but she slaughters enough nuggets for the effect to be the same. I always dug the *Family Ties* episodes where Mallory gave her little speech about not being as smart as Alex but being special in her own right, but outside the cozy Keaton sitcom set, she was D.O.A. There are two outstanding reasons for her miserable fate. One was hubris. Why would someone willingly take on the role of the firebrand front-person of a live-wire, right-in-the-socket, down-and-dirty bar band when she can't sing? When I say can't sing, I don't mean not-trained-in-the-classical-sense-but-filled-with-character can't sing, I mean the drunk-at-the-wedding-no-pitch-no-rhythm-no-control can't sing. And there's Mallory coughing into the microphone and making a starry-eyed convert of Liam Neeson, supposedly a dissolute former Grammy-winning songwriter. He even accompanies her on the piano, and when she's done trying to dislodge the piece of brisket stuck down her throat, he gives her this moist look and says, "There's nothing more I can teach you." When they were casting a leading man for *Nell,* that scene probably clinched it for the big Irishman.

The other reason for Bateman's shame: starpower. She didn't have it and Julia Roberts did. The then barely known Roberts had a grim part as the Bateman band's sex addict bass player. Horrible as her role was, the one thing you took away from the movie was the thought, "Who was that girl with the big grin?" It wasn't Justine Bateman. (It wasn't Trini Alvarado either, who emerged from *Satisfaction* with the distinction of having stunk up the screen in two movies about shitty girl groups.)

A girl group whose tempestuous history would have made a much better movie was The Go-Go's. One of their most poignant songs was "This Town," a wry testament to the strange allure of Los Angeles. "This town is our town . . ." The song doesn't appear on the soundtrack to *Modern Girls* (1986) but you sense it in every scene. As the eponymous modern girls (Daphne Zuniga, Virginia Madsen, Cindy Gibb) drift listlessly through the clubs, bars and streets of downtown L.A., you get the feeling that for these women, all of them out of school and marking time in nowhere nine-to-fives, the best that life has to offer is already over. All they have is the anticipation of going out at night in search of a mythical good time that may never arrive. When they chorus, "We never pay for parking, we never carry cash, we never pay for drinks and we never stand in line," they may hope they're giving the impression they're nightlife aristocracy, but as the night wears on it sounds like an increasingly desperate cry for help. Let me be straight here, this is a piece of shit movie, but it's one that left me in a wistful state of mind. Much like L.A. itself.

If *Modern Girls* concluded that the fun was over after 18, *Smooth Talk* (1985)—adapted from a Joyce Carol Oates story, "Where Are You Going, Where Have You Been"—stated that even when you were 15, the good times were starting to run dry. Even though Connie (Laura Dern) and her friends spend every day of their endless summer vacation scampering through the mall, smearing on makeup, trying on clothes, wolfing down meatlike products and screeching at boys, director Joyce Chopra maintains enough distance to make their days look joyless and wasted. Outside of the mall, Connie's a selfish, empty-headed, jealous brat who refuses to help around the house and complains endlessly about being bored.

Her ennui is almost at an end, though, courtesy of the hulking, tattooed psychotic figure who's been observing her throughout the movie. His name is Arnold Friend (Treat Williams) and one Sunday afternoon, when everyone is out, he shows up at her house and transfixes Connie with an epic monologue wherein he intimidates, seduces, bamboozles and ultimately lays claim to her. When she returns from an afternoon in Arnold's clutches, she's a different person: nice, caring, open and apologetic for her previous truculent behavior. The whole Arnold Friend episode is such an unexpected mood shift that once the movie's over, you find yourself hoping someone else will say, "That Arnold Friend guy was some sort of, uh, allegory. Wasn't he?" so you don't have to grapple with the nagging fear that you've just watched a film about a bitch who gets the brat fucked out of her by a psycho.

This is how wars start. A bunch of local yahoos vandalize the motorbike belonging to Binx (Christian Slater). His big sister Billie Jean (Helen Slater, no relation) remonstrates with the thugs, demanding they cough up the $600 required to get the hog roadworthy again. They laugh in her face. Hostilities escalate and someone gets shot. Big sis cuts her hair short and goes on the lam, becoming a media fixture and a voice-of-the-underdog with her spirited demands for justice and $600. What the hell was *The Legend of Billie Jean* (1985) supposed to be? Was it a modern Joan of Arc story or a parody of how a modern Joan of Arc would be embraced and devoured by the media? Was it a clarion call conceived to shake up apathetic eighties youth? Or was it an attempt to reverse the impression left by *Supergirl* that Helen Slater was a wimp? In all aspects, and especially the latter, it failed. But it was an engrossing failure.

I'm not gonna be slingin' pizza for the rest of my life," predicts Julia Roberts, quite astutely, at the commencement of *Mystic Pizza* (1988). Julia's hot-to-trot character Daisy toils, along with bookworm sib Kat (Annabeth Gish) and nutcase buddy Jojo (Lili Taylor) in the Slice of Heaven restaurant, a fixture of the small Portuguese-dominated village of Mystic, Connecticut. None of the girls want to be slinging pizza for the rest of their lives. Daisy's going to hook up with a rich guy. Kat's going to college, and Jojo's getting married.

Things don't quite work out the way they planned. Daisy's rich ticket out of her small town snail's pace existence turns out to be a messed-up little prince who uses his relationship with this mozzarella-scented temptress as a stick to beat his wealthy, icy family. Kat, attempting to make some extra college money by babysitting for an architect whose wife is in London, falls into a miserable affair with the swine. Jojo gets cold feet about marrying her fisherman boyfriend.

Girls on Film

Eventually, the trio transcend their circumstances, realizing that, like the pizza they serve with its secret ingredients, this small town they yearn to flee is what makes them and their friendship special. Or something like that. Amazingly, *Mystic Pizza* is *still* Julia Roberts' best film, notwithstanding the scene where the three girls hijack Jojo's fisherman boyfriend's truck and take off, celebrating the exhilaration of liberation by screeching—yes!—"Respect."

The most successful Girl movie, financially as well as in terms of its artistic and social influence, was *Flashdance* (1983). Adrian Lyne's dazzling fairy story was the first feature to display openly its MTV influence (the rival *Footloose* was *King Lear* by comparison), dispensing with accepted narrative practices in order to speed the plot along with a million music montages. The footless tights and off-the-shoulder top sported by the movie's heroine, Pittsburgh steel worker by day and bar dancer by night, Alex Owens (Jennifer Beals) showed up on city streets and dance floors the world over. And look how many strip joints are called Flashdancers . . .

Girls on Film

We Got the Beat

9

The Ultimate Eighties Teen Movie Mix Tape

I f you think a lame movie can't be saved by a killer theme song and a sexy video, you must be living in a gangsta's paradise. The eighties saw the dawn of synergy; if kids were too late or too lazy to sit through the coming attractions, if they never read reviews or noticed posters, chances were they watched MTV, listened to the radio or bought records. And if they participated in any of these activities, the likelihood was strong that the video they watched contained scenes from a movie, the song on the radio was the theme from that movie and the record they bought contained that selfsame song. In the eighties, movies became so sound track saturated that they made *Saturday Night Fever* seem like *The Seventh Seal.* Ironically, the majority of artists approached the chore of sound track duties with the same enthusiasm they threw into whipping up an extra track for a CD single. This brought about a situation where many groups were receiving their largest exposure with material in which they had little or no emotional investment. Never-

theless, the commingling of music and images means that some cruddy filler still has the power to swell up some throats. And if you were of a sufficiently anal nature that you felt compelled to browbeat those around you with taped examples of your eclectic taste in music, these are the teen sound track selections that I would expect to hear on your mix.

"We Got The Beat," The Go-Go's (*Fast Times at Ridgemont High*)
From its clattering drum intro to Belinda Carlisle's exuberantly nasal vocal, this new wave anthem celebrates the joys of being young, free, wild, hip and living in L.A. The subsequent movie depicts its characters missing out on almost all those joys, thus lending the tune something of a Brechtian quality.

"Johnny, Are You Queer," Josie Cotton (*Valley Girl*)

Shrill, piercing, entirely plastic and absolutely intoxicating. Cotton warbled her stupid pogomatic-pop L.A. radio hit at the senior prom. Local gay activists retorted with the equally cheesy, "Josie, Are You a Bitch?"

"Weird Science," Oingo Boingo (*Weird Science*)

Consider the dichotomy of Danny Elfman. By day, he receives fat checks and approbation as the composer of eccentric and individual scores for movies as diverse as *Pee Wee's Big Adventure, Batman, Midnight Run* and *Mission: Impossible.* By night, he's a longtime member of determinedly quirky ska-funk pranksters, Oingo Boingo. This theme to the Hughes misfire contains their trademark funny voices and stupid hooks, and as such acts as an accurate summation as to why success has continued to elude them.

"Rebel Yell," Billy Idol (*Sixteen Candles*)

Subliminally, a Billy Idol song is playing throughout the entirety of *every* teen movie. But the work of this British epitome of growing old gracefully was never more appropriately visualized than as accompaniment to the scene where Anthony Michael Hall tears across Chicago in a car for which he has no license and a zonked prom queen lying across his lap, moving her mouth towards his crotch. Like Billy said, "More! More! More!"

"Invincible," Pat Benatar (*The Legend Of Billie Jean*)

Ridgemont High boasted at least three girls cultivating the Pat Benatar look. In these lean years for tough chicks, you had to take your role models where you could. Thus, when the decision was made to cast Helen Slater as a feisty rebel, there was only one person who could set simmering female rage to music. Despite its title, "Invincible" marked the turning point in Pat's career. This was where she turned her back on the weedy guitar attack that made her name and went for something a little hipper. And that's why this defiant anthem has a strange little Talking Heads–like break in the middle of it.

"Pretty in Pink," Psychedelic Furs (*Pretty in Pink*)

These Bowie-damaged Brits specialized in sneering stories of sexual ambiguity, identity crisis and jaded hipsters in decline. Which explains why they were the perfect inspiration for a heartfelt story of true love transcending class differences. All the same, the song sounds *fabulous* as a backdrop to Molly Ringwald's early-morning assembling of her thrift-store armory.

"Hazy Shade of Winter," Bangles (*Less Than Zero*)

Here's one of those instances where the movie sank like a stone and the sound track stayed aloft. Rick Rubin put together a stellar selection of nuggets slyly designed to counterpoint the onscreen ennui. Biggest hit of the batch was the Bangles' thrashy rendition of a Simon & Garfunkel folk drone.

"People Are Strange," Echo & The Bunnymen (*The Lost Boys*)

Courtney Love's favorite group do a note-for-note version of The Doors' original, produced by Ray Manzarek. It provides a shivery intimation that All Is Not Well, then the movie proceeds to bludgeon you about the skull.

"Don't You (Forget About Me)," Simple Minds (*The Breakfast Club*)

MTV is given credit for acting as a conduit whereby European synth bands denied access to All-American airwaves could sneak into suburban living rooms. It seems to me John Hughes played an equal part in spicing up the playlists. The most extreme example of his influence is Simple Minds. These Scottish Bowie boys (once a punk band known as Johnny & the Self Abusers) had hauled themselves up the ladder as far as cult status. Hughes' appreciation for their atmospherics got them the theme-tune gig. They hooked up with Billy Idol's producer, Keith Forsey, who oversaw their rendition of a moody tune originally intended for the vocal stylings of the Sneering One. "Will you stand above me, look my way, never love me . . . ?" crooned Minds' singer Jim Kerr, echoing the questions in the hearts of moviegoers who wondered what would happen to The Breakfast Club come Monday morning. The result was an American number one.

"If You Leave," O.M.D. (*Pretty in Pink*)

John Hughes breaks another previously marginalized Brit act. Orchestral Manouevres in the Dark was a Liverpool synth act with a catalog of beautifully crafted hits. For their sound track shot, they banged out a ballad in an afternoon. In "If You Leave," singer Andy McLuskey does such an anguished job of providing the lovelorn, pleading voice of Andrew McCarthy's inner richie that the song was allowed to play out in its entirety (a rarity in the days of sound tracks stockpiled with songs that played for three seconds on screen) and beyond, stretching across the emotion-soaked final scenes like a rainbow.

"Crazy For You," Madonna (*Vision Quest*)

Madonna actually appeared in the movie performing this torrid ballad and a crashing piece of drivel called "Gambler." If you compare her appearance—tubby, squawking, dressed like a clown—with that of lead femme Linda Fiorentino—sleek, simmering, charismatic, hardbodied—you might have imagined that the actress would proceed immediately to sex symboldom and the singer would go back to the Tiki Lounge. Instead, "Crazy For You" went to number one and Linda Fiorentino went on to *Gotcha!*

"On The Radio," Donna Summer (*Foxes*)

Amid the smashups and smeared mascara of this nymphette melodrama, Donna's big disco ballad floats like a guardian angel.

"Stay Gold," Stevie Wonder (*The Outsiders*)

"Stay gold" whispered Ponyboy to Johnny, and right at the end of the movie, just when you thought you could take no more schmaltz, when you thought Coppola's glop vat was dry, along came Stevie Wonder to push you over the edge.

"In Your Eyes," Peter Gabriel (*Say Anything*)

Who can forget the image of Lloyd Dobler holding his boom-box aloft, wooing back Diane Court with the song that articulated his devotion? "Without a word, without my pride . . ."

"Endless Love," Diana Ross & Lionel Richie (*Endless Love*)

A major make-out staple, regardless of the fact it comes from a film where teen infatuation leads to madness, despair and death.

"Just Once," Quincy Jones featuring James Ingram (*Last American Virgin*)

Last American Virgin had a *bitchin'* soundtrack—Human League, U2, Cars, etc.—but in its many moments of extreme misery, this pining ballad would sob into earshot.

"Flashdance . . . What a Feeling," Irene Cara (*Flashdance*)

After she wailed "Fame! I'm gonna live forever!" and touched the desire in the hearts of stagestruck little girls of all ages and sexes, Irene Cara batted another one clean out of the park. "I can have it all, now I'm dancing for my life." Colossal performance. Whatever happened to her?

"St. Elmo's Fire (Man in Motion)," John Parr (*St. Elmo's Fire*)

Although David Foster's instrumental theme from this movie has gone on to become a Muzak standard, this big-hearted sing-along soared to number one, thus assuring that clips from *St. Elmo's Fire* were still appearing on MTV long after the movie had been booted out of theaters.

"Nothing's Gonna Stop Us Now," Starship (*Mannequin*)

Desperate to stay afloat in the eighties, many long-serving groups conceded control of their careers, handing the reins to producers and outside songwriting teams. Heart, Cheap Trick and the shifting aggregate (currently) known as Starship were the major beneficiaries of enforced commercialization. Chirpy and trite, "Nothing's Gonna Stop Us Now" was a soft-drink ad in search of a product to endorse. It was a worldwide chart topper, clearing a path for the useless Andrew McCarthy movie it themed.

"Let's Hear It for the Boy," Deniece Williams (*Footloose*)
Which song would you to choose to remember this movie by? The Kenny Loggins title tune with all the silver glitter? Or the one where Kevin Bacon teaches Chris Penn to dance? Me too.

"Old Time Rock 'n' Roll," Bob Seger (*Risky Business*)
Here's a song so bound up with a particular set of images that as soon as that thumping piano intro rolls out, even the most sober and Christian-minded among us have no recourse but hit that couch and start humpin'!

"Oh Yeah," Yello (*Ferris Bueller's Day Off*)
Never a hit, this slice of Swiss-made tomfoolery with its varispeed vocal effects and driving percussion was first used by John Hughes to illustrate the mouthwatering must-haveness of Cameron's dad's Ferrari. Since then, it has become synonymous with avarice. Every time a movie, TV show or commercial wants to underline the jaw-dropping impact of a hot babe or sleek auto, that synth-drum starts popping and that deep voice rumbles, "Oh yeah . . ."

"Soul Man," Sam Moore and Lou Reed (*Soul Man*)
Total crap, but worthy of inclusion as a prime example of that disease common to sound tracks: the Inappropriate Duet. The wish list of partners to join Sam Moore in this remake of his old chestnut included Sting and Annie Lennox. Imagine how far down that list they came, before one sound track executive turned to another and said, "*You* call Lou . . ."

"Johnny B. Goode," Judas Priest (*Johnny Be Good*)
These metal dudes spent some uncomfortable time in court, accused of corrupting young minds with the evil ideas contained in the backward-masked messages on their albums. That the band got off scot-free is no indication of their innocence, it simply shows that the prosecution wasn't on its game enough to play the jury this monstrosity.

"Who Made Who," AC/DC (*Maximum Overdrive*)

Stephen King never returned to the director's chair after the failure of *Maximum Overdrive*. My theory is that he didn't retire smarting from his wounds, but that he had achieved the ambition of having a movie scored by AC/DC. In fact, the eternal headbangers did a sound enough job to make you wish for a better framework for their cacophony.

"Infatuation," Rod Stewart (*The Sure Thing*)

Unlistenable on record or on the radio, this prime example of Rod's glaring misuse of his talent is utilized perfectly by Rob Reiner in the title sequence of his teen romance. As Rod barks and drools like a lascivious old pervo, the camera takes its time navigating the sunkissed vista of Nicollette Sheridan. Sex without love is no good, the movie tells us, and the sound of Rod working himself up into a lather over footage of Sheridan's midriff is enough to induce young voters to call for legislation permitting the automatic execution of any man over forty.

"All the Right Moves," Quarterflash (*All The Right Moves*)

Perfect song for a movie whose palette was all dark grey, muddy brown and piss-green.

"Together in Electric Dreams," Phil Oakey and Giorgio Moroder (*Electric Dreams*)

The biggest hit from a teen science movie was "The Power of Love," by Huey Lewis and the News (from *Back to the Future*), but Huey is a dark episode in all our pasts, and I wouldn't be doing anyone any good by bringing him up. Instead, from an obscure computer-age ménage à trois—boy (Lenny Von Dohlen) loves girl (Virginia Madsen) but computer (voiced by Bud Cort) loves her, too!—allow me to recommend this gorgeous pairing of bubblegum electro-elders, producer Giorgio Moroder and deadpan Human League front-cyborg Phil Oakey.

"Stand By Me," Ben E. King (*Stand By Me*)

The downside of this revived smash was the video with the

cast dopily handling each other. I mean, it was okay in the movie . . .

"Somebody's Baby," Jackson Browne
(*Fast Times at Ridgemont High*)

Not only did this peppy hit act as a lovely introduction to Jennifer Jason Leigh's character, Stacy, but it provided shocking proof that the West Coast mope was capable of penning a decent pop tune.

The Next Generation

10

Neurotics, Psychotics, Weirdos, Underachievers and Would-be Teen Idols

Shit, some of these punks got no fucking respect," seethed Charlie Sheen a while back, when the subject of the manner of men who had replaced him and his ilk as new kids on the block was raised. The Chucklehead's fury was understandable. He displayed the same insecurities we all feel when faced with intimations of mortality. One minute you're the man of the moment. Then the moment passes. Your untapped potential is all tapped out and the stampede of lackeys and strumpets that once headed your way now leaves you choking in the dust as some other happy scamp becomes the recipient of fawning, envy and expert handjobs. No one stays the wild one forever. Let's not forget that, even by the mideighties, a chasm had opened up between the Brats and their target market. When he made *The Breakfast Club,* Judd Nelson was already 26 and most of his colleagues weren't too far behind. For these actors, their tenure in the teen trenches was going to be brief. Rehab, wrinkles and the previously baffling concept of the cable movie loomed large.

Ready to retire their ailing forefathers and take over courting the under-18 audience was a whole platoon of callow, unblemished young fresh fellows (Winona Ryder and Martha Plimpton excepted, it *was* a boy's club) who seemed to be called either Josh or Corey. Among their number were kids from show-business families (Josh Brolin, Sean Astin), kids with funny names (River Phoenix, Keanu Reeves), kids with sensitive sides (Ethan Hawke, Robert Sean Leonard), kids who became movie stars (Christian Slater, Johnny Depp), kids who didn't (Patrick Dempsey, Kirk Cameron), kids called Josh (Josh Charles, Josh Hamilton, Josh Richman) and of course, kids called Corey (Corey Haim, Corey Feldman, Corey Parker).

The majority of these actors differed from their predecessors in that they had aspirations towards participating in works of value and they attempted to refrain from grabbing top billing in every witless piece of shit that rolled their way. They were inclined to gravitate towards material that would afford them limitless opportunities to cry, brood and look good next to an established star. They largely eschewed what we, over the last several chapters, have come to understand as Classic Eighties Teen Movie Fare, hoping instead to carry themselves as serious artists. Luckily, light relief was ever present in the knockabout forms of Coreys Haim and Feldman. But even these two freaks, had they a whit of self-awareness, could raise themselves up on their hind legs and state proudly, "Look, we're objects of pity and derision, our careers hang in tatters. But before it all went haywire, before madness clouded our minds, we both of us gave moving performances in films of note. Got any spare change?" Tinseltown temptation took its toll on several of their contemporaries, but in the few years they rode high, anointed as Hollywood's New Breed, most of the new school could make similar claims.

Charlie Sheen, the self-same party boy who opened up this chapter calling for the head of Keanu Reeves ("Bertolucci looks at him and he thinks 'That's my guy'?" marveled Charlie) found himself in the position of playing sympathetic protector to one of the new kids in *Lucas* (1986), a movie which is cute, cloying and hell on the tear ducts. Corey Haim is writer/director David Seltzer's diminutive, bespectacled, whip-smart, passive-aggressive, lovelorn, bug-fancying title character. Even if he hadn't been accelerated in a school where athletes are worshipped as gods, Lucas would still be perceived as an oddball outsider. With his huge glasses, backpack full of crap, love of locusts, appreciation of classical music and ability to improvise lies about his parentage, he's a walking Kick Me sign. Like Molly Ringwald's character in *Pretty in Pink*, Lucas is an eccentric out of time. In the nineties, he'd have been a Beck figure, a weirdo waif with a sharp tongue. But ten years before, he was lonely in a land of giants, either publicly humiliated by thuggish jocks or treated like a pet monkey.

Everything changes during the summer vacation when he meets Maggie (Kerri Green), a demure redhead who's new in town and stuck in the same social solitary confinement as Lucas. Grateful for a friendly face whose immediate impulse isn't to push him head first into a toilet bowl, Lucas aims the

full blast of his personality at Maggie. They become insepara-
ble over the rest of the vacation; she happily immerses herself
in his world of emerging butterflies and diatribes against the
shallowness of their football-and-cheerleading-dominated
culture. Lucas is so across-the-board strange that Maggie
doesn't question his refusal to let her visit his sprawling home
or even call him. He makes a reference to his screwed-up
workaholic parents and she and we both figure we're in John
Hughes territory and somewhere down the line, these remote
parents will *pay* for ignoring such a precious son. Sitting back
to back in a sewer underneath an outdoor classical recital,
Lucas, lost both in the sweep of the strings and the depth of his
feeling for this titian-locked angel, sighs, "I just wish school
would never start."

His bliss is to be short-lived and the reason for his wish becomes uncomfortably clear as, on the first day at assembly, a
guffawing football squad deity slings Lucas over his shoulder
and deposits him on stage to be mocked by the whole school.
Only Cappy, the appropriately named captain of the team
(Chuck Sheen), sticks up for the little feller. Lucas is humiliated because Maggie was witness to the living hell that is his
day-to-day life. She, though, is understanding and sympathetic and so, though he's too enamored of Maggie to realize it,
is a shy little girl called Rina (Winona Ryder) who loves Lucas
from afar. Although Lucas has bespectacled eyes only for Maggie, she's hung up on Cappy who, as luck would have it, is
more than a little stifled by his relationship with snitty cheerleader queen Elise (Courtney Thorne-Smith). Cappy is the victim of an unfortunate blender accident during Home Ec. When
the teacher asks if anyone would like to show the hunky football captain to the school laundry so he can soak his stained
sweater, Maggie's hand flies up so fast, she looks like she's *sieg
heil*ing. In the sweet, sexy scene that follows Maggie is so dis-
oriented by her proximity to Cappy's bare, buff torso she almost slides off her seat. For his part, he's charmed by her lack
of guile and a rambling anecdote about the plane journey
where someone threw up on her shoes. She starts to shiver and
he wraps a towel round her shoulders; they're so close and so

aware of, though unable to articulate or act on their mutual attraction that Cappy has to puncture the tension by kicking a bunch of footballs around the laundry room.

Even if you're unable to empathize with Lucas' love of winged insects or string quartets, you ought to be able to muster up a twinge over the fact that *he doesn't see it coming.* He's still floating on winged feet when he's around Maggie, unaware that her attention is entirely devoted elsewhere. When she blows off an after-school tadpole hunt to go to cheerleader tryouts, he ought to get an inkling something's up, but it takes the abortive double date he attempts to arrange between Maggie and him and Cappy and the bitter, suspicious Elise to show him the big picture. On the night of the date, Lucas shows up at Maggie's looking tragic in an outsize tux. Maggie doesn't want to go, not just because she's mortified to be seen with him, but because Cappy broke up with Elise and she feels she has to, you know, be there for him. Suddenly, Lucas gets it. He hurls wounded spite at his betrayers but they gaze back at him with eyes that are all tenderness and pity. (Don't you *hate* that?) Maggie tries to make Lucas see the light. "We were only ever friends." He rages against the process of natural selection that has sentenced him to a life as a less-favored member of the species. "Do you know how wonderful you are?" she says, attempting to salve his wounds. (Don't you *hate* that?) "Yeah," he replies venomously, "but it doesn't turn you on, does it?" Then, in a hopeless, here-goes-nothing gesture, he tries to kiss her, and after she pulls away, screams at her to leave him alone.

How do you heal a hurt that huge? In the instance of this movie, you take the insane but inevitable big-finish solution of having Lucas attempt to prove his worth to Maggie, to the school and ultimately to *himself* by trying out for the football team. His scrawny-as-a-bent-straw physique and close proximity to the ground would seem to render him ineligible. The coach, his would-be teammates and the school principal all order him to keep his skinny ass at a far remove from the field of play. Come the day of the big match, though, the school team is taking a beating. A distraction from the humiliation of defeat appears in the shape of the tiny figure swamped inside the football suit. It's Lucas! The coach rounds on him. "Get off the field you pissant." Lucas, on fire with a passion the coach could never comprehend, roars like a lion, "Don't you call me a pissant, you dumb fucking jock. If anyone's a pissant it's you. You're the second-rate coach of a third-rate team." The coach, now with a vested interest in seeing Lucas flattened and killed, gives him permission to play. He runs on to the field, inspiring derision and jeers. His humiliated teammates try to ignore his presence, but in the last thirty seconds of play, it becomes apparent that Lucas is a slippery little character, able to outrun the rival behemoths. The crowd starts chanting, "Give the ball to Lucas." He gets it, passes it and then vanishes under a mountain of flesh. When all the players are peeled off Lucas, he's an immobile cardboard cutout with cracked glasses.

Half the school maintains a hospital vigil. Maggie, Cappy and Rina go off to break the bad news to Lucas' parents. Maggie is surprised to find Cappy driving past the big sprawling house where she supposed Lucas lived a hermetically sealed life of luxury. The car stops at a trailer park where, Cappy and Rina reveal to a shocked Maggie, Lucas lives with his alcoholic father. Oh no! Back in the hospital, Lucas and Maggie repair the ruins of their friendship. When Lucas returns to school, he's suddenly the center of attention. Inquiring eyes and a constant undertow of whispering follow his every step till he reaches his locker. Quivering with suspicion, he slo-o-o-wly turns the key and there, swinging inside, is his own customized football team jacket. The dumbest of his jock tormentors begins a slow home-is-the-hero handclap. Seconds later, the whole school takes it up and if you don't have wet eyes and a thick throat at this juncture, somebody switched off your life support.

Corey Haim's name quickly became synonymous with vapidity. His subsequent film work consisted of a smirk and a prolonged bout of tonsorial experimentation. But in *Lucas,* he was just about perfect: smart, funny, vulnerable, sad, likable, infuriating. He was given a character with many colors and he brought them all out beautifully. Charlie Sheen is a prince among jocks (as, of course, was his brother Emilio Estevez in *The Breakfast Club*) and, as the girl who captures the hearts of both sporto and squirt, Kerri Green is absolutely appealing. (Sheen and Green were subsequently paired, to less-enchanting effect, in *Three for the Road,* a romantic comedy that proved to be neither.) Untainted by a technopop sound track or the flouncy fashions of the day, *Lucas* is a timeless teen story that packs enough hurt to make it seem real and enough fantasy to make you believe that every underdog will have its day. After all, the little pissant didn't get the girl of his dreams, but he had Winona Ryder as a backup option.

They may not have had a John Hughes godfather figure putting words in their mouth. They may not have had a collective moniker but the Next Generation had a quartet of ensemble movies in which to posture, bellow, screech, simper, sob and sulk. The hellish *Goonies* (1985), directed by Richard Donner with the same frenzy he brought to papering over the plotfree cracks of the *Lethal Weapon* sequels—was for a time, every babysitter's child pacifier of choice, but for the over-fives it was a full-volume endurance test. Damning evidence that Steven Spielberg would stick the Amblin imprimatur on any bloated Saturday morning serial featuring kids in peril, *The Goonies* grouped together a bunch of brats threatened with eviction by evil property developers. They find a pirate's map and set out to dig up the treasure of One-Eyed Willie (Spielberg: "One-Eyed Willie! That's genius! Whaddaya want? Thirty mil? Nah, take forty. One-Eyed Willie, you guys . . .").

Thereafter you could boil down the movie's content to one word: *Waaaaaaaaah!* The Goonies fall through trapdoors. Waaah! They're chased by the disreputable misshapen sons of the harridan also in search of One-Eyed Willie's treasure. Waaah! They fall into secret dungeons! Waaah! The open mouths doing the waaah-ing belong to a mixture of heroic guys (Sean Astin, Josh Brolin), spunky gals (Kerri Green, Martha Plimpton), a precious ethnic (Jonathan Ke Quan—Short Round from *Indiana Jones and the Temple of Doom*) and two heinous excuses for comic relief (Corey Feldman playing a precurser of Dustin Hoffman's *Dick Tracy* mumbling guy and a terrifying chubbo called Jeff Cohen shoveling junk food into his mouth at the exact same time he was going "Waaah!").

If the Goonies were incapable of shutting up for a second, the kids from *River's Edge* (1986) were too numb to care about anything. The movie opens up with little deaths-head Tim (Joshua Miller) blankly destroying his sister's doll. It's only a short jump from there to the river's edge where a big slab of a guy, Samson (Daniel Roebuck), sits beside the naked dead body of the girlfriend he just decided to strangle. His impetuous act has a galvanizing effect on his coterie of desensitized wastoids. In the mind of the group's speedfreak leader, Layne (Crispin Glover, firing on all six), the murder is a good thing, a test of the kids' mettle to which he will rise by hiding the body and protecting Samson. Matt (Keanu Reeves) is ambivalent. Samson is stowed away in the home of Feck (Dennis Hopper), a one-legged exbiker with some experience in the girlfriend-killing business who now lavishes his affection on a plastic sex doll called Ellen. Matt confides in gal pal Clarissa (Ione Skye) that he's being struck by unfamiliar pangs of something that could be conscience. Eventually, he does the right thing and calls the cops but not before his evil little brother Tim has pulled a gun on him. Any intent on the part of director Tim Hunter to issue a wake-up call to America warning it about the state of its uncaring, dysfunctional, nihilistic offspring was squashed the second he made the decision to allow Crispin Glover and Dennis Hopper to share the same screen.

A dead body also acts as the impetus for the quartet of protagonists in *Stand by Me* (1986) to assert their right to . . . well, to ogle a dead body. In the wake of Quentin Tarantino's saturation success, bilious film geeks, desperate to plunge a dagger into the back of one of their own, have compiled exhaustive lists detailing the original source of every camera movement and line of dialogue the writer/director claims as his own. Few, if any, of these *J'accuse* documents have mentioned either *Diner* or *Stand by Me* as prime influences on the pop-culture badinage which, along with copious bloodletting, has come to be seen as Tarantino's most publicly recognized stylistic trait. Rob Reiner's movie, especially, is awash with summit conferences on TV themes and comic books. "Mickey's a mouse, Donald's a duck, Pluto's a dog, but what's Goofy?" forms the core of one discussion. "Mighty Mouse versus Superman? That's a tough one" is another. The influence of *Stand by Me* can be felt further afield than Tarantinoland. When fat kid Vern Tessio (Jerry O'Connell) says, "One food for the rest of my life? That's easy, Cherry Pez. Cherry-flavored Pez. There's no doubt about it," you can almost hear those self-same words escaping from the mouth of George Costanza (the success of *Stand by Me* gave Rob Reiner the chance to start his own production company, Castle Rock, whose first dip into TV waters was *Seinfeld*). Not only can the ramifications of this movie still be felt in the rhythms of Tarantino, Jerry and George, but with *Stand by Me,* Rob Reiner solved the increasingly thorny problem of what to do with Stephen King adaptations. The movie versions of *Christine, Cujo, Cat's Eye* and *Firestarter* reeked of cheese; they were worlds away from the TLC with which *Carrie* and *Dead Zone* were treated. When Rob Reiner embarked on the act of fleshing out "The Body" (as the novella from *Different Seasons* was originally titled), he handled it like an American classic.

In their two-day trek through the Oregon woods in search of an undiscovered moldering corpse, four friends—Gordie, the sensitive storyteller (Wil Wheaton), Chris, the roughneck (River Phoenix), Teddy, the deformed looney (Corey Feldman, doing his moving performance in a film of note) and Vern, the blimp (Jerry O'Connell)—face their fears, unburden themselves of their respective angst in an impromptu therapy session and defy local hood Ace Merril (Kiefer Sutherland). Unlike *The Breakfast Club*'s chronic-inspired confessional passages, *Stand by Me* puts its kids through the wringer before letting them reveal their inner anguish. After taunting wild dogs, running from an oncoming locomotive and plucking leeches from their private parts, they're sufficiently emotionally jangled to let it all out. Gordie, always in the shadow of his elder brother (John Cusack), is ignored and despised when the sibling dies. Chris is treated like a criminal by teachers. Teddy's dad, who pressed an iron to his ear and gave him a cauliflower-shaped blemish, is in an institution and Vern . . . well, he's the fat guy. Reiner works wonders with the book but he's unable to do anything with its worst device: Gordie's interminable telling of his story about the pie-eating contest that ends in mass projectile vomiting.

Even more sensitive than the preteens in *Stand by Me* were the fully formed preppies brought out of their starchy shells and into quivering, fulminating, bongo-beating life by Robin Williams' English teacher in *Dead Poets Society* (1989). *"Carpe diem!"* cries John Keating (Williams) and so successful is he in his attempts to get his students surging with the emotion of literature and poetry that they do just that. Shy guy Todd (Ethan Hawke) flings aside his fears and does some free-form improvisation, father-dominated Neil (Robert Sean Leonard) defies the parental edict and follows his thespian ambitions and nervy smart-mouth Knox (Josh Charles) screws his courage to the mast and pursues a well-born blonde. Emotion and embarrassment bump up against each other all the way through this movie. When you're not thrilled by Keating's classroom dynamics, you're cringing at the WASPy bohemian enclave, known as the Dead Poets Society, formed by Todd, Neil and Knox. "Gotta do more, gotta be more . . . !" rage these nascent CEOs and congressmen.

By the time Corey Haim turned 15, he had amassed a body of work that included touching performances in movies like *Lucas, Firstborn* and *Murphy's Romance.* He gave every sign of maturing into a dramatic actor of some promise. By the time Corey Feldman turned 15, he had attracted attention with comic turns in *Gremlins* and *Goonies* and a more serious role in *Stand By Me.* He seemed on the verge of blossoming into a multi-faceted star. *Who Knew?* Who knew that Canuck Haim would become so entranced by his own adorability that he'd become physically painful to watch? Who knew that deadpan Cali kid Feldman would end up resembling something squishy and unpleasant from *The Hobbit?* Who knew that these two guys would end up like a Ray-Ban–wearing version of *The Defiant Ones,* chained together for straight-to-video eternity? And it all started so promisingly; their skilled goofing in *The Lost Boys* considerably upped that movie's lunacy quotient. Two funny guys with the same first names who polluted every page of *Tiger Beat* and *Bop;* a picture that paired these Coreys seemed like a no-brainer. But the first fruits of their shared labors, *License to Drive* (1988), was like an extended P.S.A. on the debilitating effect of celebrity on the young and impressionable. The film was a sporadically funny piece of nonsense about a kid (Haim) who fails his road test but boosts his grandfather's vintage jalopy to impress a date. Haim, though, was entirely free of all the residual innocence that clung to him throughout his formative movies. He fully believed he was the hot, happening guy from teenybop fanzine pages. No matter the tone of the dialogue he was called upon to deliver, every word was pushed through lips that were twisted into a combination pout and sneer (a snout?). Feldman was even weirder and even worse. His precocity had been replaced by a battery of uncomfortable affectations: the lowering of his raspy voice, the slitting of his tiny eyes and the contemplative fingers placed around his mouth.

Although both Coreys were top billed in *License To Drive,* the movie was a vehicle for Haim. The situations were reversed in *Dream a Little Dream* (1989). Wildly overdirected by Marc Rocco, this flick appeared at the very end of the teen body-swap cycle. Fred Savage and Judge Reinhold had changed places in *Vice Versa,* Kirk Cameron walked in Dudley Moore's shoes in *Like Father, Like Son.* Charlie Schlatter gave George Burns a new lease on life in *18 Again!* And Corey Feldman . . . *didn't* exactly swap bodies with Jason Robards in *Dream a Little Dream.* One of the reasons the film tanked at the box office was the fact that nobody knew what it was supposed to be about. Feldman slams his bike into local grouch Robards at the exact moment he's out in the back garden practicing Tai Chi. So their souls are exchanged . . . except they're not really. Feldman seems to be lounging around limbo and his body shows little sign of being occupied by Robards. In fact it shows more sign of being occupied by Michael Jackson, who at that time had cultivated Feldman's close personal friendship (someone thrust into the public eye at an early age, someone who *understood*). Jackson's

The Next Generation

influence was horrifyingly visible, both in the revolting state of Feldman's hair (dyed shoe-polish black, all stringy and falling into his face) and in the ghastly song-and-dance number he does to impress girl-of-his-dreams Meredith Salenger.

The Coreys had movie stardom, they had adulation, they even had a joint 1-800 number. But pride—and they had a mountain of that shit—comes before a fall. Pretty soon, Feldman got hooked on heroin and was arrested for possession. He also discovered that his parents, Bob and Sheila, had been regularly pilfering the account set up to hold his preadult earnings. (In 1993, he appeared on a Ricki Lake show whose topic was Should kids divorce their parents?). Haim, too, fell on hard times, his teen appeal strictly a thing of the past. Unable to rid himself of that snout thing, unwilling to stop dying and spiking his hair, he became one of the least-welcome denizens of the B-movie jungle. Frequently reteamed with Feldman who now emitted the oily menace of a Peter Lorre, the duo stumbled through little-seen, barely believable projects like *National Lampoon's Last Resort, Blown Away* and *Dream A Little Dream 2,* in which Feldman makes a defiant stab at proving that despite the hair and the drugs and the money, he's still a song-and-dance man. Haim, exhibiting unexpected maturity, betrays no resentment at his reduced circumstances and enforced partnership with his seminamesake: "We're like Bing and Crosby," he says, shrugging cheerfully.

Ladies love Patrick Dempsey. Young, old, rich, poor, brilliant, beautiful, eccentric, frustrated, experienced; you name them, they wanted him. That, at least, was the impression a bunch of movies strove to create. Crinkly of eye, bashful of manner, rhythmic of limb, this Dempsey character was touted as an irresistible combination of sweet-natured naif and tireless boudoir adventurer: a boy who'll do all the things your tired-ass old man won't do. *In the Mood* (1987) tells the true story of Elliot "Sonny" Wisecarver, the celebrated teenage Lothario who took full advantage of the love-starved women left behind when the boys were out fighting for life and liberty in WW2. In *Loverboy* (1989), Dempsey's supple pizza delivery boy is sliced and devoured by hungry customers like Carrie Fisher, Kirstie Alley and Barbara Carrera. In *Happy Together* (1989), a computer snafu sees him sharing a college room with Helen Slater. In *Some Girls* (1988), he's dumped by his girlfriend (Jennifer Connelly) but examined and passed around like a cuddly toy between her sisters (Sheila Kelley, Ashley Greenfield). Even her grandmother is warm for Dempsey, mistaking him for her dead husband. Dempsey's irresistibility to older women was also evident off-screen when, at 23, he married his 54-year-old agent/manager, Rocky Parker (mother of actor Corey Parker). Sadly, the only warm body from which he failed to receive torrents of affection was the audience that consistently failed to fall for him.

With his every drawled utterance, eyebrow wiggle and lascivious grin, Christian Slater sends out skyscraper-high signals that he's living his life and conducting his career as an extended tribute to an actor who embodies indulgence and mischief-making. That man is Dean Martin. Not since Dino has a performer so consistently and successfully tipped audiences the wink that however serious or lightweight the nature of the project in which he's employed, he's just picking up a paycheck. His jack-o'-lantern grin was utilized to devastating psycho effect in *Heathers*; for most of Slater's onscreen eighties, though, the eyebrows were on but no one was home.

Whether on a skateboard (*Gleaming the Cube*), on a horse (*Young Guns 2*) or in a car chase (*The Wizard*), he kept on smirking and drawling, fixating on the tall, cool one that lay in wait for him after the shoot. And also, looking forward to an after-work drink. The notion of this affable dude as a voice through which the alienation, despair and unfocused rage of a generation who felt abandoned and trapped in a world they never made could scream seems batty. But there he is in *Pump Up the Volume* (1990), a film as sincere in its treatment of teen angst bullshit as *Heathers* was scornful. He plays a high schooler who is a mumbling misfit by day, but behind the console of the shortwave radio transmitter in his basement he is a howling, horny, caustic truth-teller and social satirist. He is Hard Harry, the pirate DJ who stirs a school out of its apathy. "Do you ever get the feeling everything in America is fucked up?" he asks. "I'm a member of the why-bother generation my-self," he sneers. Religion, government, music, school, conventional expressions of rebellion: Hard Harry pours scorn on them. And the kids listen. They blow up their radios, they flout convention, they ask the killer question, Why? And then one of them kills himself. (Talk about ahead of its time. The last five years' worth of Buzz Bin bands probably cribbed their lyrics from Harry's tirades.) Suddenly, the school wants to shut down this spreader of sedition. But, as they cart him off to be deprogrammed, he throws out the challenge to the kids he has awakened to carry on his good work: "Talk Hard!"

Written and directed by Allan Moyle, previously responsible for the frightful *Times Square*, *Volume*'s big mistake was having Harry get tangled up in a suicide. An *Over the Edge*-style display of mindless violence and destruction would have been much more appropriate and satisfying. As it is, the film falls apart in its third act, turning into an extended kids-outrunning-cops chase sequence. But during the time it isolates Slater behind that microphone, gasping his masturbation fantasies ("Here it comes! Another gusher!") and smirking at the hopelessness around him, it gives this self-satisfied actor his finest hour.

Take Ted Danson in *Dad*. Take Tom Selleck in *Runaway*. Take Shelley Long in *Hello Again*, Bill Cosby in *Leonard Part 6*, David Caruso in *Jade*, Don Johnson in *Harley Davidson and the Marlboro Man*, Roseanne in *She-Devil* or Ed O'Neill in *Dutch*. None of these TV stars' failed attempts to translate their small-screen success into movies—not even Julia Sweeney's *It's Pat*—was the all-out abomination that Kirk Cameron's *Listen to Me* (1989) was. The idea of putting *Growing Pains'* clown-faced young heartthrob into a movie that treated college debate with the same passion that a sports film would treat football seemed like it might be ripe with comic potential. And ripe it was, but with melodramatic dementia.

Cameron, with his beaming little button eyes and red lips, looking like a ventriloquist's dummy that's broken free of its terrified owner, is Tucker Muldowney, the country boy from Oklahoma who gets into a California college on a debate scholarship. "This chicken farmer's son," as he ingratiatingly and endlessly refers to himself, is one of only two students to get such a scholarship. The other lucky recipient is Monica Tomanski (Jami Gertz, ending the eighties on a note of ignominy), a Chicago girl with a dark secret. Coach Charlie Nicholls (Roy Scheider) schools his debating rookies in the practice of turning on a dime to deliver either side of an argument, kissing up to the judges and, after delivering a heart-wrenching story of his poor old mother's abuse at the hands of a back-street abortionist, the power of a really good lie. The team's best liar is Garson McKellar (Tim Quill), scion of a Kennedy-like political dynasty. But the pressure of living up to the family name is beginning to tell on Garson. He wants out of the team. "How do you just walk away from debate?" asks a mystified coach. "Because I don't love it like you do," says the golden boy.

After Garson is killed, saving Tucker from an oncoming car, the chicken farmer's son and the Chicago girl, who have been sparring around with that old unresolved sexual tension thing, are paired together to go to Washington and represent their school in the National Debate Tournament in front of a selection of Supreme Court judges. They take on a pair of cold-blooded killers from Harvard who look set to steamroller them on the Abortion Is Immoral issue. They've got the facts, they've got the arguments, they've got the logic. But what they haven't got is someone who's had an abortion and never told anyone till that minute. Monica delivers a teary-eyed repudiation of Roe v. Wade and the responsibility it puts on women. She does such a powerful job that a crippled girl stands up and applauds. Then the chicken boy wraps up the argument. Pacing the floor in his shirt sleeves, his button eyes sending laser lights of truth into the souls of the potential baby-killers in the audience, he works himself up into a frenzy, bemoaning the moral breakdown of the country, climaxing with a quote from "my good buddy Dostoevsky." The Harvard men are crushed under this tide of righteousness and the movie ends with the chilling image of Tucker and Monica running down the steps of the Supreme Court, making their way toward the White House. Help!

End of
an Era

11 Slackers, Students,
Pre-teens, Post-twenties,
Kids and *Clueless*

A funny thing happened on the way to the nineties: the generation who cheerfully accepted cynical cinematic representations of themselves and their lives grew up and rejected movies that attempted to depict them in a realistic and sympathetic light. Though Richard Linklater's *Slacker* (1991) played—along with Nirvana, the Lollapolooza mudbath and Douglas Coupland's bumper-sticker compendium *Generation X*—a crucial part in the cultural confluence that forced Motley Crue into hacking off their hair and attempting to cultivate goatees, films aimed at a young-ish audience found few takers and much derision. Why should this have been? Weren't the legions of Americans between the ages of 18 and 29 pop-culture fluent to the extent that they were more comfortable in the presence of a small screen radiating images of *The Brady Bunch* than they were around their own fractured families? Perhaps. But a quick glance down the shopping list of accepted Gen-X characteristics reveals, nestling between minute attention spans, heavy irony, heavier ennui, fear of the future and resentment

of the wasteland of a world bequeathed to them by their stoner parents, distrust of the very same media that suckled them.

Commercials, sitcoms, rock videos, news shows and movies; they were all the same. They all wanted to sucker you in, spray soft drinks down your throat and stick sneakers on your feet. The ridicule and disgust that greeted the first, faltering attempts to market products to suit the perceived needs of the almost-growns proved that the unthinkable had occurred: the audience had got smarter. In fairness, it has to be said that the advertising campaigns in question (Subaru's "It's like punk, except it's a car!" and Coke's experimental fizzy drink, OK, with its Dan Clowes artwork) would have been laughed off screens and left on shelves by consumers of any generation and any culture in any stage of civilization at any time. Ever. Add to this lingering mistrust of the media the fact that of the approximately 45 million Americans included within the parameters of the Gen-X definition, probably over 75% were either oblivious to or resentful of the label and it becomes apparent why movies claiming to speak for the frustrations and aspirations of twentysomethings were greeted with no little suspicion.

Ben Stiller's film *Reality Bites* (1994), whose origins bore no taint of contrivance, appeared in its finished incarnation as if it had been assembled by cyborgs programmed to display Gen-X traits. It featured overeducated eggheads (Winona Ryder, Ethan Hawke) failing to hold down joke jobs, it featured ironic worship of seventies kitsch (courtesy of Janeane Garofalo, the peevish woman of pop culture), it featured dysfunctional families, distrust of the demon media (as personified by Stiller's faux-MTV exec who is innocently complicit in the co-opting of videomaker Ryder's untarnished vision), flannel and goatees. The movie poster featured its three stars posing somberly in front of a wall spattered with graffitied buzzwords: sex, love, jobs, money. Though the film was charming and well written (plus, it took Winona Ryder out of crinolines and into contemporary mode), its assumption of generational commonality turned off more than it attracted. In fact, it turned them off to the degree that the majority of the audience who might have been relied upon to give *Reality Bites* a profitable opening weekend put their money down for the movie that came out at the same time, *Ace Ventura: Pet Detective*.

A similar fate, in terms of low turnouts, greeted Cameron Crowe's *Singles* (1992)—which was based in grunge mecca Seattle, featured an entire rehab ward's worth of lumbering rock acts and Matt Dillon in the part that should have been his Jeff Spicoli. All of those ingredients failed to gel (though the center-staging of straights Campbell Scott and Kyra Sedgwick didn't help much) and the movie quickly fizzled. As did the likes of *Threesome* (1994), *With Honors* (1994) and Richard Linklater's brilliantly realized exploration of the origins of the slacker species, *Dazed and Confused* (1993). In fact it wasn't till the release of *Pulp Fiction* (the *Porky's* of its day in as much as it altered the notion of what could be put onscreen in the name of entertainment and its influence could be felt in lesser works for years to come), that the twentysomething audience fully and completely embraced a movie as something that spoke to them. Here was cynicism, here was pop-culture overload but without the we're-all-in-this-mess-together overtones that made some viewers think they were attending a college reunion with all the people they'd tried to avoid the first time around.

If the audience leaving their teens behind were less than thrilled by the movies that mirrored their progress, the kids entering double-digit–hood—and there were far fewer of them than there were in the eighties—were pretty much bereft of films designed to flatter, scare, move or amuse them. *90210* gogo boys Luke Perry and Jason Priestley, huge, internationally recognized teen stars, couldn't pull their screaming legions of fans off the couch and into theaters for *Buffy the Vampire Slayer* (1992) or *Calendar Girl* (1993). *Married . . . With Children*'s Oomph Girl Christina Applegate had modest success with *Don't Tell Mom the Babysitter's Dead* (1991), an eighties movie out of time if there ever was one. Ethan Hawke, discomfort radiating from his every pore, found himself stranded in Corey territory with *Mystery Date* (1991), an *After Hours*–ish I-just-wanna-get-laid-why-is-this-shit-happening-to-me disaster. Christian Slater let his eyebrows do the talking one time too many in *Kuffs* (1992). Patrick Dempsey, after years of failing to get past first base with the female audience, tried his hand at action in *Run* (1991), notable for being one of the few movies to climax with its villain impaled on a mechanical rabbit. Slater and the aforementioned Dempsey starred in *Mobsters* (1991), which did for gangland what *Young Guns* did for the Old West, i.e., nothing. Fellow mobster Richard *Booker* Grieco, with his satanic eyebrows, committed big-screen suicide with *If Looks Could Kill* (1991). Sean Astin led a bunch of military academy brats against an unsuspecting mob of terrorist scum in *Toy Soldiers* (1991). The newly clean and sober Drew Barrymore's panties fell off in *Poison Ivy* (1992).

But while these movies were collapsing like undercooked souffles, the early nineties saw a sudden boom in an area that had been a dead zone in the previous decade. *House Party* was pretty much the only black teen movie of the eighties. But, in the wake of *Boyz N the Hood,* a glut of gangsta pics increased employment opportunities for young black actors.

The other growth area was in preteen movies. Just as he had been at the helm of the adolescent explosion, so John Hughes was the king of the kindergarten. His first teeny titan was Macaulay Culkin, plucked from his deadpan scene-stealing in *Uncle Buck* and given *Home Alone* in which to run rampant. From there, Hughes' nursery school expanded to take in Alison Porter in the hideous *Curly Sue* (1991), Mason Gamble in the horrifying *Dennis The Menace* (1993), Mara Wilson in the unnecessary *Miracle on 34th Street* (1994) and a couple of gurgling tots in the miserable *Baby's Day Out* (1994). Rumors that he's auditioning his next star via sonogram remain unconfirmed. Hughes' success in the under-10 market flooded multiplexes with a new squad of child stars. Elijah Wood, Christina Ricci, Jonathan Taylor Thomas, Brian Bonsall, Tina Majorino, Mara Wilson, Jesse Bradford, Jason James Richter, Thora Birch, and Gaby Hoffman were among the kids who could cry on cue.

Then, in 1995, 10 years after *The Breakfast Club,* two movies were released that hinted at a Teenpic Renaissance. Larry Clark's *Kids* was 24 hours of drinking, drugging, fighting and fucking in the lives of a group of thoughtfree Manhattan scumbags. Its exact opposite was Amy Heckerling's *Clueless,* a pastel-shaded delight that was crafted to seem as if it had been stored in suspended animation since 1984. *Heathers* through the looking glass, *Clueless* asked the revolutionary question: what if the pretty, rich, popular girl wasn't the evil witch? What if she was *really, really* nice? What if she didn't make it her mission to lacerate the hopelessly uncool and uncoordinated new girl, but saw it as her civic duty to spread the wealth of her knowledge, friendship and taste? Not since *Pretty in Pink* has a teen film been graced by a star performance as accomplished as Alicia Silverstone, as Cher, delivers in *Clueless.* Whether throwing herself at the perfect new boy in school whom everybody but she realizes is gay or mocking her square stepbrother's taste in "complaint rock," Silverstone makes her every minute count. While the *Kids* ensemble is numbed by experience, *Clueless*'s Cher is like a beautifully accoutred, still shrink-wrapped toy doll; she doesn't drink, doesn't drug, doesn't smoke, doesn't drive and doesn't . . . well, just doesn't. They were the dark and light sides of teen movies. *Kids* attracted controversy and lengthy critical wrangling. *Clueless* was an unexpectedly big box-office hit, scaring up an opening week take only a few pennies short of Kevin Costner's unwieldy *Waterworld.*

In the wake of those two films, 1995 saw a brief accompanying burst of teen movie activity. *Angus* was a fat version of *Lucas. Hackers* was to cyberspace what *Breakin' 2: Electric Boogaloo* was to hip-hop, i.e., nothing. Kevin Smith's cruddy *Mallrats* tried to be both smart and stupid; unfortunately, the smart bits came off stupid and the stupid bits . . . okay, that's not gonna work. The stupid bits *were* stupid but they weren't . . . you know what I'm saying. *National Lampoon's Senior Trip* was a doomed attempt to reanimate the Grossout corpse. *Now and Then,* the teenage female seventies *Stand by Me*, had a cute cast but scared off its audience with publicity material that indicated Christina Ricci was going to grow up to be Rosie O'Donnell.

So, 1995? An indication of increased activity that will one day bloom forth into a whole new cinema of teen? Or an isolated burst of movies that happened to come out at the same time and target the same demographic but exhibit no tendency to spearhead a trend? Probably the latter. It'll be a long time before there's a teenage audience voluminous enough to dictate the direction of Hollywood, and it may be even longer before so many kids exhibit so little discrimination.

Whether you look back on it with fondness or anguish, whether you reveled in the food fights and crying jags or winced at the onslaught of shallowness, stupidity and affectation, you probably won't live through another time like it. The eighties was the period when parents were away for the weekend for an entire decade, leaving the kids in charge of the movie industry. Suckers.

End of an Era

Don't You Forget About Me

Where Are They Now?

We're probably more *au fait* with the personal and professional lives of Tom Cruise and Demi Moore than we are with those of our own families. The same goes for Sean Penn, Nicolas Cage, and Tim Robbins. But what of some of the others names mentioned in the preceding pages? Have the Nineties been good to them? Did they ever work again? Are they eligible for parole any time soon? The following list may help to confirm your worst fears.

CURTIS ARMSTRONG
Still playing Booger in *Revenge of the Nerds* movies. (*Revenge of the Nerds: The Next Generation* and *Revenge of the Nerds: Nerds in Love* which revolves around Booger's marriage). His non-Booger employment includes roles in Tom Arnold's awful *Big Bully* and Leslie Nielsen's shameful *Spy Hard*. He supplies the voice of one of Savage Steve Holland's animated *Terrible Thunder Lizards*.

SEAN ASTIN

Responsible for inflicting Pauly Shore on a mass audience in *Encino Man,* tugged at heartstrings in *Rudy.* He appeared in a supporting capacity in the highly-acclaimed *Courage Under Fire.*

SCOTT BAIO

Scott was most recently seen presenting the series *Before They Were Stars* and in Dick Van Dyke's *Diagnosis: Murder.* His catalogue of small-screen work includes the short-lived *Happy Days* spin-off, *Joanie Loves Chachi,* series such as *Charles in Charge* and *Baby Talk* (a *Look Who's Talking* TV ripoff), and the TV movie *The Boy Who Drank Too Much.*

JUSTINE BATEMAN

She's done various TV movies and currently appears in the U.S. adaptation of the scuzzy British sitcom *Men Behaving Badly.*

DAVID BEAIRD

The director of *The Party Animal* attempted to create a *Northern Exposure* of his own with the quickly-extinct Fox series *Key West.*

JENNIFER BEALS

Won critical plaudits for her performance in husband Alexandre Rockwell's film *In the Soup.* She received no such acclaim for her work in Rockwell's segment of the anthology movie *Four Rooms.*

JOSH BROLIN

Appeared in David O. Russell's *Flirting with Disaster.*

PHOEBE CATES

Married Kevin Kline. Her best film this decade remains *Drop Dead Fred.*

KIRK CAMERON

Went on to warm hearts in the WB sitcom *Kirk.*

Don't You Forget About Me

BOB CLARK

The *Porky's* auteur went on to establish a formidable body of work including *Rhinestone, Turk 182!, From the Hip,* and *Loose Cannons.*

CHRISTOPHER COLLET

Turned up as a rollerblading bad guy in the nutty Corey Haim wheeled-fascist fantasy *Prayer of the Rollerboys.*

WES CRAVEN

The veteran horror director's name and reputation continue to thrive despite such titles as *Shocker, Vampire in Brooklyn,* and *The People Under the Stairs.* He'll next attempt to skewer his *oeuvre* with *Scream* (formerly titled *Scary Movie*).

JON CRYER

0 for 2 as far as sitcoms are concerned. Bombed on the highly-regarded *The Famous Teddy Z,* went down for the count on the *Friends* clone *Partners.* Wrote, co-produced and acted in little-seen but excellently-titled indie effort *The Pompatus of Love.*

PATRICK DEMPSEY

Divorced the manager/wife who was some 30 years his senior. Directed the movie *Ava's Magical Adventure.* Appeared in movies *Outbreak* (the monkey bit him and he spread the virus) and *With Honors.* Portrayed the young JFK in miniseries *Reckless Youth.*

SHANNEN DOHERTY

Where you do start? *90210.* The tantrums. The sulks. The *"I Hate Brenda"* campaign. The terrified ex-boyfriends. The blink-and-you'll-miss-it, too-late-it's-gone marriage. The affair with Judd Nelson. The attempt to convert her into an icon of ironic cool in *Mallrats.* The failure of *Mallrats.* This one will run and run.

ANTHONY EDWARDS

Currently welcome in living rooms the world over as affable, dedicated Dr. Mark Greene on *ER.*

EMILIO ESTEVEZ
Married and divorced Paula Abdul. Found a franchise that will keep him in work for life in *The Mighty Ducks.*

COREY FELDMAN
Keeps on churning out the cable hits. He was a stalker in *Evil Obsession.* A cursed student in *Voodoo.* A bad guy with barely credible kickboxing skills in *A Dangerous Place.* 1996 marked his triumphant return to the big screen in *Tales From The Crypt Presents Bordello of Blood.*

DEBORAH FOREMAN
The *Valley Girl* herself. A Deborah Foreman Film Festival would include such titles as *Lunatics: A Love Story, Lobster Man from Mars, Sundown: The Vampire in Retreat, Waxwork, Destroyer,* and *Friends, Lovers and Lunatics.*

JAMI GERTZ
Still gorgeous. Played the light relief in *Twister* as Bill Paxton's prissy, princessy therapist fiancee.

JENNIFER GREY
Entirely failed to consolidate on the worldwide goodwill garnered by her role as Baby in *Dirty Dancing.* A subsequent nosejob rendered her completely unrecognizable. Most substantial role to date has been one appearance on *Friends* as Rachel's ex-best friend, Mindy.

COREY HAIM
Cable fans will be almost religiously aware of the dopey *Fast Getaway* movies he made with high-kicking Cynthia Rothrock. Like his partner in Coreydom, he keeps churning out the straight-to-video fillers (latest entries: *Life 101, Demolition High*). Unlike Feldman, no triumphant return to the big screen in his immediate future.

ANTHONY MICHAEL HALL
Grew into such a behemoth that he was perfect casting for the psycho jock boyfriend in *Edward Scissorhands.* Turned up as

Will Smith's mark in *Six Degrees of Separation.* Directed his own movie *Hail Caesar* featuring cameos from Robert Downey Jr., Judd Nelson, and the old black man accent he used in the John Hughes movies.

JOYCE HISER
Even though *Just One of the Guys* is broadcast so often that its star Joyce Hiser seems like a familiar face, her only notable work in the past decade has been a recurring role on *L.A. Law* and a part in the Michael J. Fox dud *Greedy.*

SUSANNAH HOFFS
To date, she hasn't made another movie.

SAVAGE STEVE HOLLAND
Hitched his wagon up to the Fox network, producing for them, first the short-lived live-action teen spy series *The Adventures of Beans Baxter,* the longer lasting cartoon shows *Eek! The Cat* and *Terrible Thunder Lizards,* which evolved into *Eekstravaganza,* featuring the vocal talents of his most frequent collaborator, Curtis Armstrong.

C. THOMAS HOWELL
A major cable presence, usually playing some poor schlub who strays into the web of a panting seductress who bamboozles him into offing her rich, brutish husband. Briefly starred in the Aaron Spelling vampires vs. cops flop *Kindred: The Embraced.*

JOHN HUGHES
Devoting his energies to producing remakes of much-loved family favorites. On the way: *101 Dalmations* and *The Absent-Minded Professor.* Fans of his 80s work are continually tantalized by rumors of a *Breakfast Club* sequel, though it would have to be a Next Generation, because the only way *that* crew would ever be together again would be in rehab. Also reportedly met with Matthew Broderick about the possibility of a *Bueller Part Deux.*

MICHAEL LEHMANN

The *Heathers* director went on to helm *Hudson Hawk, The Applegates,* and *Airheads.* He was not to see another positive review until 1996 and *The Truth About Cats and Dogs.*

ROB LOWE

Turned himself into the butt of the joke. Played yuppie villains for Lorne Michaels in *Wayne's World* and *Tommy Boy.* Garnered some good reviews for his role as a deaf-mute in the gargantuan miniseries adaptation of Stephen King's *The Stand.*

RALPH MACCHIO

His last role of any note was in *My Cousin Vinny.*

KELLI MARONEY

For anyone interested in mounting a Kelli Maroney Retrospective, the giggly, gun-toting little sister from *Night of the Comet* starred in such films as *Transylvania Twist, Not of This Earth, Big Bad Mama II, Chopping Mall,* and *Slayground.*

ANDREW MCCARTHY

The *Weekend at Bernie's* movies saved his bacon. Transformed, in the nick of time, into a surprisingly effective character actor. Turned up in films like *The Joy Luck Club, Mrs. Parker and the Vicious Circle,* and *Mulholland Falls.* Recommended among his battery of cable movies is the supersadistic *Night of the Running Man* in which his feet are boiled in pots of scalding hot water.

ILAN MITCHELL-SMITH

The little raspy-voiced star of *Weird Science* has been laying low since the TV series *The Adventures of Superboy.*

JUDD NELSON

His nineties movie work includes *New Jack City, Airheads,* and *The Dark Backward* wherein he portrayed a failed stand-up comedian who got a career boost when a third arm suddenly grew out of his back. Notable amongst his cable work are *Blindfold: Acts of Obsession*—his and Shannen Doherty's *Postman Always Rings Twice*—and *Flinch,* in which he plays a failed actor forced to make a living portraying a shop-window mannequin. Currently seen by his biggest audience this decade in the Brooke Shields vehicle *Suddenly Susan.*

JERRY O'CONNELL

Stand by Me's snivelling blimp Vern Tessio shed pounds, shot up—in height, I mean—and starred in the Fox series *Sliders* and the MTV movie *Joe's Apartment.*

JASON PATRIC

Things have turned out well for this late bloomer. Of late, he's been in *Rush, Sleepers, Speed 2*, and Christy Turlington.

JUDGE REINHOLD

Seemed stuck in the same Nice Guy career bind that briefly bedevilled Tom Hanks and Anthony Edwards. But while they found their places in the firmament, Reinhold is still in a holding pattern. Last role of note was playing Ned Flanders to Tim Allen's Homer Simpson in *The Santa Clause.* Should never again appear in public sporting a moustache.

MOLLY RINGWALD

Had a lead role in *The Stand,* and now stars as Carrie on the ABC sitcom *Townies.*

CLAYTON ROHNER

The befuddled male from *Just One of the Guys* and *Modern Girls* most recently turned up in the nightmarish Pamela Anderson cable movie *Naked Souls.*

ALAN RUCK

Had a couple of failed sitcoms, and kept the spirit of Cameron Frye alive as the snivelling tourist on the bus in *Speed.* Also appeared as one of Helen Hunt's troupe of goofball meteorologists in *Twister.* Currently appears in the Michael J. Fox sitcom *Spin City.*

MIA SARA
Did a few miniseries and appeared with Jon Cryer in *The Pompatus of Love.* Most memorable role to date: Dr. Kronk's transsexual girlfriend in *Chicago Hope.*

ALLY SHEEDY
Last appeared on the big screen opposite a genetically-engineered killer dog in *Man's Best Friend.*

CHARLIE SHEEN
Provided years of laughter and entertainment. Moving on to an entirely separate subject, his movies have included *The Chase, Terminal Velocity, The Three Musketeers, The Rookie, The Arrival,* the *Hot Shots* films, the *Major League* films, and *All Dogs Go to Heaven 2,* where he provides the voice of Charlie. He currently has a relationship with God.

CRAIG SHEFFER
Played Brad Pitt's brother in *A River Runs Through It.*

NICOLLETTE SHERIDAN
Narrowed her eyes and pouted her lips for seven seasons as Paige Matheson on *Knots Landing.* Played Leslie Nielsen's love interest in *Spy Hard.* The dissolution of her relationship with *L.A. Law* actor Harry Hamlin landed her in a real-life *War of the Roses* scenario, marooned in her half of their spacious mansion.

HELEN SLATER
Last seen in a remake of *Lassie.*

CATHERINE MARY STUART
Sadly, her most prominent role to date remains the female lead in *Weekend at Bernie's.*

KRISTY SWANSON
Appeared in *The Phantom, Higher Learning, The Chase, The Program, Buffy the Vampire Slayer, Hot Shots,* and *Mannequin Two: On the Move. Somebody* must like her . . .

Don't You Forget About Me

DANIEL WATERS

The *Heathers* screenwriter went on to pen scripts packed with dazzling wordplay and baffling plots for *Hudson Hawk, The Adventures of Ford Fairlane, Batman Returns,* and *Demolition Man.*

DAPHNE ZUNIGA

Featured in *Spaceballs, The Fly II,* and *Gross Anatomy.* Best known for her four tumultuous years as Jo on *Melrose Place.*